W9-BZF-570

LIFE ON THE LINE

PHILIP D. CHINNERY

LIFE ON THE LINE
Stories of Vietnam Air Combat

St. Martin's Press
New York

THIS book is dedicated to all the pilots who were killed in South-East Asia between 1961 and 1972 and to those MIAs who remain unaccounted for. They are not forgotten.

If you are able,	*Take what they have left*
save for them a place	*and what they have taught you*
inside of you	*with their dying*
and save one backward glance	*and keep it with your own.*
when you are leaving	*And in that time*
for the places they can	*when men decide and feel safe*
no longer go.	*to call the war insane,*
Be not ashamed to say	*take one moment to embrace*
you loved them,	*those gentle heroes*
though you may	*you left behind.*
or may not have always.	

Major Michael Davis O'Donnell
1 January 1970
Dak To, Vietnam

On 24 March 1970 Michael O'Donnell, a helicopter pilot, was killed in action in Cambodia whilst attempting to rescue a Special Forces team that was about to be overrun.

This poem is reproduced with the kind permission of the New York Vietnam Veterans' Memorial Commission and was first published in the book Dear America: Letters Home from Vietnam edited by Bernard Edelman for the New York Vietnam Veterans' Memorial Commission and published by W. W. Norton & Company (cased) and by Pocket Books (paperback).

LIFE ON THE LINE. Copyright © 1988 by Philip D. Chinnery. All rights reserved. Printed in the United States of America. No part of this book may be used or reproduced in any manner whatsoever without written permission except in the case of brief quotations embodied in critical articles or reviews. For information, address St. Martin's Press, 175 Fifth Avenue, New York, N.Y. 10010

Library of Congress Cataloging-in-Publication Data

Chinnery, Philip D.
        Life on the line.

        1. Vietnamese Conflict, 1961–1975—Aerial operations,
American.   2. Vietnamese Conflict, 1961–1975—Personal
narratives, America.   I. Title.
DS558.8.C47 1989   959.704'348   88-29838
ISBN 0-312-02599-8

First published in Great Britain by Blandford Press.

First U.S. Edition

10 9 8 7 6 5 4 3 2 1

CONTENTS

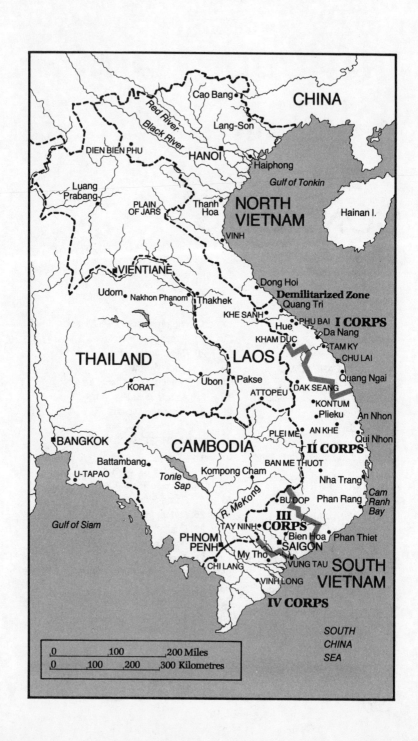

INTRODUCTION

*T*HE idea for Life on the Line *came from a strong desire to know more about the experiences of pilots in Vietnam. I had written a series of ten articles on the air war over Vietnam for* Aeroplane Monthly *magazine in 1986, and had contacted a couple of pilots to add some colour to the series with a few 'war stories'. Having served eight years in the British Army, I was well aware that every ex-serviceman has a story or two to tell, but after reading Phil Marshall's account of how he was wounded during a medical evacuation mission and John Morgan's tale of being shot down during a combat assault, I realized that I had stumbled upon the tip of an iceberg. Two things soon became apparent: first, most pilots in Vietnam faced danger and possible death on a daily basis; second, the experiences of the majority of these pilots are known only to their families and close friends.*

The objective of this book is to ensure that the experiences of the pilots are preserved for posterity and to make the public aware that while the 'grunts' humping the 'boonies' may have suffered most of the casualties and received most of the publicity during and after the war, the pilots have a story to tell as well.

Locating and interviewing the three dozen pilots whose stories appear in the book was an experience in itself. I sat with former Army Warrant Officer Phil Marshall at the Vietnam Helicopter Pilots' Association annual reunion at the Hilton Hotel in Washington and, as inebriated 1st Cav veterans threw each other in the pool, talked about the night he was shot. Colonel John Aarni related the story of his shoot-down and rescue when I met him at the Third Air Force Headquarters in the Suffolk countryside in England. Patricia O'Donnell McNevin, the sister of the late Major Michael O'Donnell, rang one night from New York to thank me for the copy of the story a friend of her brother had sent to me: she informed me that it was the first time in fourteen years that anyone had told her exactly where and how her brother had died.

Day after day, the pilots in Vietnam flew into murderous barrages of anti-aircraft fire over North Vietnam and Laos, or into withering clouds of small-arms fire at landing zones throughout the South. Often they were required to act above and beyond the call of duty and to lay their lives on the line, so that others might live. Many paid the final price. Some, still listed as prisoners-of-war or missing in action, may still be paying it.

The day I paid my respects at 'The Wall' in Washington, a Dustoff pilot advised me that 'The only difference between a fairy story and a war story is that a fairy story begins "Once upon a time" and a war story begins "This is no sh**"'. Well, *the stories in this book are all true. They are exciting, 'hairy', interesting, tragic and humorous – as indeed is war itself. The intention is not to glorify the Vietnam War, but to pay tribute to the brave men who flew in it. When the reader has come to the end of this book, he will indeed know that Vietnam was a lousy war fought by brave men. And that 'is no sh**'!*

Philip Dennis Chinnery
Middlesex, England
October 1987

AUTHOR'S NOTE

Letters from Pleiku *Is the title of Michael Davis O'Donnell's collected Vietnam poetry and is used as the title for this story by kind permission of Michael's sister, Patricia. The work that Michael wrote before he went to Vietnam,* Ice Cream Sundays, *is yet to be published. An ode to Muleskinner: the poem was given to Mike Ryan, Gary Roush's hooch mate, by Major Dutcher. We sincerely hope that the Major survived the war and has the chance to see his poem in print. The full story of Peter J. Giroux's wartime experiences can be found in a report he wrote for the Air Command and Staff College at the Air University, Maxwell AFB, Alabama. The report number is 82-0920 and is entitled 'Fifty-Two Days in Hanoi: A B-52 Pilot's Perspective'. The material quoted from the report has been used with the kind permission of the Air Command and Staff College.*

PART ONE: EARLY DAYS

ALTHOUGH the United States officially became involved in the Vietnam war in August 1964, following the approval by Congress of the Tonkin Gulf Resolution, American servicemen had in fact been fighting in Vietnam for years. American advisers had begun to arrive in the country as the French withdrew after their disastrous defeat at Dien Bien Phu in May 1954. Later that year Vietnam was divided along the 17th parallel into a communist North and a non-communist South, pending elections to decide the issue of reunification.

The elections due to be held in July 1956 never took place, so in 1957 the communist supporters in the South, known as the Viet Cong, began to carry out terrorist attacks against the regime of South Vietnam's President Diem. In May 1959 the communist leader in the North, Ho Chi Minh, announced that the country would be reunified by an armed struggle and prepared to send units of the North Vietnamese Army (NVA) to South Vietnam.

Rather than sending their troops and supplies directly across the ten-mile wide demilitarized zone (DMZ) that divided North and South Vietnam, the North Vietnamese leadership ordered the construction of an infiltration route through Laos and Cambodia to South Vietnam. Unlike the Americans, the North Vietnamese were no respecters of international frontiers and soon their troops began the long journey down the interconnecting tracks and roads that made up the Ho Chi Minh Trail, to fight alongside the Viet Cong in the South.

As the insurgency gathered momentum, American military support was increased. More advisers arrived to train the Army of the Republic of Vietnam (ARVN) and to organize surveillance camps along the border, manned by local tribesmen under Special Forces leadership. At the end of 1961 the first American air support arrived, thinly disguised as the 'Farm Gate' training detachment. Hot on their heels were the first Army helicopter companies, flying their ageing, banana-shaped CH-21 Shawnees. They were soon replaced by the first Bell UH-1 Hueys, and the stories contained in this book will show just how drastically the new helicopter changed the rules of jungle warfare – and, indeed, warfare in general.

At this stage of the war, 1961–63, the 'Farm Gate' detachment and the various helicopter units were present solely in support of the ARVN Divisions. As the pace of the conflict in Vietnam increased and civil war broke out over the border in Laos, American reconnaissance and, later, strike aircraft were deployed to South Vietnam and Thailand.

In August 1964, attacks (both real and imaginary) on American destroyers in the Gulf of Tonkin off North Vietnam led President Johnson to put the Southeast

Asia Resolution before Congress. The approval of this crucial and controversial document effectively gave the President and his advisers the power to direct an undeclared war against North Vietnam.

At that point, the civilian leaders in Washington should have turned the whole matter over to the military, with clear instructions to stop the flow of men and arms into South Vietnam and to destroy Hanoi's ability to support operations against South Vietnam. Unfortunately, the Johnson Administration favoured a campaign of gradually increasing military pressure, rather than the short, sharp air campaign that the Joint Chiefs of Staff recommended.

History has shown that the controls and restrictions imposed by the White House hampered, and eventually bogged down, any hope that the military had of a successful conclusion to the war. In the meantime, American pilots continued to give their all, for a war that they would never be allowed to win.

The six stories in this chapter show the lives of typical pilots during these early years, up to the arrival of the first American combat troops in the autumn of 1965.

FARM GATE

1. Bien Hoa Air Base

*I*N 1961 the Viet Cong began to intensify their guerrilla war against the regime of President Ngo Dinh Diem, and it became obvious that the United States had substantially to increase its military aid to South Vietnam. It was also obvious, however, that the United States Armed Forces had little or no knowledge or expertise in the art of counter-insurgency warfare, and this applied particularly to the Air Force.

President Kennedy ordered that new units be formed to deal with this type of conflict, and in April 1961 the Air Force established the 4400th Combat Crew Training Squadron (CCTS) at Eglin Air Force Base in Florida. The unit was codenamed 'Jungle Jim' and was tasked with learning and developing counter-insurgency tactics, using aircraft more suitable to the conditions prevailing in countries like Vietnam.

In November 1961, with the situation in South Vietnam worsening daily, Detachment 2A of the 4400th CCTS, designated 'Farm Gate', left Eglin for Vietnam. It took with it four SC-47 Skytrain cargo aircraft, eight T-28 trainers and four Douglas B-26 bombers. The bombers were listed as RB-26 reconnaissance aircraft, to stay in line with the Geneva Agreement which forbade the introduction of bombers into Vietnam. The T-28s and B-26s were, however, modified for the ground attack role, and all wore South Vietnamese Air Force markings.

It has proven impossible to track down any of the members of the 'Farm Gate' Detachment, but an advertisement in The Retired Officer magazine caught the eye of retired Major James O. Henry, who was attached to the unit in a unique position which allowed him to view the war and the workings of the first Air Force unit in Vietnam.

My experience with the Farm Gate T-28s came as a requirement by the 13th Air Force Headquarters at Clark Air Base in the Philippines for a tactical analysis of the T-28 and B-26 in Vietnam. They wanted two jocks from the field to do it, so I volunteered from a nuke alert pad in Korea, where I was stationed with the 531st TFS, the same squadron I went to Bien Hoa with in 1965. I proceeded to Clark to work for the Director of Special Operations, 13th Air Force, and my compatriot, who worked on the B-26 project, arrived from the 5th Air Force in Japan.

The reason for the analysis was, I suppose, inter-service rivalry. The Army were claiming they were not receiving the close air support they desired and therefore were embarking on a programme of funding to provide their own close air support. The Air Force viewed this as an encroachment upon a portion of its long standing mission; also, if the Army were successful, it would more than likely divert some Air Force funds for its enactment.

Below: Armed with bombs, rockets, machine-guns and napalm, the Farm Gate T-28s wore South Vietnamese Air Force markings. (via James O. Henry)

As a result, I spent about four months with the Farm Gate detachment at Bien Hoa Air Base, researching their data and compiling it into a 47-page report on the T-28B. I also flew on some supply and training missions with the Farm Gate C-47s. They supplied outlying ARVN troops and Montagnard (Mountainyard) tribes. Much of their cargo at that time was Second World War automatic weapons such as 9mm Schmeissers, Swedish Ks and 45-caliber American Thompsons. I went on a couple of humorous training flights. One was taking a new group of VNAF recruits up on a familiarization flight. I think it was the first time most of them had been on an airplane. We had just gotten airborne when one of them got sick, started throwing up and caused a chain reaction, all of them puking rice and fish all over the aircraft. On another flight, an American Army Captain was taking a group of ARVN Rangers on a low-level night jump. They were to jump from 800 feet and the Captain, a bit concerned about the jump altitude, came up to the C-47 pilots and myself, prior to boarding the plane, and just said 'Would you please be on your altitude, I would hate to have to run 100 yards before my chute gets open'.

The T-28s had been modified with a more powerful engine, self-sealing fuel tanks, armor plating around the seats and fuel sump tank and with the addition of underwing ordnance-carrying stations. The stations were capable of carrying 50-caliber machine gun pods, napalm, general-purpose and fragmentation bombs, rocket launchers and parachute flares. They were rugged aircraft, requiring a minimum of maintenance and capable of operating from relatively unsophisticated airfields. The T-28 and B-26 missions were varied and included close air support, interdiction, visual reconnaissance, armed reconnaissance and armed escort and cover for ground operations. In the ground attack role, each aircraft had different advantages over the other: the B-26 could carry more ordnance, but the T-28 was more maneuverable and presented a smaller target to the enemy on the ground.

Almost without exception, the T-28's targets were either small boats (sampans), wood structures or personnel. Due to the hit-and-run, highly mobile tactics of the Viet Cong, these targets were seldom found in large concentrations. Viet Cong troop concentrations were rarely more than one or two attack companies and the structures no more than ten to fifteen small huts; these were ideal-size targets for a flight of two T-28s. Occasionally, four or more aircraft would be used against a small enemy supply or ammunition concentration, with the size and nature of the target determining the number of aircraft required.

The T-28 pilots discovered by experience that two 500-pound napalm tanks are extremely effective against wood structures and hidden or dug-in troops, while 120-pound fragmentation bomb clusters are very good against scattered troops. The rockets with their high degree of accuracy are better utilized against spot targets such as sampans, while the 50-caliber machine guns combined with the T-28's maneuverability are better employed against highly mobile ground targets.

The techniques used to deliver the ordnance were basic air to ground tactics, modified slightly to adapt to the COIN environment of high jungle and obscured target areas. When employed against ground targets the T-28s would always attack in flights of two, three or four aircraft. This provided a continuous delivery of ordnance and hopefully forced the enemy to keep their heads down, thus improving pilot survivability. Normally, when an attack was begun, the heaviest ordnance (bombs and napalm) was expended first. This was to give the enemy a heavy shock and disrupt his defence, and to lighten the aircraft and allow greater maneuverability. The follow-up attacks would be made with the flight in trail formation, with each succeeding aircraft coming on target as the previous aircraft broke off. Each attack would be made from a different angle to avoid a pattern that would enable the enemy to anticipate the next attack, and the angles and airspeeds would also be varied, according to the ordnance delivered.

Napalm would be delivered in a 20- to 30-degree dive angle with the run beginning at around 2,000 feet and leveling off before the drop was made at 300 to 400 feet, with the aircraft staying low until clear of the target area. A rocket-firing dive would begin with a 30-degree angle of attack, with the rockets being fired at around 1,200 feet and the aircraft pulling out at 500 feet.

The restrictions on ordnance delivery specified that all in-country strikes be made under the direction of a VNAF Forward Air Controller, who usually flew a Cessna O-1 Bird Dog and would approve and mark the target with smoke for the attacking T-28s. The system at this early stage had many failings, as these extracts from two 3 January 1963 pilot mission reports illustrate:

'Mission 044. Victor flight of T-28s arrived in the area and rendezvoused with FAC Skylark. Victor heard calls from ground, both American and Vietnamese speaking English, requesting the T-28 give support to them as they were under heavy ground fire from the enemy. Skylark did not acknowledge. Victor asked Skylark if he was getting these calls and asked if they could strike in support of the ground troops. Skylark indicated he heard the calls, and then continued to circle the area without going to the aid of the troops. The ground troops laid out ground panels and put out smoke and again asked the T-28 flight for assistance.

'After about twenty minutes Skylark went to the ground troops, looked the area over and finally dropped smoke and directed Victor to make two passes, with rockets and guns. After making these two passes

Above right: Napalm, a very effective weapon against troops in the open or inflammable structures. (via James O. Henry) Right: Farm Gate T-28s attacking a Viet Cong position with napalm. (US Air Force)

Skylark ordered Victor to climb to 2,500 feet and remain for air cover. Victor informed Skylark they still had frags, but Skylark repeated his instructions to orbit. Victor orbited the area until relieved by Arrow Blue. Victor was disturbed that the ground troops continued to ask for strike but were ignored by Skylark, and when strike was finally authorized all ordnance was not expended before Victor again had to climb out.

'Mission 045. FAC Delta Papa and Skylark. Friendly troops were taking refuge in a village while under attack from VC force. Papa marked VC position with white smoke but did not ask for air strike. Artillery fire was used instead. Friendly village was between the VC force and the friendly

Right: Major James O. Henry (left), having flown his 2,000th hour in the F-100, during his second tour in Vietnam with the 531st TFS. Lieutenant Howard (right) was later killed flying an F-4 with the 'Thunderbirds' display team. Colonel White (centre) now flies for United Airlines. (via James O. Henry)

artillery, making it necessary for the artillery to fire over the friendly village. Artillery was adjusted but this fell short of the VC and directly into the friendly position. Approximately fifteen rounds hit the village, destroying approximately one dozen structures. One round barely missed one of the helicopters on the ground that had been shot down the day before.

'When X-Ray (the cover T-28s) departed the area, friendly choppers were removing the friendly dead and wounded from the village. X-Ray 2 heard two helicopter pilots talking over the radio. One asked the other if the mutiny was confirmed and the other answered in the affirmative. No other conversation was heard on this subject. X-Ray felt that an air

strike would have been more appropriate against the VC concentration, especially in light of the fact that the artillery had to fire over the friendly position. X-Ray was relieved by Arrow Violet and returned to Bien Hoa without expending ordnance'.

The air support organization clearly had a way to go to become an efficient and effective contributor to the war effort. Change was coming, however, and the summer of 1963 saw the 'Farm Gate' detachment reinforced and then replaced by the 1st Air Commando Squadron. As time went by, dozens more squadrons arrived, and in 1965 James Henry returned to Vietnam again to spend a year flying the F-100 Super Sabre out of Bien Hoa. He returned home in one piece and can now look back objectively on the war and the reasons why it was not won.

I think there are several causes of failure.

1.   The field commanders were not allowed to run the battle. When targets are directed from Washington off aerial photos and bomb run headings are prescribed so as to avoid orphanages and other humane obstructions in preference to the avoidance of SAM sites, it is, without question, an invitation to failure. On many of our missions in the south, one aircraft in the flight carried an elaborate camera pod mounted on the centerline, with fore-and-aft-aimed 16mm color motion cameras, activated with the gun trigger and bomb/rocket button. This film was sent to Washington so the bureaucrats could attempt to keep up with what was going on.

2.   The refusal by Washington to allow the cut-off, by interdiction, of the supply of NVA troops and equipment coming down from the North. This should have been done prior to it becoming a flood in the 1968–70 time frame, by leveling Haiphong first and Hanoi second.

3.   The media coverage that turned American opinion against US involvement. The majority of the civilian populace will not relate to burned bodies. I would not quarrel with media coverage, but to neutralize public opinion we needed equal coverage to come from the enemy side of the line to show equal atrocities of war, if it would have been possible.

4.   The war dragged on so long, experience of personnel became a factor. When I left Vietnam, I returned to Luke AFB, Arizona, and was instructing in a squadron training replacement pilots for SEA. I was distressed by the caliber of the replacements we were working with – pilots who had little or no fighter experience, and older pilots, some with three or four years to retirement and most who had no desire to go to SEA.

If failure to win had to be attributed to one person, my vote would go to Robert McNamara and his insatiable desire for numbers, statistics and control. His commitment against delegating authority in any form was quite evident.

UP THE RIVER UNDER THE CLOUDS

2

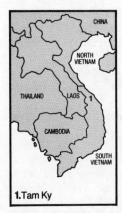

1.Tam Ky

O NE of the more pleasant discoveries made by the author during his research was that a good number of former Vietnam pilots are either writing their autobiographies or intend to. One person who has begun the task is William E. McGee, who flew Hueys and fixed-wing aircraft in Vietnam during the early days of 1963–64. A heavy work load has post-poned further work on his autobiography, but Bill has kindly sent one of his stories for inclusion in this book because, as he says, 'It is more important that the story be told than who tells the story'.

Log book entry: 3 January 1964. Nobody likes to work on Saturday even in Vietnam, but there we were at 0500 hours in the mess hall, forcing down scrambled powdered eggs and slightly soggy toast. Our briefing had been short and simple: be at the soccer field at Tam Ky at 0600 hours to take an ARVN Province Chief and his American adviser to inspect their line units. CWO Kirkham and I ate early chow in the empty mess hall along with the two gunship pilots. We seldom flew single-ship missions and this was no exception.

Kirk looked through the screens into the pre-dawn darkness and sighed, 'This is a helluva way to spend a Saturday morning!' Someone else said, 'Well, it still counts toward your thirty years.' We laughed.

I estimated thirty minutes' flying time from Quang Ngai to our pick-up point and fifteen minutes for the aircraft pre-flight inspection, which left us enough time for another cup of coffee. We refilled our mugs and returned to the table. I reached for the bottle of chloroquine tablets. The freshly brewed coffee was hot and helped wash down the quinine taste. The chloroquine was supposed to prevent malaria, but about half the unit was only pretending to take the tablets in the hope of contracting malaria and being shipped home early.

I checked my watch and slugged down the rest of my coffee: 'Time to go.' One of the other pilots came out with the old John Wayne cliché, 'Saddle up and move 'em out,' as we grabbed our helmet bags and slung on the bulky flak vests. As we walked out the screen door of the mess hall, also known as 'Chez Louis,' Kirk called out, 'My compliments to the chef.' The sleepy GI who had served the meal flipped us a bird once our backs were turned. 'Smart-ass officers,' he mumbled under his breath and returned to his thoroughly worn, six-month-old Playboy magazine.

The four of us walked silently in the damp darkness across the PSP apron to the Hueys. Our pre-flights were slowed because we had to use flashlights. About halfway through the inspection, the rain started. It came pelting down in sheets across the runway, chasing us inside the Huey. We dove inside, slamming the door behind us. The crew chief and gunner were halfway between the maintenance shack and the other side of our Huey when the rain hit. They were both drenched by the time they tumbled into the chopper. 'Beautiful day, isn't it?' grinned Sergeant Malone, our crew chief.

The gunner, Corporal Young, was a new guy from the 25th Infantry Division in Hawaii. 'Does this mean they'll cancel the mission?' he asked hopefully.

'No way, Jose,' said Kirkham. 'This is the rainy season. We'll be in and out of this stuff all day long. Lots of fun.'

'I completed the Daily Inspection just before you got here,' offered Sergeant Malone. 'If you'll take my word for it, this bird is ready to fly.'

'I'll take your word because you're flying with us, Sergeant,' was my reply. 'If this Huey falls out of the sky, it's your ass as well as ours.' I would have taken his word anyway. Malone was the best crew chief in the 117th, a real quality individual.

The control tower was closed, so we taxied out to the runway and made a slow, hovering, 360-degree turn to clear ourselves for take off.

Kirk said, 'Looks OK to me. Hell, anyone with any sense is still asleep in the sack, not out flying at this time of day.' He was right too.

I glanced over my shoulder and got 'thumbs up' signals from Malone and Corporal Young. The gunship called in ready to go too. I pulled pitch, holding forward pressure on the cyclic stick, pointing us down the runway. The two Hueys gathered speed and climbed out together heading north. We reached a safe altitude and followed the coastline flying in a loose formation.

Kirkham broke the silence. 'My, but it sure is a beautiful morning now that the rain has stopped. Look at that sunrise!' We all nodded and continued enjoying the coming daylight and the rhythmic vibration of our rotor blades slapping the humid air. I turned out over the South China Sea and pressed the mike button: 'You guys want to fire a few bursts at the water just to see if those M-60s still work?' It was Corporal Young's first mission and he nervously pulled off more rounds than necessary. What the hell – after a few more rides he'd settle down. The gunship called in that their weapons checked out OK. We were all set for whatever lay ahead.

Kirkham was flying now and turned the formation back to the coastline. The low clouds and fog hung in the valleys like white lakes amid green hilltops. After another ten minutes, we saw our checkpoint and turned, flying west until the hamlet of Tam Ky came into view. Our landing area was the soccer field, identified by jeeps and ARVN troops around its perimeter. Someone on the ground threw a smoke grenade, which was standard procedure but today was entirely unnecessary. At least it indicated the wind direction.

After landing, I shook hands with the American adviser, Major Smith. Smith then introduced the pilots to his counterpart, the ARVN Trung Ta (Lieutenant Colonel). He was all business and quickly pulled out his map, pointing to the location of the strike force he wanted to visit. Kirkham and I noted that it was up a river valley, and, from the closeness of the contour lines, the hills on each side of the river were steeply sloped right down to the water. In good weather it would be an easy flight in and out with a steep landing descent into the strike force camp. Today would be another story, because we would have to fly low-level under the clouds that still hung in the valleys.

I motioned Major Smith to one side and outlined the situation concerning the clouds and the terrain. 'It will be a hairy ride up that twisting valley. We will be more vulnerable to ground fire at the slower speeds we'll have to fly. The walls of the valley are so close on each side of the river, we won't be able to make a flying turn. I don't know if the base of the clouds gets lower as we go farther up-river. If we lose visual contact with the ground, we'll be in deep trouble. My advice would be to wait for an hour and see if the clouds lift.'

The Major just smiled and said that he didn't think that we would chicken out on him – that would cause him to lose face in the eyes of his ARVN counterpart. 'Whatever happened to completing the mission, Captain?' I was being baited and challenged, and I knew it. I reminded him that you couldn't complete a mission if you flew your aircraft into a mountain, killing everyone on board. 'Let's wait for half an hour and maybe the sun will burn off the clouds.'

He just smiled, shaking his head, and walked back to explain the delay to the Trung Ta. The ARVN Lieutenant Colonel excitedly reminded Major Smith that they would be late for his inspection tour. Smith's explanation about the weather fell on deaf ears as we were standing in the sunlight under a nearly cloudless sky. Besides that, the MAAG had been telling the ARVN that Americans were invincible. The Vietnamese probably thought that we could walk through walls. Hell, flying in the clouds up a narrow river valley should be a piece of cake for these Americans!

I returned to the two flight crews. 'OK, we're supposed to get this ARVN Lieutenant Colonel and Major Disaster up river to an encampment within the next half hour. I'm of a mind to wait for a while and let the ground fog burn off, but Major Disaster wants to go now. We'll fly in trail formation; don't follow too closely. We might get surprised coming around one of those river bends. If we start getting stitched by heavy ground fire, I'll give you the word and we'll climb into the clouds at max rpm, OK?' My ship will climb straight ahead maintaining our last heading. Gunship, you can turn ten degrees left or right of our last heading, your option, but maintain that heading until we break out of the clouds on top! Any questions?'

Everybody collectively muttered an 'oh sh**' to himself as we walked to the Hueys. I signalled to our passengers, who came immediately, smiling. 'I knew you'd see it my way, Captain,' smiled the Major, as they strapped themselves into their seat belts.

Malone stood out front with a fire extinguisher in his hand. I yelled to him 'Rotors clear?' Malone yelled back 'Clear' and circled his hand overhead – clear to start engine. As soon as we had power, I keyed the mike button and said to Kirkham, 'I really let us get conned into this one. I'll fly in, you fly out, OK? Keep on that map so we don't overfly the ARVN camp. They'll have panels on a sandbar and will throw red smoke as a recognition for us to land. Even though we'll be going slowly, yell out as soon as you see their signals.'

Malone jumped into his seat and strapped on the seat belt, then gave me a thumbs-up. The gunship called in ready and off we went. The UH-1 Huey has a powerful turbine engine, which can carry huge payloads and allows for spectacular take-offs, but was deadly unforgiving to pilots who didn't plan ahead or fly smart. Keep ahead of the aircraft was what we were told in training.

Navigation would not be our problem today. The river was right there for us to follow. As we gained altitude, the white clouds in the river valley became apparent. I leveled off at 50 feet and shot a quick glance over my shoulder at our passengers. The impact of the situation still hadn't quite registered with them. I headed to the middle of the river and decreased our altitude to ten feet above the water; our airspeed was 80 knots.

We were about to enter the cloudy tunnel of the river valley when we struck a wire strung across the river. It slapped the windshield and skipped upward until it hit the airscoop, which cut the wire. It had happened so fast we just barely had time to realize what had happened when we hit another wire. This one caught the skid. Malone later said we pulled up a pole before the wire finally snapped. The Hueys raced forward, skimming the water. What more could happen, we wondered?

The staccato of Sergeant Malone's M-60 jerked me a little higher in my seat. I hadn't noticed the muzzle flashes of ground fire, but we were under fire from the left river bank, now rapidly diminishing behind us. Kirk called to the gunship behind us who laid down some neat stitching of their own. 'Young, remember the location of that fire – it'll be on your side on the way out', I called into the intercom.

As we swerved around the curves of the river, I noticed three things that tightened the knot in my stomach: the river was getting narrower, the sides of the mountains closer and the cloud ceiling lower. I called back to the gunship, 'Reducing speed to 70 knots, acknowledge.' They called back, 'Roger, leader. 70 knots.'

We jumped a waterfall, swerved around another curve and suddenly there was the sandbar and the red smoke billowing. I flared the Huey and keyed the mike simultaneously: 'We're here!' The gunship had to swing to our right and flared sideways. They kicked rudder and we both settled onto the wet sand together, just as if we had rehearsed the maneuver a hundred times.

Our two passengers bounded out of the Huey, bent over, holding onto their hats until they passed out from under the still spinning rotor blades. Kirkham and I just sat there for a minute in silence before we could start the shut-down sequence. The eight flight crew members gradually gathered as the main rotor blades finally stopped turning. Malone tied down the big blade and began checking his ship for damage. I may have flown that ship occasionally, but emotionally it was Malone's ship. I wouldn't have had it any other way either.

Kirk had found an ARVN with coffee for us. Oh man, just what we needed! Each of the flight crews grabbed a cup and everyone began talking at once. Funny, but our voices were a little higher than usual and we were jabbering at a rate three times faster than we normally talked. The coffee was hot and, even though not particularly good, really hit the spot. We started to relax, and out came the cameras. First someone would take a picture of the ARVN camp, then someone would take a picture of him taking the picture, and I took a photo of everyone taking everyone else's picture. This had to be the most photographed war in history.

Finally our passengers returned and the knot in my stomach tightened. The clouds had not burned off – they had probably lowered. No telling what was happening on top or back at the sea coast either. Well, we made it in – we can make it back out!

Major Disaster smiled at me and said, 'I just knew you could make it if you gave it a try'. It suddenly occurred to me why most enlisted men hate most officers. What a complete jerk! 'Well, hold on, sir. The ride out may be a bit hairier, because those VC down river know that we have to come out the same way we went in. We can't go any higher, but we're sure going out faster than when we came in!'

It was Kirk's turn to fly. We all strapped in and tightened the chin straps of our flight helmets. The gunship called 'Up', and we both lifted to a hover. 'Adios, muchachos!' said Kirk as he nosed the Huey forward out over the river. Both ships gathered speed and we whipped around the river bend, heading downstream. Kirk kept us low, skimming the water at high speed. The anticipated lifting of the clouds had not happened. As we approached our attack point, Corporal Young let loose with his M-60, the bullets hitting the water. Using them as a reference, he deliberately brought the deadly trail upward toward the tree line on the river bank. Good boy! Keep them down. Now we're past. Home free . . . oh-oh! There's a tall tree about half a mile ahead. No, we can't go over it and the valley is too narrow to go around it. I wasn't sure what I would have done, but then I wasn't flying. I wondered what Kirkham had in mind.

A quarter of a mile away and closing fast. Still we haven't varied our speed or altitude at all. Closer . . . If we continue like this, the body of the Huey will miss the tree, but the main rotor blades will hit it about ten feet down from the top. I didn't think we would come out on the winning end of that meeting. Closer . . . I didn't think that Kirkham was suicidal. I wonder if he used to play 'chicken' in hot rods on Saturday nights back in Oklahoma? Closer . . . A glance over my shoulder showed two very concerned and somewhat terrified passengers. Closer still . . . Airspeed 100 knots and closing fast. I told myself to keep my hands off the controls – Kirkham must have a plan.

We were almost in the branches! Kirkham made a fast lateral movement of the control stick and as we passed within two feet of the tall mahogany tree, our main rotor blades are skillfully tilted to an angle to allow us to shoot past without ruffling the feathers of a perched bird! Suddenly we were past the terrible Huey-eating tree and the sunny plain of the sea coast lay ahead.

The soccer field came into view and Kirk landed slowly and gently. I keyed the mike to ask, 'Where did you ever learn that maneuver?'

'Oh, it just seemed like the right thing to do at the time,' he said. Sergeant Malone helped the two passengers out of the aircraft. Their faces were as white as chalk. As they hunched their way out from under the spinning blades, I called to the Major. 'Just call us anytime you need a ride.'

He yelled back, 'Don't hold your breath until I call.' Sergeant Malone's voice came over the intercom. 'I'm holding my breath already, sir. I think they sh** their pants when we passed that tree back there.'

FIRST BLOOD

3

1. Korat Royal Thai Air Force Base
2. Plain of Jars, Northern Laos

*I*N July 1964, as the air war in South-East Asia was starting to hot up, the 36th Tactical Fighter Squadron was deployed to Korat Royal Thai Air Force Base with its Republic F-105 Thunderchiefs. The pilots were eager to try out their skills with the 'new' -31 variant of the 'Thud' which they had received a year earlier, and by August they were champing at the bit.

Korat was a hot, muggy, desolate place, where the main activity, if not flying training sorties, was drinking at the Officers Club. To pilots like First Lieutenant Dave Graben the waiting around for something to happen was becoming unbearable. Graben had worked his way through North Dakota State University by giving flight instruction and flying charter in light planes. After graduating in 1960 he entered the Air Force Pilot Training Program and finished first in his class in primary, basic and gunnery courses. He had also won the Daedalians Orville Wright Achievement Award, and with a record like this it was no surprise to find him in the forefront of the action when the 'scramble' was sounded.

Within minutes the standby flight of four F-105s was accelerating down the 9,000-foot runway at Korat, en route to the Plain of Jars in Laos. The Flight Lead was Captain Jack Stressing (now deceased) and his wingman was Dave Graben.

When we arrived in the target area an Air America T-28 was there, acting as a Forward Air Controller. We had some trouble finding the exact target position because of scattered cloud and the lush green jungle all looking the same from 15,000 feet. Jack finally pinpointed the target area where a 37mm gun site had been causing problems for the T-28s.

Jack put us in trail and rolled in with a 'Let's see if we can wake them up.' I was about 1,500 to 2,000 feet behind Jack and watched as he opened

Left: William E. McGee with his UH-1B, painted in a camouflage scheme unique to the 117th Aviation Company and armed with 2.75-inch rockets and the XM-6 Quad machine-gun system. (William E. McGee)

up with his M-61 gatling gun. As I came into gun range the 37mm gun site opened up and red 'golf balls' began to float up at me. I broke right and simultaneously felt a thump as a 37mm shell struck home. I called 'Two's off and I'm hit,' jettisoned my fuel tanks and ordnance and lit the afterburner. As I started a left climbing turn a fire warning light came on. It was well known at the time that a fire in the aft fuselage would almost always end up in a catastrophic explosion. My selecting the afterburner aspirated the tail area and kept the fire from going forward under the aft fuel cell and causing an explosion. The Thud was later modified with an air scoop that kept the air flow going from the front to the rear along the outside of the engine.

Right: An F-105 Thunderchief firing a pod of rockets at an enemy target. (US Air Force)

Jack searched for me and started a rejoin as I climbed out to 39,000 feet. When I leveled off and assessed my situation, the engine, a Pratt and Whitney J-75, was running fine and the fire warning light was out. I had lost my utility hydraulic system but P1 and P2, the flight control hydraulic systems, were in the green. I had no speed brakes, the in-flight refueling probe had extended without my command and I would have no flaps or hydraulic brakes on landing.

I could extend the landing gear via the emergency system, so I concluded that a landing could be pulled off at Korat with a high degree of success. Controllability was checked after Jack 'came aboard' and described the damage to my tail section. A large, two-feet-square

Above: Lieutenant Dave Graben after safely landing his damaged F-105 (US Air Force)

hole had been blown in the leading edge of the left stabilator, and the aft fuselage had been riddled with shrapnel holes. There also appeared to be a large hole in the bottom of the aircraft, near the exhaust pipe. However, I touched down slightly fast at Korat and deployed the drag chute, coasting to a halt with room to spare. Afterwards I was recommended for a Distinguished Flying Cross (DFC), but could not receive it because we were not at war at the time!

The F-105 'Thud' had received its baptism of fire and brought its pilot home, despite the damage. In the years to come many more pilots would be brought home by their battered, leaking Thunderchiefs as they began to carry the war north, to Hanoi.

Between 1964 and 1972 a total of 334 F-105s were lost in combat, and a further 63 were lost for operational reasons. 'Combat losses' were aircraft shot down by MiGs, SAMs or anti-aircraft fire; 'operational losses' included aircraft running out of fuel on the way home and mid-air collisions. With such a reputation, it was no wonder that Robert B. Piper was a little apprehensive when he was notified of his posting to Vietnam to fly the Thud.

I was a student at Air Force Command and Staff College when I first received word that I had been volunteered for a tour in Thuds in Vietnam. The week before I received this news, Rand Corporation gave a briefing to the class on their analysis of the Thud missions to date. Their conclusions were that, during a 100-mission tour, one should expect to be shot down twice and picked up once! They were trying to convince HQ Air Force that the tour should be shortened to 75 missions over the North. Needless to say, this did not give one a great deal of enthusiasm for the assignment. A standard Thud joke defined an optimist as a Thud pilot who gives up smoking . . .

Fortunately the Rand Corporation were working with an incomplete data package when they did their study. By the time I arrived in Vietnam, the Thuds had improved their survivability by a combination of a change of tactics and the use of a jamming pod to make the SAMs essentially ineffective.

The 'Catch-22' atmosphere continued . . . When I arrived at the squadron in Thailand, I was greeted by the old-heads (pilots with 20 or more missions over the North) with the expression, 'If I had to fly 100 missions over the North, I'd shoot myself'. This turned out to be the standard greeting for the new guy.

I was assigned a hootch, and when I walked in I found my roommate asleep on one bed and a large box (six feet by three feet by three feet) occupying most of the rest of the room. My new roommate woke up long enough to say hello and explain that the box contained his ex-roommate's stuff. His roommate had been shot down and they were collecting up his stuff to send home. I felt like Yossarian and wondered if I was going to have 'the missing man in Yossarian's tent' experience.

Flying combat was not anything like I expected. We are spoiled by the movies and TV. In the real world there is no background music, the flak does not make loud noises (unless it hits you) and, particularly in Vietnam, the missions did not accomplish much. The first missions were the scariest. One was worried about making a mistake and thereby getting oneself killed or captured.

After a few missions, one realizes that it is a big crap-shoot. There were, or course, things you could do wrong, but generally it was a random selection process that determined who got hit and who didn't. Pilots would get shot off your wing doing the same things you were doing. Their only error was being in the piece of air where the shell exploded. I was always amazed at how many times we flew through all the flak and SAMs with no one getting hit. My training in statistics told me that this was possible but not probable . . .

One interesting anomaly that did surface in Vietnam was superstitions. Thud pilots were, or became, very superstitious. They would have established routines that they would go through before a mission and it was almost worth your life not to interrupt these routines – a special seat on the van that carried the pilots to the aircraft (I saw a pilot throw another pilot off the van because he would not give him his seat), giving a special 100-mission hat (an Australian bush hat) to the crew chief before getting in the aircraft (a fight broke out when a pilot took the hat as a joke), or wearing a special artefact or item of clothing (a scarf, religious medal, special pin, etc.).

When I arrived, our squadron had not had anyone with a mustache shot down, so I started a mustache. Vietnam is hot and humid and the mustache, particularly in the oxygen mask, is uncomfortable, so I shaved mine off. The next mission I took my only hit in 100 missions. Knowing full well that it was just a coincidence, I grew back my mustache, and didn't even trim it, after that. As I used to say, 'I'm not superstitious . . . I'm not superstitious . . . I'm not superstitious.' There, I said it three times.

Left: Robert B. Piper wearing the moustache that protected him during his 100 combat missions in the F-105. The World War One helmet was worn on the last flight. (Robert B. Piper)

EARLY DAYS 4

1. Tan Son Nhut Air Base
2. Ban Me Thuot
3. Plei Me

THE summer and autumn of 1965 saw the beginning of the American build-up in South Vietnam. No Division-sized units had arrived yet, but several Brigades and huge numbers of support troops were making processing centres, à la World War Two Repodepots, necessary. A handful of helicopter units had arrived, and Captain William H. Zierdt was on his way to join one of them, the 155th Assault Helicopter Company.

My first arrival in Vietnam was 11 September 1965. The charter flight had been from Travis Air Force Base via Honolulu and Clark Air Base in the Philippines. My recollections are of saying goodbye to my parents, wife and children on the tarmac at Friendship Airport (now Baltimore-Washington International) and of arriving in Saigon. The time between those events is a complete blank, though we must have gotten from San Fransisco Airport to Travis by bus and the stops in Honolulu and Clark must have had some interest, as I had never before traveled west of the coast. Certainly we were processed at Travis, and military processing is usually unforgettable.

Taxiing to the terminal provided a rush of excitement – after all, my entire productive life had been spent preparing to go to war, and this was it! Tan Son Nhut was wall to wall airplanes. They were mostly F-4s, F-100s, C-123s, C-130s, A-1s and Hueys. A separate apron had a collection of World War Two transports with strange or no markings. A lonely Caravelle and the DC-8 we were arriving on were the only non-combatants in sight.

As the door opened we were struck by the famous aroma of Indo-China, so revolting initially but rapidly an unnoticed part of daily existence. The civilian crew was over-anxious to get us off, a new load on, and be on their way back to Clark. The military crew meeting us were no less obnoxious in their desire to get us out of the terminal and into the hands of whoever was to process us.

The 200 of us were, rapidly and literally, herded onto flat-bed trucks encircled with wide mesh wire. Benches ran down both sides and the center, but standing was more comfortable for the seemingly endless but only two-mile trip to Camp Alpha.

The Field Grade officers were immediately separated from the group and, as soon as the baggage arrived, were moved somewhere else. Company officers, non-commissioned officers and enlisted men were aimed at three separate rows of SEA huts, the plywood, screen and corrugated metal buildings with which the US Army endeavored to cover Vietnam.

An hour later there was an announcement that our processing and first 'in-country briefing' was about to begin. Processing amounted to our personnel folders being collected; the briefing was a thing of beauty. A Lieutenant Colonel, CO Camp Alpha, informed us that there would be a work formation each morning at 0730 hours and threatened various horrible punishments for infringements of the never elucidated regulations of Camp Alpha. He was followed by a bored, monotonous enlisted medic who spent thirty minutes assuring us that sexual contact with 'indigenous personnel' would result in immediate and disastrous consequences with long-term implications. End of first 'in-country briefing'. So much for motherhood, apple pie and baseball. It took about ten minutes to find a cab to the Rex Hotel.

In September of 1965, Saigon was swollen with refugees, but not completely inundated nor overwhelmed with the later American presence. Away from Tan Son Nhut, the Embassy and a few headquarters areas, foreign influence could be avoided. Decent food was still available in restaurants, and the beauty of the city had not been completely eroded. Ships were still being unloaded onto lighters in the river; legitimate shops were still functioning in competition with the black market. A few months later none of this would be so.

The view from the cab was my first of the Far East. The view from the roof-top bar of the Rex was European: the Caravelle Hotel, a Renault dealership, a cobblestone roundabout, a street of banks of French architecture, tiny yellow and blue Renault cabs, Vespas everywhere. Part way through my first San Miguel a classmate showed up.

Bertie and I reminisced through the afternoon, catching up on our separate doings for six years. He was on his third 'short tour' with the Special Forces and knew Saigon particularly well. We had dinner at an Italian restaurant in some back alley. The staff and decor were all Corsican, the food excellent and the clientele European. I never found it again.

.Assignments were still not available – 'officers be back in the morning'. As the senior inhabitant of Camp Alpha, I appointed myself to visit the commander and inquire what could be done to get us all on our ways. He was still, or again, drunk, but listened to my concern politely, made a phone call and assured me that our processing was being expedited. It appeared that Camp Alpha was using a delayed reporting scheme to hold the labor they needed to complete building the facilities. It took a further week and a visit to Headquarters, Military Assistance Command Vietnam to discover what our assignments were.

Other than actually verifying my assignment and saying that the company to which I was being assigned was not in its base at Ban Me Thuot, the 52nd Aviation Battalion Liaison Officer was supremely uninterested in my presence or desire to get to my unit. He did not know where the unit was, how to get hold of it, or when or how I could get transport. He suggested I wait at Camp Alpha until processing was complete.

On the ninth day, frustration was running high and I appropriated a jeep, loaded my footlocker and parachute bag and went over to the ramp of unmarked aircraft. I wandered around operations and the ramp inquiring as to whether anyone was bound for Ban Me Thuot. Eventually, a C-123 pilot of unidentifiable nationality allowed that he would be passing over and could drop me in Ban Me Thuot. The aircraft was completely without markings, the crew was nonidentifiable and seemed to be of different nationalities, and there was no communication among them throughout the flight. The crew chief helped me load my bags and promptly went to sleep, the two pilots climbed into their seats, and I swung the jumpseat out to sit between them.

We passed over what I later learned was Bien Hoa on takeoff and proceeded over Dalat, then north to Ban Me Thuot. Much of the flight was on top and rather fewer than half the instruments seemed to be working. In about two hours we landed on a seemingly deserted airstrip where I had been assured that I would find a complete Assault Helicopter Company with supporting units. In a few hours I would know the difference between Ban Me Thuot City airport, where my company was based, and Ban Me Thuot East airport, where I had just been dropped.

There were a few Regional Force/Popular Force guard towers with sleeping teenagers who were not too interested in my arrival or isolation. Finally, one placed a call on a field phone and about an hour later a jeep arrived from the MACV advisory team to the 23rd ARVN Division. I explained my situation to the driver and he drove me to Ban Me Thuot City airport where I found a small tent city and what passed as the rear echelon for an absent Assault Helicopter Company. It was then designated A Company, 1st Aviation Battalion, having been detached from the First Infantry Division at Fort Riley, Kansas, some seven months previously. It was shortly to be redesignated as the 155th Assault Helicopter Company, a part of the 52nd Aviation Battalion in Pleiku, another hour's flight to the north.

It was believed that the company was in Bien Hoa and that there would be a maintenance run in the next few days. 'Find a bed and settle in.' I fell asleep wondering whether the young privates at Camp Alpha knew that the whores across the street were 'indigenous personnel'. Within a day or so the maintenance run arrived to drop off some people ready to return home and pick up some spare parts. I returned to Bien Hoa with the flight, had my 'in-country check-ride' en route and discovered that the unit was about forty miles from Tan Son Nhut. During the entire time that I was trying to get to them, they were a couple of hours by jeep away. The company was laagered on a short airstrip north of Bien Hoa, at the confluence of what were referred to as War Zones C and D – the Iron Triangle. We were in direct support of the Royal Australian Regiment and the New Zealand artillery units supporting the Aussies.

Upon joining the 155th AHC, I found a field-dwelling helicopter company. The Darlac Plateau, or Central Highlands, where Ban Me Thuot was located, was generally free of military activity. Other than a few Viet Cong hospitals, staging areas and infiltration routes, there was essentially nothing going on between Di Lin and Pleiku. What little activity there was, was being watched by several widely spread Special Forces camps. Located in the middle of this, we spent most of our time supporting operations in other parts of the country. In the first three months we were functioning from Ca Mau in the Delta to Quang Tri by the DMZ.

Much time was spent along the central coast from Nha Trang to Qui Nhon and some of the valleys on the east side of the mountains – Ben Cat, Ben Tre. On this operation I just joined, the entire 52nd Aviation Battalion – 117th, 118th, 119th and 155th Assault Helicopter Companies – was attached to the 145th Aviation Battalion, based at Bien Hoa. They went home at night; we slept in the helicopters and ate C rations.

I was linked up with an experienced and older warrant officer for breaking in and building time in the helicopter. He was killed on a subsequent tour in a Sikorsky Crane that was shot down. Shortly after dark we settled down with the aircraft, set for a quick start. When operating from unprotected areas we went through a full pre-start right up to pulling the starter trigger and then turned off the master switch. In the event of attack we could turn on the master, pull the trigger and depart on a planned course, blacked out. We only used the procedure a few times, but were always ready.

The enlisted crew – crew chief and door gunner – were on perimeter security with most of the others. At the northeast end of the clay strip, which barely held two companies, was a Regional Force/Popular Force (Ruff Puff) installation of some sort. They were responsible for local security but were fully a kilometer away. We posted ours.

About 0200 hours, the ruff puffs opened up with machine guns in all directions – including ours. Chuck dove out one side of the helicopter and I the other. We ran into each other at the nose. He was loading a belt into an M-60 and screaming 'What's the immediate action on this son of a bitch?' He had not been flying long enough to forget the basics.

The perimeter settled down, we wiped the mud off and sat and talked the rest of the night. In the morning all the helicopters were well checked for damage. Our gunship had a round lodged in a rocket pod. They were parked hot, too, and had it gone it would have been right up the tail pipe of another gunship. Essentially no damage.

Above: Captain William H. Zeirdt with waitresses from Ban Me Thuot Officers Mess in January 1966. (William H. Zeirdt)

The next day was my first combat assault or GRF (Grand Rat F***) as they were popularly called. It was a two-battalion affair with artillery but no air support. Five sorties for two aviation battalions into about three different landing zones. The troops were the 173rd Airborne Brigade and the Royal Australian Regiment. We had the Aussies and stayed with them for several weeks. There were no Chinooks in-country yet and I do not know how the artillery moved. Probably by road after the assaults.

The pre-mission briefing had an impressive array of intelligence information. It ended with the statement that no friendlies had ever operated in the area previously. Chuck and I flew left wing on the lead 'V' of the lead company. On the first landing, we were immediately beside a wrecked H-21. This was the first indication that perhaps the institutional memory was somewhat scrambled by rotation. I never again took the intelligence reports too seriously – even on my second tour as G-2 of the 101st Airborne.

It was a fairly quiet day. There was light grazing fire on the landing zone of the first lift, but it was quiet for the next four. It was a good training day for me with quite long legs to practice formation flight. We were done by mid-morning and began to resupply and support in single-ship missions. We worked with the Aussies and Kiwis for several weeks and found them to be competent, pleasant and easy to work with. The only problems were fights over who got the Budweiser and who got the Swan lager. We would load only the Swan for them – we reasoned that if they made the stuff, they could drink it.

During this several weeks we rotated our ships through Bien Hoa, where our maintenance was set up, for 100-hour inspections. Intermediates we did in the field, but we did get a chance to clean up occasionally and visit. This was still a time when most commissioned aviators knew most others. It would still be a year or more until Fort Rucker would be cranking out 800 pilots a month and even then most would be warrants.

We returned to Ban Me Thuot in late October for a few weeks of maintenance of birds and crews. The flight home was one of which I

Left: These UH-1s with white bands and black diamonds on the nose are from Bill Zeirdt's 155th Assault Helicopter Company and were photographed in September 1965. (William H. Zeirdt)

still have many pictures. Mostly VFR formation on top among towering cumulus with a radar vector into Ban Me Thuot. We landed in formation on the runway and hopped one at a time over fences into our pads. It was a safety officer's nightmare, but we had no trouble during my year there.

During this time in BMT the word came to turn in our Bird Dogs. Each helicopter company had two O-1s. Sometime early in helicopter thinking, it was decided that each helicopter company should have two airplanes. They were intended for artillery spotting and staying at altitude to vector the low-flying helicopters to their targets. Placing two reciprocating-engine airplanes with 26 turbine helicopters proved to be a logistics nightmare. Simply put, who cared about them? Most new aviators were rotary wing qualified only, anyway.

I volunteered to take one to Nha Trang though I had not flown an airplane for more than a year and these two birds had not flown for a couple months. There were only three of us qualified and the company commander would not get near them. A started pre-flight inspection showed that which would only scare me. We drained a quart or so of water from each tank, hand propped it and off I went. The left magneto wasn't quite right and everything electrical stopped before I crossed the mountains.

The descent through the clouds was about three miles out to sea – faster than the Hueys, surprise! I put on an air show until the tower got the picture and gave me a green light and then had to ground-loop it to stop on the maintenance ramp – no brakes. It was painted grey and given to the Air Force for Forward Air Controllers.

About six months later in Saigon I ran into a FAC from Ban Me Thuot who had 'pressing business' and asked me to take his plane back for him. Rather than wait for a ride, I jumped at the chance. It was the same airplane. The Army did not pay much attention to the niceties of flight plans, weather clearance etc, but the Air Force did. I filed for Ban Me Thuot but before I got started an irate Air Force Colonel arrived on the ramp, announcing that I was not 'qualified' to fly Air Force aircraft. Had he stood on regulations, I may have been persuaded; on qualifications, it was a challenge. I taxied off with him diving away from the empennage. The brakes and alternator had been fixed and it was a beautiful flight. I never again flew an O-1, though they occupy that warm spot any pilot has for his first solo airplane.

Our time was spent in support of the several Special Forces camps around the Central Highlands, the 23rd ARVN Division, sometimes USAID and bootleg time to a missionary group who operated in Ban Me Thuot. The 23rd Division missions were usually dull and, we suspected, meaningless. They used us mainly for taxi service.

This was the fall that the First Cavalry Division (Airmobile) arrived and set up permanent quarters at An Khe – thirty miles or so east of Pleiku along the main road to the coast. Their Mohawks and Caribou moved into Pleiku with the 52nd Aviation Battalion. History tells us that the North Vietnamese wanted to test them, and we figured prominently in that test.

We received orders one morning to proceed to Pleiku, pick up some of the headquarters equipment and move to the coast. The 119th, the company in Pleiku, was proceeding that morning. We had to gather birds off other missions and did not start out until late that afternoon. We arrived in Pleiku in lousy flying weather. We refueled, continued on, and were back in less that an hour. The An Khe pass was socked in and there was no other reasonable route for an entire company. We stayed the night in Pleiku intending to proceed at first light.

That night Plei Me was hit. No one realized that the largest battle since Dien Bien Phu had begun. The weather cleared on the plateau and we flew all night. It did not clear on the coast for a week and we were the only helicopter support for the first five days of the Plei Me–Ia Drang Valley operation. Memories of that first night are mostly of tracer fire that you could land on. The camp was being attacked in waves. Our guns flew a steady shuttle from Pleiku – reload and back on station. We matched up slick pilots with gun pilots to keep up the pace.

During the night an American A-1 Skyraider was shot down a few kilometers north of the camp. We could see his strobe on the ground, but every time an approach was begun all hell broke loose. There seemed no way through the blanket of tracers. He finally came on his VHF emergency radio and reported movement all around him. My wingman was flying a

Hog – a UH-1B with 48 2.75-inch folding-fin aerial rockets. He ripple-fired the entire load and went into autorotation without a call. We thought he had been hit, flipped out or both. He completely disappeared through the tracers. We got occasional glimpses of his landing light. About two minutes later he climbed up through the tracers, blacked out, reported simply 'We got him,' and returned to Pleiku.

The attack caught a patrol operating outside that had no way to get back to the camp. About 0300 hours we got a call from a familiar sergeant who was leading the patrol requesting all the guns we could muster. He had six Americans and about 50 Montagnards with him. They were hit at the same time the attack began on the camp. They were all in hand-to-hand combat when he called us. He marked the ends of his patrol with flashlights and asked us to 'Hose down everything in between.' We emptied everything we had in the air, reloaded, but never regained contact. The South Vietnamese Rangers found the site of the battle a few days later, but the Americans were never recovered.

The days were not much different from the nights. There seemed to be constant activity for about 48 hours, then it became paced with no relief for the camp for over a week. The Air Force attempted low-level drops from C-123s, the Army from Caribou; we attempted landings, drops and anything else that might get ammunition into them. The Air Force missed the camp; the Caribou took intense fire; we got our asses shot off.

One morning I went on station with a Frog – a UH-1B armed with fourteen rockets and a 40mm grenade launcher in the nose, and the camp was getting resupplied. There were South Vietnamese H-34s sitting serenely in the middle of the camp unloading! We called Pleiku and pre-loaded ships were immediately launched. The H-34s departed with hardly a shot. Our Hueys arrived and caught hell.

The Vietnamese did a great job of getting into the camp from about the third day and kept them in ammunition. We never did find out where they were coming from, but they had the markings of the VIP flight detachment at Bien Hoa. They got more supplies in on four-hour turnarounds from Bien Hoa than we did on one-hour sorties from Pleiku. We never did figure out how they seemed to operate with impunity. Maybe they did not.

The Vietnamese also inserted a Ranger Battalion and attempted to get an armored column through to the camp. Both probably served a tactical purpose in diverting troops and giving the attackers something else to think about. In the short term, both elements simply gave us more to do. Both units started screaming for resupply immediately; both were hit hard as soon as they got into the area and the 155th was the only outfit around that could do anything about it.

.Medevac missions seemed endless, and the II Corps hospital was filled to overflowing. We did notice that they had a unique triage procedure: the Vietnamese troops were taken immediately to surgery, while the Montagnard troops were allowed to die on the lawn. Then the local tribes were called to get rid of the bodies. As a unit, and as long as I remember, we ever after took Montagnard troops to American medical facilities.

Throughout this week we had no intelligence or operational briefings beyond the immediate task of supporting Plei Me. Five enemy regiments were surrounding Plei Me and the 1st Brigade of the First Cav was cranking up to meet them. Hell, we were just the warm-up and the strangle hold on Plei Me merely the bait to get the First Cav involved.

On the sixth day, the 119th got back from the coast and the First Cav opened up the Ia Drang Valley operation. From An Khe to the border, the sky was filled with helicopters. The pressure was off and Plei Me had held. The Rangers and the tanks got through. We took a few supply runs in and had a few drinks with the team leader, Charlie Beckwith, who was later heard from at Desert Base Alpha during the abortive American attempt to free the hostages in Iran.

The commitment of the First Cav relieved the pressure on the camp immediately, partly because they interposed themselves between Plei Me and the border and partly because that is what the North Vietnamese were waiting for. The battle of the Ia Drang Valley is, however, another story.

THREE TALES OF THREE TAILS

5

1. Marble Mountain
2. Vung Tau

*I*N the world of aviation literature there are certain types of aircraft that receive little attention. If they are not glamorous types such as the F-4 Phantom or exotic types such as the SR-71 Blackbird, they are generally ignored. One such type is the Grumman OV-1 Mohawk, which first flew in 1959 and it still is use today.

Designed as a two-seat battlefield surveillance aircraft for the Army, the Mohawk appeared in Vietnam as early as the summer of 1962, when six OV-1As from the 23rd Special Warfare Aviation Detachment arrived to support ARVN forces. They performed railroad surveillance, convoy observation, artillery adjustment and night illumination as well as general visual and photographic reconnaissance missions, and produced a wealth of intelligence information. Hundreds of structures, most of them camouflaged, were detected in Viet Cong base areas, and with the detailed familiarity of the crews with the local areas and activities it was easier to identify insurgents amongst the populace.

As the war progressed, a number of aviation companies were sent to Vietnam to fly three variants of Mohawk, the OV-1A, B and C. The OV-1A was fitted with a belly camera capable of vertical or oblique coverage and obtained aerial views of small targets such as fortifications, road junctions and hamlets – the kind of detail needed by ground commanders. They were also armed with machine guns, officially for self-defence. Later, 2.75-inch smoke and high-explosive rockets would also be carried, much to the annoyance of the Air Force who considered armed aircraft to be their ballpark and objected to others playing in it.

The OV-1B carried side-looking airborne radar. The antenna was housed in a long pod beneath the forward part of the fuselage. This model could fly over South Vietnam, but still carry out stand-off night-time surveillance of waterways and roads in Cambodia or Southern Laos. The SLAR equipment could scan either or both sides of the aircraft and fashion a near-real-time radar map that could be reproduced photographically and studied while the aircraft was in flight.

The OV-1C was different from the A and B models and carried infra-red detection equipment and a forward-aimed panoramic camera, as well as the same belly camera used in the A models. As the enemy relied heavily on the cover of darkness to move men and supplies around the countryside, this model was particularly useful. Eventually a D model would be produced, allowing either SLAR or IR gear to be installed in a single airframe.

Carl A. Weaver was associated with the Mohawk in Vietnam from his early days with the 73rd Aviation Company, Aerial Surveillance, in 1965, until 1968 when he took command of the 245th Surveillance Airplane Company at Marble Mountain near Da Nang. He has written a trilogy entitled 'Three Tales of Three Tails' to describe the aircraft and the people who flew them. The first two stories are from 1965 and the third from 1969.

A Titillating Tale

Mack was a hot-sh** pilot and a practical joker. He was also a high self-tester who possessed an air of invincibility. He had been flying JOV-1A Mohawks in Vietnam since the gunships arrived in early 1964. Flying guns on fixed-wing aircraft was very demanding, but there was an element of fun associated with the two-ship, daylight photo and visual reconnaissance missions that pilots of other types of aircraft did not enjoy. The high degree of maneuverability of a gunship Mohawk, along with the freedom to generally operate as a visual reconnaissance pilot saw fit, provided a catalyst for friendly competition for the limelight among surveillance pilots in general.

Competition began in earnest the day that the 4th Aerial Surveillance and Target Acquisition organization arrived. This was a unit with two platoons of night fliers whose infrared and side-looking airborne radar planes offered a new dimension to combat aerial surveillance. The planes that came with the 4th ASTA were different than the gunships. Both the B and C models had huge 150-gallon fuel tanks under each

Below: A view from above of an OV-1A Mohawk at Vung Tau. (Bob Livingstone)

wing. Furthermore, the B model had a large cigar-shaped radar pod slung under the fuselage. Its protrusion forward of the nose of the aircraft provided the illusion that the B model was a male Mohawk.

The night pilots were also a cocky lot. Flying night surveillance was every bit as demanding as visual surveillance. But unlike the gunships, the single-plane night missions were preplanned in great detail, very precisely executed, lonely and, in the case of the SLAR, boring.

Mack, the VR platoon leader, and Jimmie, his wingman, had just returned form a VR mission in the Delta. It was almost seven o' clock in the evening. The two had parked their A models in front of their respective berms. The crew chiefs were hastily servicing the aircraft so that the tug could push the planes into their protective enclosures.

Mack and Jimmie hurried to operations to close out their flight. Getting to the club in time for the movie was foremost on their minds. *The Green Berets* was playing, and Jimmie wanted to see John Wayne make the sun set in the east at the end of the movie.

Walt had just stepped out of the operations shack as Mack and Jimmie walked up. Walt was the SLAR platoon leader and had come over with the 4th ASTA. He was trying to light a cigarette when he heard Mack say, 'Going out to fly your big pecker around on autopilot all night Walt?' Walt mumbled back without thinking, 'Afraid to fly single ship at night?'

Walt let the incident pass as he had all the others, but thought privately to himself, 'It sure would be nice if I could get one of those bastards out on a low-level IR mission one night. I think they'd change their tune.' But Walt was in a hurry to finish his mission tonight. Tomorrow the Chief of Staff of the Army was coming to visit the 73rd. A full-dress dog and pony show had been planned and Walt was to brief on SLAR operations and display a B model.

Recently the Army Chief had heard that there were guns on Army fixed-wing aircraft despite his order to the contrary. An old roles and mission controversy with the Air Force had been revived and the Chief was livid. Obviously there were combat needs and an agreement between the Commander in Vietnam and the Chairman of the Joint Chiefs that overrode the Army Chief's desires. Nevertheless, the Army Chief was coming to see the guns first-hand and the 73rd Commander was scared stiff. Everything had to go right or else.

It was the day of the visit. The Chief's helicopter was due any moment. The CO was scurrying around like a lost puppy. He was not particularly conversant with the inner workings and hidden mechanisms of electronic surveillance. And, in particular, he was not a night pilot. Because of the competition in the unit, he was afraid that one of the night pilots was going to make a fool of him in front of the Chief. Unfortunately for the CO, his gun pilots didn't exactly like him either, and they were just as prone to a prank as anyone else.

The CO heard each of the three briefings numerous times and was unable to find fault with them. Consequently, he concentrated his final efforts on the static display of aircraft. One of each type was on line in front of operations where the Chief was to be escorted following the briefings. The CO made a final check of the line. The A model stood tall with two General Electric 50-caliber machine gun pods slung under the inboard pylons. The outboard pylons each had 2.75-inch rocket pods mounted on them. The CO looked over the A model with pride. He knew that he could answer any question that arose.

Next in line, a C model stood with its electronic bays open to reveal the sophisticated infrared surveillance system. As the CO glanced in the main bay, he said to the IR platoon leader, 'I hope you know more about this contraption than I do. If the Chief asks me any questions about this stuff, I'll stall out!'

Just as the CO finished looking over the C model and before he could check the B model, the familiar whopping of a Huey's rotor blades could be heard in the distance. The CO turned and quickly started to walk to the landing pad near operations. As he hurriedly passed in front of the A model, Mack, the visual platoon leader, shouted, 'Better check your six, Major!' Even though the Chief's helicopter was touching down in the distance, the familiar voice caused the CO to stop in his tracks. Instantly he spun around and quickly glanced down the line. The incident he had

Left: A Grumman OV-1B Mohawk, easily distinguished by its Side-Looking Airborne Radar (SLAR) boom. (via Jim Wood).

feared loomed before his eyes. Someone had stretched a weather balloon over the end of the SLAR boom.

A Tale of Termination

Hawk two-three was a tired bird. She was one of the original Mohawks to go to Vietnam in the early 1960s. When she arrived, she was only a few hundred flying hours out of the factory. Hawk two-three's skin gleamed in the in the bright Asian sunlight as she began flying combat missions in the Mekong Delta. On her very first flight, a small-caliber round penetrated the right elevator, leaving two small holes in her skin.

The maintenance crew worked hard to patch up the holes. Since the type of paint used on Mohawks was hard to come by, the riveted patches were merely sprayed with zinc chromate. This left two pale yellowish green spots on her elevator, one underneath and one on top.

The months that followed saw Hawk two-three on more than 500 missions. The pilots that flew her felt safe because she always brought them home. Hawk two-three became well known though, because the number of zinc chromate patches increased at a noticeable rate. There were only a few flights that did not result in a hole in the aircraft. Fortunately, as luck would have it, none of the antiaircraft fire ever penetrated a vital part of the plane. Her wounds were superficial, but there were a lot of them.

Over time, Hawk two-three became the flight line favorite. The pilots and crews began referring to her as 'Ole Yaller.' Ole Yaller was known throughout the Delta and became a familiar and comforting sight to the troops on the ground. The popularity of her splotchy yellow coat caused the maintenance officer to decree that she should never be repainted to her original color.

One clear June morning, Ole Yaller and her crew of two set out on a visual and photo mission in the Delta. Her destination was on the south-ernmost tip, a very hostile place to say the least. When they arrived in the mission area, there was a lot to see and photograph. Numerous enemy sightings were made, especially on the many canals in the area. The crew did not notice any ground fire. This is normal because small-arms fire is difficult to detect in the daylight unless you happen to be looking right at the muzzle of a rifle when it flashes.

For the crew, the mission was relatively quiet and uneventful. When Ole Yaller's fuel tanks became low, the crew headed the plane to home base at Vung Tau. After about twenty minutes of flying, the pilot could see across the water to the cape where the home airfield was located. The crew were happy: in a few moments they would be in a jeep on their way to the club for a couple of beers and some relaxation. The pilot planned on working on his 'going home tan,' a ritual that all short-timers engaged in. There were only two weeks left to perfect his bronzed body.

The pilot called the tower: 'Vung Tau, Hawk two-three is ten miles south on an extended right downwind for landing.' 'Roger two-three, you're cleared to land runway one-eight. Winds are one-niner-zero at one-five.'

Ole Yaller hung out her dive brakes and slowed down as she entered the downwind leg of the traffic pattern. Once at traffic pattern speed, the pilot lowered the landing gear. 'I've got a gear,' said the pilot as he looked in his rearview mirror. 'I don't have one!' shouted the observer in a panicky voice. The pilot quickly looked down at the gear indicator on the instrument panel. Only the nose and the left main gear were showing green. The right main gear was showing red. First the pilot recycled the useless gear handle. Nothing happened. Then, almost immediately, the pilot pulled the emergency gear handle to activate the pneumatic gear blowdown system. Still nothing happened!

The runway surface at Vung Tau was made out of pierced steel planking and this made a crash landing out of the question. An alter-native would have been to go to Saigon where the runway was paved, but Ole Yaller was very short on fuel. The crew had only one alternative remaining – eject.

The pilot slowed the plane down to 120 knots and made a pass over the field in a straight line. The observer ejected safely and descended to a sandy open area in the vicinity of the operations shack. The pilot turned the plane around and started a pass across the field so that Ole

Yaller was pointed out to sea. By this time, the entire population of the field had turned to watch Ole Yaller terminate.

The pilot was as cool as a cucumber. He trimmed Ole Yaller for level flight, an error that would soon seal the old plane's fate. When he was over the exact center of the field, he reached up and firmly pulled the face curtain out from its recess. The seat fired and the pilot was hurled above Ole Yaller in an instant. As the chute opened, the pilot watched Ole Yaller drone off toward the sea with two of her legs dangling below like a wounded dragonfly.

Ole Yaller was not ready to terminate. With the pilot and ejection seat gone, the trim settings were now wrong and Ole Yaller's nose was light. Slowly she started a gentle climbing turn to the left. Her climb continued for a few moments until the lift under her wings gave out. The nose fell through like slow motion and Ole Yaller started back for the field, picking up speed as she dove. 'That old bird is coming straight for me,' the pilot thought to himself. Ole Yaller passed by the pilot and his chute in a proud salute. The people on the ground watched in awe as Ole Yaller, with her engines purring in unison, passed across the field. At the field boundary, Ole Yaller started a climbing turn again. It was beautiful and graceful. As she turned in the sun, everyone could see her yellow splotches gleaming. Ole Yaller did not want to die.

One more pass across the field was made before the pilot reached the ground. Then, Ole Yaller made a very steep climb. She pointed her nose to the sky. Her engines were struggling to keep aloft. The steepness of the climb was too much for the tired lady. Lazily, Ole Yaller turned over on her left wing and started downward. The pilot knew that this was the end for his friend. Ole Yaller started to scream as her speed built up. The dive became straighter. There was intense anticipation on the faces of everyone. Ole Yaller was on her way out, but she was not going to go without a final hurrah. For you see, Ole Yaller terminated herself in the aircraft salvage yard.

A Tale of Terror

Pete was an excellent pilot. It was near the end of his third tour in Vietnam. On a previous tour, he had been shot down twice, once in an O-1 Bird Dog and once in a U-1 Otter. On this tour, Pete was flying OV-1 Mohawks. For the previous nine months he flew side-looking airborne radar missions. These were long, dull flights that lacked the kind of challenge and excitement that Pete was used to. In my view, Pete was a tired man who needed a change.

Fortunately for Pete, his turtle came early. A turtle is a replacement, and they are called by this name because they are often very slow in coming. Pete's replacement was an experienced combat pilot and I took the opportunity to give the new man Pete's SLAR platoon right away.

Pete's desire was to fly daylight visual and photo missions for the rest of his tour. At the time, the visual platoon leader's slot was vacant, so I conceded to Pete's wishes. As can be expected, the Vietnamese jungle looks very different in the daytime, and Pete required several orientation rides over our area of operations before he could be sent out on his own. One sunny, bright, and very clear day, Pete and I and our two observers set out in two A model Mohawks on a routine photo and observation mission. The first target assigned by our intelligence officer was an abandoned airfield about 100 miles southwest of Da Nang on the edge of the mountains. About six months previously, the airfield, then occupied by the Air Force, had been overrun by the Viet Cong and had been evacuated.

Since that time, there had been considerable activity around the field. It was suspected that the base was being used as a center of operations against the Third Marines about twenty miles to the northeast and against the Army Americal Division approximately fifty miles to the east.

We entered the area at 1,500 feet above the ground, cruising at just over 200 knots. Pete's plane was to my right rear at about 100 meters and slightly above me. My observer was one of the trained enlisted men from my company. Pete's observer was a Special Forces sergeant who was on his last day in-country. He was a personal friend of Pete's and had also been operating on the ground in the mission area for the past six months. His knowledge was important to getting Pete oriented.

I instructed Pete to circle at our original cruise altitude and cover me while I went down to take a look at the area more closely. While maneuvering, I was describing landmarks to Pete. I made three photo runs and each was uneventful. As I climbed up from the last one, Pete asked me to cover him while he went down for a closer look. I circled to the left so I could watch the ground more closely for any signs of ground fire.

Pete made one pass through the centre of the area on a gently curving line. When he was about a third of the way across the area, he suddenly pulled up in a steep climb and leveled off in front of me. Pete called 'Mayday' over the guard channel and said that he had taken a hit behind the cockpit. I could see smoke trailing from just above the wing root; it was thick and brown. I told Pete of the smoke and he replied that he could see flames over his left shoulder, inside the aircraft, through the lightening holes in the aft cockpit bulkhead. I told him to get out before the flames burned his chute.

Pete's mayday was heard by a CH-53 Jolly Green Giant between us and the coast. Immediately, two Skyraiders were despatched to provide covering fire for the Jolly Green Giant, but they had a long way to come as compared to the rescue helicopter. All I could do was wait.

Pete pointed his A model toward the coast and put all the balls to the firewall. I suppose that he was trying to get some distance behind him before punching out. His distance run did not last long though. In a matter of seconds, I saw the observer eject. His chute opened immediately.

Pete was right behind him. When Pete's chute opened he was about 200 meters from the observer.

As I watched these events unfold before my eyes, I was awestruck by the clarity of the air, the stillness of the landscape, the rich blueness of the sky, and the brilliant green of the jungle. It all looked very artificial. I also was struck by the fact that everything was happening in what seemed to be slow motion. The entire sequence of events only lasted a few seconds, but the whole incident was displayed before my eyes slow enough for me to notice every detail. During the entire event, one thought kept recurring – this is just like the movies!

The sergeant observer landed in a small clearing that had plenty of vegetation in which to hide. Upon hitting the ground, he immediately got on his survival radio and made contact with us. The Jolly Green Giant heard his radio also. Pete, on the other hand, landed in some water at the bend in a small river. At first, we did not hear Pete on his survival radio. We could see him going toward the outer edge of the curve in the river. He disappeared from view as he went under the bank where the swift-moving water evidently cut an overhang.

A few moments went by before I saw an enemy soldier with a dog approach the bank. He and the dog stood there a moment, looking over into the water. As suddenly as they appeared, the soldier and the dog disappeared. Still no word from Pete over the radio.

As I circled, I tried to see the bank, but it was to no avail. After several passes, the fuel low-level light on my enunciator panel became illuminated. Under normal circumstances, this is an indication that about 20 minutes of fuel is remaining in the tanks at cruise power. I notified the Jolly Green Giant that I was departing and he said that they were about three to five minutes out. The Skyraiders were still about ten or more minutes out. As I leveled off on a course for home base, I saw the rescue chopper below me and to the right about two miles out. It was a terrific sight to say the least. But Pete was still not on the radio. It was not too long before the entire mission area was out of my sight.

About a minute later, I heard the segeant directing the chopper to his position. Shortly thereafter, the Jolly Green Giant reported that they had rescued one soul and were searching for the second one. I was elated when I heard Pete ask the rescue pilot if he had room for another soul on board. The radio conversations that followed were Pete directing the chopper to the bend in the river. As the rescue pilot said over the radio that the second soul had also been picked up, the Skyraiders reported that they were entering the area. 'Don't need ya,' said the chopper pilot. 'OK, we're on our way back,' said the Skyraider leader.

Pete and the sergeant were being flown to a nearby field hospital. The sergeant was none the worse for wear, but Pete, on the other hand, passed out during the helicopter ride. His body was covered with leeches. They were in every soft area of his body, his arm pits, his inner elbows, behind his knees and in his groin. They had been sucking on

Above: A big drink for Carl A. Weaver after completing his last combat flight for the 245th Surveillance Airplane Company on 24 June 1969. (Carl A. Weaver)

him for about three quarters of an hour.

As he laid there on the stretcher, the corpsman noticed that Pete was gripping something in his hand. It was the ejection seat face curtain and handle that had started the sequence of events that saved his life. Gently, the corpsman removed the handle from Pete's grip and placed it into a cloth bag with Pete's other belongings. Later when I saw Pete in the hospital, he complained bitterly that some Air Force son of a bitch stole his handle. Of course we ribbed him about his wild imagination and tried to convince him that no one had ever had enough presence of mind to hang on to the handle through an ejection and a rescue. After a while, Pete began to believe us and surmised that he had indeed lost the handle in the excitement.

Since Pete was on his third tour of duty in Vietnam, it was easy for me as Company Commander to secure an early release for him. When he got out of the hospital the next day, we threw a grand party for Pete. At the end of the evening's drinking and celebrating, I called Pete to the front of the room. I presented him with a set of going-home orders. He gave a half-hearted speech, thanking all of us for our support. But, he said, he was leaving Vietnam without his most valued possession. I followed his talk with a few remarks about how he should be more careful with his belongings. As he looked down at the floor in a sullen way, I pulled my other hand from behind my back and handed him his ejection seat handle and curtain, mounted on a wooden plaque. Pete cried.

THE SAVING OF BU DOP CAMP

6

1. Tan Son Nhut
2. Bu Dop

O NE of the many coincidences that occurred during the research of this book was that some of the pilots actually knew each other. Two cassette tapes dropped on to the author's doormat one day from Norman M. Turner, a retired Air Force Lieutenant Colonel. It transpired that he had served his second tour of duty in Vietnam with the 390th TFS at Da Nang and knew Jake Sorensen and Mike Aarni, whose story appears in the book as 'Guess You Are On Fire'.

When Norman Turner joined the 390th to fly Phantoms he was already an old hand. He had spent six months flying F-100 Super Sabres out of Saigon's Tan Son Nhut Air Base. He was a fighter pilot through and through, and by the time he retired in 1976 after twenty years' service he had flown 2,000 hours in the F-100 and 1,800 hours in the F-4 Phantom. By the end of his second tour of duty in Vietnam he had flown 335 combat missions, 127 in the F-100 and 208 in the F-4. Of the 208 missions in the F-4, 100 were over North Vietnam.

Turner joined the Air Force in 1956 and checked out in the F-100 in 1958. He was therefore fortunate to have had seven years' experience in the aircraft before having to fly in combat. At that time he was also a graduate of the Air Force Fighter Weapons Instructor School at Nellis Air Force Base, the Air Force version of the Navy's Top Gun school.

In 1965 Captain Turner was flying with the 481st Tactical Fighter Squadron of the 27th Tactical Fighter Wing at Cannon Air Force Base in New Mexico. In June they flew non-stop using KC-135 tankers to Honolulu, where they spent the night. The next day they went on to Andersen Air Base on Guam and the following morning continued on to Clark Air Base. After a week at Clark they flew on to Saigon, and Turner took off on his first combat mission on 1 July 1965.

When we first got there we had no bombs. In fact for the whole of that first tour ordnance was a problem. At first we got 750-pound bombs and we used these for a month until we ran out of them. They then dredged up some old 500-pound bombs that were either Korean War or Second World War vintage. They were certainly not designed to be carried on our aircraft, and new lugs had to be welded on to make them fit.

Above: Captain Norman N. Turner of the 481st Tactical Fighter Squadron, whose superb airmanship helped prevent the Bu Dop Special Forces Camp being overrun. (Norman M. Turner)

We also carried napalm, and at that early stage of the war it was mixed up on the spot, whereas later the napalm would come ready in sealed containers. We were required to unscrew a cap on the early napalm bombs and inspect the mixture. It looked like 200 gallons of snot, but consisted of gasoline and naptha to jellify the mixture. This early bomb was called a BLU-1 (Bomb Live Unit). The later type was called a BLU-27.

On each end of the can is an igniter containing a fuse. The igniter is filled with white phosphorous, which burns in contact with the air. When the bombs hit the ground and broke up spraying napalm through the air, the fuse would explode the white phosphorous, which in turn would ignite the napalm. A burning sheet of jellified gasoline would cover the ground, sticking to and incinerating anything in its path.

We (the pilots of the 481st) all lived in a villa in Saigon and would drive to the airport to go to work and return again at night. The first few weeks were uneventful, but then we started standing alert 24 hours a day in a trailer by the operations building. Two pilots would be on call and on my first alert, on 19–20 July, I flew the hottest mission of both my two tours. It was to a place called Bu Dop.

Bu Dop was a border surveillance camp near the Cambodian border approximately 100 miles north-east of Saigon. On 19 July 1965 it was occupied by six Special Forces enlisted men under Captain Nugent, eight LLDB (their Vietnamese counterparts) and 289 Stieng and Vietnamese CIDG troops.

At 0100 hours in the morning of 20 July, the first mortar and recoilless rifle rounds began to fall inside the camp perimeter, seriously wounding Captain Nugent and damaging the camp radio and generator. The Viet Cong assault teams dashed forward, bridging the moats and barbed wire with bamboo ladders. They overwhelmed the north-west bunker, killing the defenders at their posts, and raced into the camp, decimating the CIDG troops with machine gun fire and flamethrowers. Two Special Forces Sergeants defending the supply building were killed and the

Below: *An F-100 Super Sabre dropping napalm on enemy positions. (via First Lieutenant M. J. Kasiuba)*

third wounded as the camp radio operator and light weapons Sergeant engaged the Viet Cong in hand-to-hand combat at the mortar pit.

The LLDB camp commander reorganized the defences as close combat raged throughout the camp. He shifted reinforcements to the south-eastern corner bunker just in time to kill dozens of Viet Cong as they tried to cut through the wire. Pandemonium reigned as the darkness was broken by grenade explosions and streams of tracer fire and ghostly shadows flitted across the ground as the sky was lit by enemy signal flares.

Back in Saigon, the two pilots of the standby flight of the 481st Tactical Fighter Squadron tried to sleep in their trailer. Captain Turner and Lieutenant Paul Watson had flown during the day and had also launched once already that night. They lay slumbering in their G suits until the hand-cranked field telephone woke them with instructions to scramble. They left the trailer at a dead run.

As they gained altitude in the clear night sky they could see their destination, lit by flares on the horizon – Bu Dop Special Forces camp. Their F-100 Super Sabres would be needed there, with their loads of two 750-pound bombs on the inboard wing stations and 19-shot rocket pods on the outboard stations.

When they arrived on station the Forward Air Controller instructed them to hold while some A-1 Skyraider aircraft dropped napalm on the attackers. Soon afterwards the FAC had to leave owing to low fuel, and the pair of F-100s had to wait around fifteen minutes for Viper Seven, the relief, to arrive. In the meantime a C-123 flareship flew in a racetrack pattern over the camp, dropping flares to assist the defenders and the fighters waiting to go into action. However, it started to get hazy and by the time Viper Seven arrived it was undercast and the pilots could not see the ground.

The FAC contacted the camp and relayed the information to the F-100s that, as the weather began to close in, the enemy had renewed their assault and were now coming over the walls. 'I don't know if you can get in, but they really need you now', said Viper Seven.

By now the clouds were as low as 500 feet and glowing as the flares from above floated down. Beneath the undercast, the enemy knew that the camp had lost its air support and renewed the attack with vigour. Men were dying down on the ground and the F-100 pilots knew it.

The choice for the orbiting flight was difficult. To try to fly under the clouds in the dark, at a height of just a few hundred feet with no visual references and 100-feet-high trees below, was virtually suicidal. However, eight enemy machine gun nests were positioned at the edge of the jungle and were firing across the airstrip at the camp. Something needed to be done and right away. Fortunately, as occasionally happens in war, the right man was in the right place. Captain Turner decided to go down.

I told Paul to hold high and went out to the west to get clear of the clouds. I was not going to be able to use my bombs, so I set myself up with the gun trigger hot and the buttons on the control stick set to fire the rockets.

Above: An F-100 Super Sabre firing a pod of rockets at an enemy target. (US Air Force)

As it was dark I couldn't see much of anything, except the thin grey line of the clouds lit up by the flares. On my first try I got down as low as I could, but I flew into the clouds and had to pull up and go around again. I decided that this time I was going to get down low enough or hit the trees. I couldn't see the trees, but I could see the cloud deck above me and I could see a white light in the haze in front of me, and this gave me enough of a visual reference to keep the airplane right side up. I remember thinking to myself 'I am probably going to die tonight' as I skimmed the trees at 400 knots and came out too far to the left, with the camp at three o' clock.

Next time I overcompensated and flew past on the other side of the camp. On about my fifth attempt I flew directly over the camp, but I was going in the wrong direction, from the tree-line to the camp. I tried to maintain my heading as I flew out from under the clouds and did a whifferdil turn, which is what the display teams do to try to go back down the same path along which you came.

I broke out over the camp and found that I was lined up perfectly. Now there is no set method of delivering weapons in conditions like that: I was in about a one-degree dive, almost straight and level. I rolled up into a 90-degree right turn and aimed at the left side of the tree-line by the runway and hit the pickle button twice.

There was a blinding flash as the nineteen rockets in the left pod fired and another from the right wing as the rockets left their pod and hurtled towards the ground with their motors sparkling behind them. I was still moving horizontally across the ground, and as the rockets disappeared under the nose I pressed the trigger and watched as each of my four guns spewed 1,500 rounds per minute of 20mm high-explosive toward the tree-line. I walked the guns along the tree-line until I was down to about 100 feet and felt like I was about to hit the ground, then I rolled the wings level and pulled out.

The FAC told me that all the machine guns had stopped firing, so I rejoined my wingman and cleared him to go down. Paul eventually got down and put some ordnance on the ground, but I am a bit vague as to what he actually did. We didn't get much time to discuss it and he was killed a couple of days later when he flew into the ground on a napalm run. The FAC said that we had saved the camp, and we got something in writing to that effect about two weeks later.

The surviving defenders of the camp spent the rest of the night fighting in close quarters both inside the camp and along the walls. The last enemy attack across the airfield was thrown back at 0800 hours and the tired defenders raised a South Vietnamese flag at the east gate. By midday reinforcements had arrived. The total allied losses in the attack were 70 killed, including two Special Forces, and 39 wounded. A body count put the number of Viet Cong dead at 161.

Captain Turner was awarded the Distinguished Flying Cross for his actions at Bu Dop. By the time he completed his second tour of duty flying Phantoms, he had been awarded a total of four DFCs, a Silver Star, twenty-one Air Medals and the Vietnamese Cross of Gallantry. Upon retirement from the Air Force Turner completed law school and passed the California Bar Exam on the first attempt. At the time of writing he is campaigning for election as a Judge at the Riverside Municipal Court in California.

PART TWO:
FIGHTING THE WAR

*T*HE build up of American air power began right after the Tonkin Gulf incident in August 1964 and continued throughout 1965. By the time the first Marines of the 9th Marine Expeditionary Brigade began to wade ashore at Da Nang on 8 March 1965, Navy and Air Force aircraft had flown their first missions against the Ho Chi Minh Trail infiltration route through Laos and Cambodia and the 'Rolling Thunder' air campaign against North Vietnam was underway.

Rolling Thunder began on 2 March 1965 and continued, with various pauses, until the end of 1968. It was not to be the short, sharp, all-out campaign that President Johnson's military advisers preferred, but rather a slow, gradual programme of attacks, increasing in intensity over the months, with the aim of persuading North Vietnam to negotiate an end to its insurgency in the South.

In April 1965 the first Marine Corps squadrons arrived. Although they were there primarily to support Marine operations in the South, they were soon flying missions to North Vietnam and Laos as well. In the same month that they arrived the Navy anchored an aircraft carrier at a position known as Dixie Station, off the coast of South Vietnam, and began to fly close support missions in the South. This took the heat off the Air Force until they could move enough squadrons to South Vietnam and Thailand to handle the workload on their own. It also gave the Navy crews some experience in the comparatively peaceful southern war zone, before going North into the world of surface-to-air-missiles (SAMs), MiG fighter interceptors and an anti-aircraft defence system which would eventually become the toughest in the world.

In May 1965 the first Army combat unit arrived in South Vietnam, raising the number of US servicemen in Vietnam to over 50,000, including 10,000 from the Air Force. By the autumn the newly activated 1st Cavalry Division (Airmobile) had arrived, bringing with them 15,800 men and 434 helicopters and aircraft. Unfortunately, the civilian war managers never would agree to give General Westmoreland, the commander of United States Military Assistance Command, Vietnam, the troops he needed to defeat the Viet Cong and the North Vietnamese troops within South Vietnam, and neither would Westmoreland be allowed to attack the enemy in their sanctuaries over the border in Laos and Cambodia. Search and destroy became the name of the game, as troop-laden helicopters filled the sky in search of the enemy.

The peak years of the war, as covered in this chapter, were 1966 to 1968. Seventeen of the thirty-two stories in the book took place during that three-year time period and they describe the ferocity of the fighting during those years.

There were, in effect, three wars going on at the same time, although each was interrelated. The ARVN units took a back seat as the American Marines and Infantry, ably assisted by South Korean and Australian troops, spread out through the four Corps Tactical Zones into which South Vietnam had been divided and sought to bring the elusive enemy to battle.

The air war continued inside Laos itself and along the border with South Vietnam, where the tentacles of the Ho Chi Minh Trail fed into the jungles of the South and where the North Vietnamese Army units rested in their sanctuaries. This air war was unofficial at the time, as were the Special Forces intelligence gathering operations into Laos and Cambodia.

The third war was taking place over North Vietnam, as Air Force aircraft from Thailand and South Vietnam and Navy aircraft from the carriers on Yankee Station in the Gulf of Tonkin attempted to destroy the enemy supply and communication systems. Their task was not a little difficult. The whole of North Vietnam had been divided into six route packages, three of which were under Navy control, two belonged to the Air Force and the sixth split between the two. To compound matters, the Johnson administration imposed a thirty mile radius restricted zone and a ten mile prohibited zone around Hanoi, and similar zones of four and ten miles around Haiphong. To this was added a thirty mile buffer zone along the northern border with China. Permission to strike targets in these zones had to be obtained from Washington and it was seldom given. The American pilots could see the North Vietnamese MiGs taking off from Phuc Yen airfield near Hanoi, but had to wait until they were in the air before engaging them – the airfield was out of bounds.

The war continued throughout 1966 and 1967, with American casualties increasing and the public back home becoming impatient as the war dragged on. On 21 January 1968, the North Vietnamese began to lay seige to the Marine combat base at Khe Sahn, and nine days later all hell broke loose as the Tet Offensive began. Viet Cong and North Vietnamese forces attacked nearly every important city, provincial capital and military installation in South Vietnam. Although the offensive caught the Allied forces largely by surprise, they soon regained control and inflicted massive losses on the Viet Cong, who had borne the brunt of the fighting.

The major effect of the Tet Offensive was felt not in South Vietnam but in the United States. Television screens showing armed military police trying to root out a VC suicide squad from the US Embassy in Saigon, and pictures of Hue, the ancient capital of Vietnam, being reduced to rubble as Marines fought house-to-house to clear the city did little to inspire public confidence in the Johnson administration.

In March 1968, President Johnson announced a halt to all bombing north of the 19th Parallel and decided against a second term as President of the United States. On 1 November, he ordered a halt to all bombing of North Vietnam on the advice of his peace negotiating team in Paris. Although the ground war in the South and the air war over Laos would continue, American bombers would not return to the North again until 1972.

TREE STRIKE ON THE HO CHI MINH TRAIL

1. Thakhek (Laos)

*L*AOS, at the height of the 'Secret War', was a place where one could meet anybody. The US Special Forces were there, together with the CIA and its clandestine airlines and anonymous pilots. The North Vietnamese and Viet Cong were also there, as were their own communist advisers from China and Russia. This was quite apart from the people who actually lived in the country and were engaged in their own three-way civil war. Mercenaries were present, as were personnel from various 'friendly' nations. One of the latter was British. His name was John Pote, and surprisingly he was not there to try to kill anyone. Let us join him now: the date is 1966, and the place an Air America H-34 helicopter.

As we spiraled down in a lazy, unbanked turn, the air became warm again. All around us, only a few hundred yards away, were the vertical limestone cliffs, the view repeating itself every minute or so. Below was a small group of untidy shelters, a soldiers' encampment. An orange 'T' was in a small clearing. This was Ban Na Khen.

Close to the ground we straightened up to run into a slightly larger clearing, passing alongside a small outcrop. From my seat in the cabin my forward view was limited, but I could see an isolated tree in our 2 o' clock. I watched in disbelief as we turned towards it, the rotor striking it half way up its 10-metre trunk. There was hardly any impact, but as the crown of the tree fell through the rotor disc the blades smashed it to matchwood, which poured in through the doorway along with the dusty debris of many tree ant nests complete with their angry occupants.

If the impact with the tree had been mild, that with the ground was not, as we rolled to a stop over the small sharp ridges that had been paddy boundaries. As the dust cleared, so did my mind. This valley was accessible only by air or by an arduous journey through the gorge. I was in a Choctaw loaned to the CIA and we had crashed a long way inside Viet Minh territory. I was potentially in serious trouble because I simply could not refuse any opportunity to fly.

It was 1966 and, just out of school, I was working with a small medical team at Thakhek, beside the Mekong River in Central Laos. When I returned to England I would take up my place at medical school, but for that year I worked on the medical team, initially with just one doctor, later with two doctors and a nurse. We provided what medical care we could, both in Thakhek and along the Mekong valley wherever the military situation allowed. The hospital was rebuilt during my stay and my function in the team was one of general assistance – keeping the vehicles running, obtaining supplies and working with local craftsmen. I had the chance to become involved with the aircraft in Laos and to fly often.

Just to the east, in the Annamite mountains, lay the networks of the Ho Chi Minh Trail. Through a pass wound the trackbed and bridges constructed by the French for a railway to the port of Vinh (in 1966, a part of North Vietnam) although the rails were never laid. Beyond K15 (15 kilometres out of Thakhek) this track was considered to be in Viet Minh territory. A few miles to the west, across the mighty Mekong into Thailand, was Nakhon Phanom Air Base. When I arrived in September 1965 there were only Kaman HH-43 Huskies based there, but soon I saw my first Jolly Green Giant and its attendant Skyraiders, used for rescue work over Laos and North Vietnam. When scrambled, the Skyraiders would thunder over Thakhek in a loose finger-four, followed shortly by the slower HH-3E. Depending on the distance to the downed pilot, they would eventually be back, the Skyraiders not far in front of the HH-3E which they had escorted back to friendly territory. Occasionally the HH-3E would turn back whilst still in flight. I never knew whether this was because the downed pilot had been rescued another way, or had been seen to be killed or captured. Either way, it brought a lump to my throat. Before I left in August 1966, there was the unforgettable sight and sound of B-26K Invaders of the 606th Air Commandos, festooned underwing, in close formation over the tree-tops. Dien Bien Phu lay 300 miles to the north, just across the border. As far as that towards the south lay Cambodia, soon to become equally tragically familiar.

We relied heavily on the Americans for transport of our supplies from Vientiane, although the 360-kilometer Route 13, widened to form airstrips for Caribou or Skytrains at odd places, was a rewarding if arduous drive in the dry season. Air America provided most of the aircraft, Continental Air Services a few. Both were openly talked of as Central Intelligence Agency sub-contractors. Their fleets were a mixture of Skytrains, Commandos, Caribou and Providers. For smaller tasks there were Pilatus Porters, Helio Couriers, Dornier 28s and Sikorsky UH-34Ds. During my year there, they lost at least twenty aircraft. I saw the wreckage of six. The management never complained, for the CIA paid well, but the crews were sometimes very unhappy.

Thakhek was a small westernized town of a few thousand people, with a dozen expatriots. It had some metalled roads to its outskirts. Nearby were many villages of Lao and other ethnic groups, many of them refugees. Despite the influx of refugees, there was no shortage of land for paddy fields, with unused land between one village and the next. A monument by the river told of the massacre of the entire French population of twenty by the Japanese, late in World War Two. Daily one could hear shellfire in the distance and the sound of Thunderchiefs overhead, bound for North Vietnam. The area had known war since 1942 and had another decade of it to come. Thakhek had two airstrips, K2 on the outskirts and K6 a little way into the scrub. K2 was the base of EC 2/596 of the Vichy Air Force, who flew Morane MS.406 fighters against the Royal Thai Air Force in the Franco-Thai war of 1940–41. For its trouble K2 was bombed several times by Thai Vought V-93S Corsairs and several aircraft were destroyed near the town before hostilities ceased. Later on it was an Imperial Japanese Air Force base. The strip was just 800 meters of laterite, sun-baked earth. Because K2 flooded in the monsoon, K6 had been built more recently for the wet season. K6 had not a single facility, not even a fence to keep the buffalo off. The fuselage of a yellow Cessna Bird Dog, ex 51-12650, c/n 23374, late of the Royal Lao Air Force, lay at one end. K2 boasted a wooden shelter, some 50-gallon drums of avgas for the Choctaws and some scattered munitions boxes still containing bazooka rounds.

Wednesday 27 April 1966 started routinely enough, warm and dry. The monsoon was months past and even the effects of the mango rains of March had disappeared. I went for lunch at 'Chez Louis,' an orderly restaurant run, indeed, by Louis, a veteran of the French army. There I sat with Val Petersen, a USAID official I knew well. Casually, he said that he was riding an H-34 to check out security at a place on the Nam (River) Ca Dinh, landing at Ban (Village) Na Kenh to discuss the military situation with a Colonel of the Royal Lao Army. There would be a spare seat and I was welcome.

Val was a large and quiet man, whose overt work was with USAID and the refugee programme. However, after eight months of working alongside him when our respective work coincided, I knew full well he also had a covert role. One might disagree totally with the American role in Southeast Asia, but there were many fine people carrying out that unfortunate task and Val was one of the best. His idea of the interests of Laos was foremost in his mind, whatever the price to him or others.

At K2 airstrip were three Sikorsky UH-34Ds of Air America. All were olive drab and bereft of all markings bar a white serial on the tail pylon. H-36 and H-38 left immediately, heading east. H-22 was our aircraft, an old airframe now used for less demanding sorties. A year or so ago it had been brought down by ground fire and repaired at Udorn Air Base in Thailand. A number of riveted patches resulted from less dramatic encounters with the feared 12.7mm machine guns of the Ho Chi Minh Trail, or from its previous Marine Corps service in South Vietnam. We hand-pumped 120 gallons of avgas from the drums, filtered through chamois leather on which a lot of dirt remained.

I strapped in just aft of the door. A locally recruited crew chief had the single seat in front of the door, where a gunner would have sat had the customary 50-caliber machine gun been mounted. Val rode up front in the left-hand seat. The nine-cylinder Wright R-1820 radial fired, a clattering din. Soon the rotors were turning and we taxied out for a rolling take off in a cloud of dust. Climbing only slowly, we turned northeast towards the Annamite mountains. The door was wired open for easier escape – in South Vietnam the doors were actually removed. Any protection the fuselage could have offered from gunfire was in the mind only. For the same reason, those who had vest armor usually sat on it except when close to the ground. Just to the east I could see the brown scar of the heavily bombed pass at K15 on the road to Mahaxay and the old rail route to Vinh. It was rather hazy, but North Vietnam, 80 miles east, would not have been visible anyway. We flew in small clouds at 1,000 meters, bitterly cold in tropical working clothes.

Below passed many landmarks, each bearing some memory – the red scar of Route 13 to Vientiane, the grey stone road to the old French tin mine of Phontieu and, as we left the last track behind, intermittent traces of twin tire tracks, made by our medical Land Rover weeks before as we drove to Ban Tanah for a clinic. From above it looked gentle, but I remember only too well its mud, ruts, thorns, rocks and crude bridges, all conspiring against the vehicle. Then below was the 300-meter tower of limestone which John, the team's doctor, and I had climbed. We chose the easy side, but even so over half the ascent required ropes. Quite possibly we were the first people on the summit, desperately hot and dry and surrounded by strange tree cacti, but the view that day compensated.

Passing over Ban Tanah, the furthest I had previously traveled, we reached Ban Na Koke, the last village on the Mekong flood plain before the Nam Hin Boun entered its gorge. We spiraled down to about 200 meters, whereupon the Choctaw straightened into a shallow dive, accelerating rapidly. Only a few meters from the ground we pulled sharply up, completing a wing-over as the speed decayed and again running in low and fast to complete a rolling landing in a small paddy field. Ban Na Koke was no longer visible through the scrub. Soon Lao people appeared nervously from the scrub and Val talked to them in Lao. A soldier appeared, dwarfed by his M-1 Garand rifle and pack. He asked for a lift back to Thakhek, the pilot agreeing, and I personally checked that the breech of his M-1 carbine was clear. Once, when I asked a soldier if he had 'one up the spout' as he got into my Land Rover, he replied 'Of course not' and pulled the trigger. The look on his face when he discovered his error compensated for the repairs to the Land Rover.

Soon we were airborne again, climbing to 1,000 meters before we penetrated the Hin Boun gorge. The gorge almost defies description. It is over 1,000 meters deep, but very narrow. From rain-forest-clad peaks, the walls drop sheer to the river, foaming below. We flew in deep shadow between the cliffs, huge caves on either side. The Choctaw seemed like a tiny insect in a large dark crevice. There was a temptation to fly into the larger caves, a feat I witnessed in a Prestwick Pioneer (XL665 of No 209 Squadron, on loan to the British Military Attache in Vientiane). On that occasion, having flown low and slow over the Karst (the precipitous limestone ridges) we flew along beside a cliff to where a vast overhang formed the roof of a cave system. The pilot turned gently towards the back of the cave until we were in shadow beneath solid rock, before turning sharply away and back into open air. When we returned to K6 he made a short landing. I measured the tire marks at 24 meters – about three times the length of the fuselage. A wonderful aircraft – even the Choctaws usually had a longer landing run.

Soon we emerged into a bowl a kilometer or two across. The river ran along the east of the floor and reentered a similar gorge beyond. The walls of the bowl were vertical and the few huts of Ban Na Khen were the only sign of human presence. It was here that we spiralled down to our rendezvous with that tree. . .

I unstrapped and ran out from under the rotor disc. The engine noise reverberated on the cliffs, so I moved to the edge of the clearing, hoping perhaps to be able to hear incoming gunfire that the crew might not. With relief I saw them greeted as friends by our new passenger. I walked up to them and was welcomed by a short but well-built man, bare to the waist, long hair down his back. His handshake was painful and his bearhug more so. This was 'The Colonel'.

Only later did I learn that he was Japanese and had arrived in the area during the Second World War with the Imperial Army. Cut off from his unit, he had lived rough well into the late '50s, when he had finally contacted the Americans. He was told his war was many years over, but was asked if he would help his former enemies. Knowing no other life, he returned to the jungle, was supplied by the Americans and now used his hard-won survival skills for surveillance on the increasingly important Ho Chi Minh Trail. Mostly he reported by radio, but the true purpose of our sortie was to collect the written records he also compiled and to bring him such supplies as he needed. He was officially 'missing in action' in 1945, and I feel sure he would have stayed on after the fall of Southeast Asia and must surely now be dead, but I have no idea if he ever passed any messages to his family in Japan.

The reason for our collision was simple. Spiraling down in a long, steady, unbanked turn, one loses the sensation of turning. When the turn ceases, there is a sensation of turning the opposite way. Our pilot had 'corrected' this apparent yaw, disbelieving what he saw, and had turned into the tree. The crew chief sat up on the horizontal stabilizers as the pilot moved each blade in turn to him for inspection. One was bent up at 15 degrees close to the tip, two were dented, the fourth untouched. The pilot then tried a low hover, and although the damage

H-22

DANGER ← KEEP AWAY

Above: Following the tree-strike while landing at Ban Na Coke, the Air America crew-chief climbs up to inspect the damage to the rotor blades. Left: He found three out of four rotor blades damaged, but UH-34D H-22 still managed to fly John Pote back to safety. (John Pote)

caused a great deal of vibration, we decided that to fly out was the least dangerous option.

The flight back to friendly lines was tense at first, but the vibration got no worse and the rotor stayed with us. By three in the afternoon, as the midday break ended, I was back at work in our little hospital. It was probably a minor incident in the history of UH-34D H-22, but to me it was a flight the interest and excitement of which I would never forget.

Twenty years later, I fly as a doctor in the Search and Rescue Wessex helicopters of No 22 squadron, Royal Air Force. The sound of the Gnome is very different from that of the Wright radial and the vibration much less, but the airframe and cabin are identical. Luckily, there are very few trees over the sea.

THE CHI LANG BIRD DOG

1. Chi Lang
2. Vung Tau

*T*HE *author looked hard at the black and white photograph that lay on his desk. It was a picture of an Army Cessna O-1 Bird Dog, sure enough, but in contrast to the usual white phosphorous target marking rockets carried by the O-1 Forward Air Controllers, this one was armed with two XM-157 rocket pods, each containing seven 2.75-inch high-explosive rockets.*

The O-1 had many uses: its mission included forward observation for mortars and artillery, forward air control for air strikes, convoy escort, radio relay, medevac, bundle drops, command and control, and liaison. Another role could now be added to that list – attack.

The eventual fate of the aircraft in the photograph is unknown, but its pilot survived his twelve-month tour of duty and then returned for a second tour eighteen months later. The pilot was Alfred F. Schwinghammer and this is his story.

During the US build-up in South Vietnam in 1965 the Army sent four companies of O-1s, one for each of the four Corps areas. The 221st Reconnaissance Airplane Company was stationed at Soc Trang in the south of the country in IV Corps, and its platoons were scattered in four other locations. Basically, one O-1 pilot and his aircraft were assigned to each province and lived at, or near, an airstrip in that province. At platoon headquarters there were several pilots assigned to support the ARVN Divisions. Sector pilots flew their province every day and learned to recognize the movements and habits of the people. Virtually every trail, rock, muddy canal or field, anything which would indicate the presence of the enemy, would be learned by the sector pilot. A wisp of smoke rising from a distant treeline or activity on a trail far from a village would require closer inspection. The pilot's mission was primarily reconnaissance, and he reported all intelligence to the Province and Corps S-2.

Because of the claim by the Air Force to the virtual monopoly of the fixed-wing ground attack role, only two O-1s in IV Corps were authorized to carry the XM-157 system. The others were mounted with a pair of tubes carrying a maximum of four 2.75-inch white phosphorous

Above: Al Schwinghammer with his
0-1 Bird Dog armed with two seven-shot XM-157 rocket
pods. (Alfred F. Schwinghammer)

marking rockets. The two armed Bird Dogs were allocated to the areas
adjacent to the Cambodian border. This was mainly due to the extra
time it would sometimes take to get an immediate air strike approved
through channels and out to the target area.

The technology involved in arming the O-1s was, to say the least,
basic. The maintenance platoon reinforced the wing racks with channel
iron in four places. The channel iron had four large bolts acting as set
screws, to tighten down the pods firmly and to give some degree of
boresighting to the modification. The sighting device for the pilot was
very sophisticated – three black grease-pencil marks near the center of
the windshield. The center mark was equivalent to the crosshairs on a
regular sighting device. The top and bottom lines, about an inch apart,
were ranging lines. After firing the first pair of rockets at a target, the
pilot would observe where the rockets hit and make a trim adjustment,
if necessary, to put the center line on a point reference to the target.
After seeing the second pair hit, a final trim adjustment could be made
and if the target was worthy another pair, or up to seven pairs, could be
unleashed. This could deplete the arsenal, but with home base usually
only five to fifteen minutes away it would not take long to rearm and
return to the target area.

The pilots were issued with parachutes and flak vests, although the parachutes were left back at base. They were much too uncomfortable to wear in a cramped cockpit and if the aircraft were hit they felt safer just riding it down. Apart from that, the normal recce altitude was 1,500 feet, and in an emergency there would be minimum altitude remaining to bale out anyway.

The flak vest was folded neatly on the pilot's seat for protection of the important parts while in level flight. Protection during a rocket run consisted of one piece of plexiglass and one jungle fatigue uniform. A rocket run on an enemy position would begin at 1,500 feet, and if firing only one marking rocket the pilot would break off at about 1,200 feet. When firing seven pairs of the XM-157 rockets, the dive would be broken off as low as 600 or 700 feet. This usually caused the neighborhood to become quite angry, and they would turn their attention to the source of the problem. The defending grunts on the ground loved this sharing of attention.

One of the armed Bird Dogs was stationed at Chi Lang, near Nui Cam (Nui meaning Mountain), in the Seven Mountains region of Chau Doc Province. The province lies along the Cambodian border, west from the Mekong River to the Gulf of Thailand. Much of the province is at sea level, with rice paddies in the east, mangroves in the west and, in the center, the Seven Mountains which rise to between two and three thousand feet. The Chi Lang airstrip was made of pierced steel planking and was 1,900 feet long. It was located just inside an old French minefield, which served as the northern boundary to the Chi Lang National Training Center.

Chi Lang was a basic training center for ARVN recruits and was also used for annual battalion retraining. Visits by 'Charlie', the nickname for the Viet Cong, would help indoctrinate the new recruits, and sometimes members of the Viet Cong would surrender and then receive training at Chi Lang. Several times small groups, and on one occasion a company-sized unit, mutinied. They killed several friendlies before departing with their weapons and ammunition, returning to their former allegiance.

In May 1966 Al Schwinghammer flew into Chi Lang to take over as the resident sector pilot. He continues his story:

The ARVN basic training company hooch was immediately next to the American hooch, which housed seventeen American advisers and training cadre, one Air Force FAC, and one Army sector pilot – me. It was a comfortable place as far as Vietnam went. Termites ate the ammunition crate furniture, rice paddy rats would visit when fresh care packages were opened, and water for showers was trucked in from a muddy canal two miles away, using an old Second World War gasoline tanker. Mail usually came in twice a week with the IV Corps courier. The local Vietnamese and Cambodians were struggling and hard-working people who always smiled and were pleasant. In 1966 we really wanted to help them and their country, and to make things better by building schools, dispensing medicines and taking care of Charlie. Charlie had been around a long time. He was well established in Chau Doc and the Seven Mountains. Locals said that he had battalion- and company-size units in the mountains, unmolested for decades. Well, somebody had to check it out. The numbered ARVN divisions were established and operating in the populated areas in central and eastern IV Corps. However, Chau Doc Province was inhabited by many peasant Cambodians who were of minimal interest to the government of South Vietnam. The government's method of dealing with the Seven Mountains was to mark three large free bomb zones around the three largest mountains, Nui Cam, Nui Giai and Nui Coto

In January 1967, Task Force 489 of the Fifth Special Forces Group (Airborne) initiated the first mobile guerrilla operation in the Delta – Blackjack 41 Red. Captain George Maracek and his Mike Force of Khmer Kampuchea Krom (KKK) were given the task. The KKK were local Cambodian troops commanded by American Special Forces officers and NCOs. Their original task was to link up with local Khmer Kampuchea Krom Viet Cong leaders in the Seven Mountains and convince them to join the Special Forces as a permanent guerrilla force in the area. After numerous contacts using female agents, the Mike Force was sent to the Seven Mountains to flush out uncooperative Viet Cong, and to assist negotiations they decided to check out Nui Cam first, by infiltrating to the top on foot, using rough trails and making their own where required. They carried enough supplies with them to last two to three weeks but planned to stay as long as thirty days if necessary. The Mike Force moved quickly and quietly, but on the third day all hell broke loose. Al Schwinghammer continues the story:

It was a bright, sunny day with high clouds, about 5,000 feet and 90 degrees Fahrenheit. I had just returned from flying the border. It was about 1400 hours when the Air Force jeep came tearing down the road to the airstrip. I thought something was really wrong for the jeep driver to be going that fast. My crew chief Charles Prochaska, Captain Maracek and an Air Force radio operator pulled up and said that the Mike Force had just walked into an enemy base camp and were in heavy contact. We armed the XM-157 rocket launchers and Captain Maracek climbed into the rear seat of the O-1. Prochaska said he would prepare more rockets. Take-off with fourteen rockets and a rear-seat passenger was all the O-1D could muster. Breaking ground at the end of the 1,900-foot runway and clearing the four-foot wire fence used all available power from the 213-horsepower engine. The throttle was firewalled, over the red line, until 500 feet, and we then climbed at approximately 200 feet per minute until 2,600 feet, where we turned in over the mountains and made radio contact with the Mike Force.

Captain Maracek talked to his commander on the ground and the radio clatter in the background gave evidence to the ongoing battle. Charlie was trying to regain his base camp and drive back out the intruders. As we passed over the densely treed area, the ground force commander said he would pop smoke. I was not in position to make a rocket run at that point, so I asked Captain Maracek to have his man hold all marking efforts, but to give us the azimuth and distance to the enemy and wait for my request to pop a smoke grenade.

I continued to finalize the approach to the target area and flipped the firing switches to 'on.' Fully realizing how close the two forces were to one another, I had great apprehension on how close to fire the ordnance. The radio operator on the ground called 'Shotgun One-Eight, azimuth One-Four-Zero degrees, meters One-Zero-Zero.' I had begun my descent and said 'Pop smoke.' A few seconds later yellow smoke began to rise up out of the trees. I saw large boulders in what I felt must be the target area and called the ground: 'Yellow smoke, are you near the large boulders?' He responded, 'They're all over those rocks.' By this time the altitude for the rocket run was a third gone and I was at about a thousand feet above ground level and closing when the first pair of rockets hit the target area. I felt so sure about the accuracy that I squeezed off all seven pairs.

As the last pair of rockets left the tubes there was about 500 feet of altitude remaining. Breaking hard right, I began to resent having fired all the rockets. What if I had hit friendlies? Nothing is worth the cost of that. Deep depression set in: I didn't want to hear this next call. And then those beautiful words came over the radio: 'On target!' Captain Maracek gleefully beat me about the helmet and shoulders and told his ground commander that we would be back in fifteen minutes with more rockets. The descent from the mountain to the airstrip put us past the yellow range on the air speed indicator and as soon as we came to a halt the crew chief and radio operator arrived in a cloud of dust, with the jeep's rear seat and hood stacked with more rockets. Reloading took only a few minutes and then we were on our way back to the top of Nui Cam again.

We made four more trips that afternoon and after the second one Bart Nine-Five, Captain John McKenna, the Air Force FAC, had fast movers – Phantoms, dropping heavy ordnance onto the enemy positions. The last run for me that day was at dusk, on the suspected escape route down the southwest corner of the mountain. No ground fire came from this area until the first pair of 2.75s hit the trail they were obviously using. As an angry retreating Viet Cong pointed everything they had at a lonely Bird Dog, the number of muzzle flashes that lit the evening sky confirmed for me the ground commander's initial estimate of over 300 Charlies.

Puff the Magic Dragon came to maintain the force on the mountain that evening and Charlie departed gracefully to another mountain. He knew we'd stay there a few days or weeks and then he could have it back, free gratis. Eventually the other six mountains were attacked too, by B-52s, air strikes, artillery and gunships.

Looking back now I remember many things from those days: the night a Sergeant went off his rocker and tried to kill a First Sergeant; the Sunday a field grade officer ordered a Captain off Chi Lang, never to return as long as he was there. The Captain's crime? He had been out of uniform and was repairing a trailer wearing shorts and shower shoes. I got food-poisoning twice from eating with the Vietnamese soldiers, and I remember the thousands of rats that scoured the landscape at night. One day a UH-1 with two new pilots, right out of flight school, landed on the wrong side of the minefield fence and set off an old French mine, destroying their helicopter. Their crew chief and gunner, who had already run out of the minefield to safety, ran back again to unstrap the startled green pilots.

One day the Special Forces camp at Ba Xoai was attacked by a large force. After the assault was beaten off by air strikes, their new commander and a small force went out to get a BDA, a bomb damage assessment desired by the Air Force to check how many enemy, if any, had been killed by the strikes. The force returned with the commander wounded in the back of the head: the camp defenders had known VC in their ranks. I offered to land on the road to medevac the Lieutenant out, but the camp replied 'It's too late.' The next morning I found out his name was Lieutenant Major. We had served together three years before as Sergeants in the Tenth Special Forces Group (Airborne) at Bad Toelz, West Germany.

Al Schwinghammer left Vietnam at the end of his twelve-month tour in May 1967. However, the shortage of pilots led to his return for a second tour of duty in December 1968. This time he was flying with the 54th Utility Airplane Company 'Big Daddy' out of Vung Tau. The Company flew nineteen De Havilland Otters all over III and IV Corps and had one more on temporary duty in Thailand, which was used to fly people and supplies from Bangkok International Airport to dirt strips all over the country. Al Schwinghammer recalls this second tour of duty:

I got to fly in Thailand for two weeks in September 1969. What wonderful people and a beautiful country too. A tremendous change from Nam – I thought I had died and gone too heaven! I quickly learned, after two elephants walked out of a treeline right in front of my aircraft, that elephants have the right of way – period. One afternoon on a return flight, we located and circled the 'Bridge on the River Kwai': that was very memorable and special. And yes, I did get back to Chi Lang

In February 1969, I landed at Chi Lang at around eleven in the morning for a one-hour layover. It was like old home week. The Vietnamese camp commander and many of his cadre came to the runway, all smiling and happy to see an old face. They showed me my old room, number ten, and told me that, two months after I had left, a mortar round had landed in it during a mortar attack. Then they added 'Number ten Dai Uy, number ten!' In Vietnamese, number one is the best and number ten the worst. Dai Uy is Captain, pronounced Dai-wee. They then laughed and giggled like we all do when fate is cheated. Chieu, the Chinese cook, was there too. He shook hands and said 'Hello, Dai Uy.' He looked older, like thirty-seven going on sixty-seven, and his eyes moistened while I recalled all the evening meals he left in the oven for me when I was out on operations and reconnaissance. Its amazing how hard it is to converse during such moments, especially when trying to blink back something that just landed in both eyes. By the time I returned to the aircraft, about a hundred people had shown up to smile and give regards. That congregation was the only public welcoming committee I experienced, but at least I experienced one!

ALONE, UNARMED AND UNAFRAID

9

1. Udorn
2. Vinh
3. Hanoi

THERE are a number of variations on the motto of the photo-reconnaissance pilots, generally at odds with the claim of 'Unafraid'. However, the undeniable facts are that their aircraft were unarmed, they usually flew alone and their job was extremely hazardous to say the least.

At this stage of the war most of the Air Force daylight photo-recon missions over North Vietnam were flown by the RF-101C Voodoo; the RF-4C Phantom flew most of the missions at night. The flights were essential to obtain pre- and post-strike photographs of a target, and a number of squadrons were allocated to the task. By the end of 1965 it was the turn of the 20th Tactical Reconnaissance Squadron (TRS) at Shaw Air Force Base in South Carolina. They took up residence at Tan Son Nhut Air Base between December 1965 and January 1966 and were assigned to the 460th Tactical Reconnaissance Wing. They moved in March to Udorn Royal Thai Air Force Base.

One of the pilots with the 20th TRS was Captain Edward W. O'Neil Jr., known to his friends as 'Fast Eddy'. He served with the squadron at Udorn from 1 July 1966 until he flew his last mission to Vinh on 18 September 1966. At the end of his tour with the squadron he wrote down his thoughts and described his experiences whilst flying photo-recon missions in the Voodoo. Entitled 'Flying in the Barrel' and reading as a virtual guide to the art of flying recon missions over North Vietnam, the words of 'Fast Eddy' were not declassified until December 1974. They were written in the hope that they could bring back safely other RF-101 pilots, but were classified and never read by those who might have benefited from them. The recollections are reproduced here at last, by kind permission of 'Fast Eddy'.

Flying in the Barrel. Summer 1966

This is not meant to be a thesis, although it might appear to be one. It is just a compilation of some thoughts and some knowledge I gathered while flying some 59 missions with the 20th Tactical Reconnaissance Squadron at Udorn Royal Thai Air Force Base. I am writing it while it is fresh in my mind and some of it, or maybe all, you may not agree with. We are all individuals, and in recce it is the individual we must rely on from take-off to landing. While these ideas were good for me during July,

Above: 'Fast Eddy' O'Neil, RF-101 pilot, photographed just prior to his arrival in South-East Asia, wearing a 'Voodoo One-O-Wonder' patch on his right shoulder. (Edward W. O'Neil, Jr)

August and September of 1966, while flying deep into hostile territory, they may not be good in October. It is the day-to-day updating of knowledge that keeps one coming back with the fragged mission.

I do not believe the people who came back were lucky, but I cannot help thinking some of the people who did not return were unlucky. The

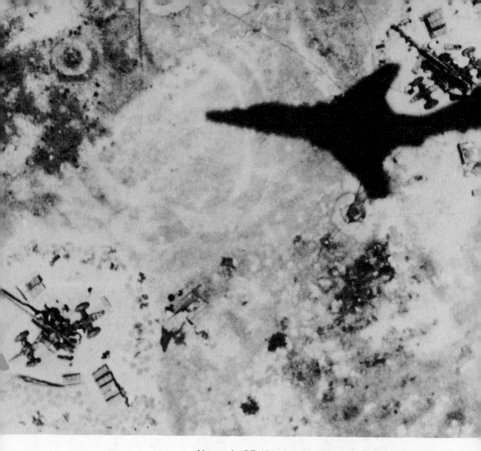

Above: An RF-101 photographing a North Vietnamese 57mm gun emplacement captures its own shadow in the picture. (U.S. Air Force)

atmosphere was hostile, but relatively free of MiGs; however, during this time we lost three crews, very competent crews, each with over sixty missions. We lost them to something – if only we knew.

My experience and the missions I flew resulted in some flights over all areas of Route Packages V, VIA and VIB, north of Hanoi, I have never been to the area within ten miles of Hanoi, or immediately south of that city. I have never executed a sea entry or escape and I have never been in Route Package IV or VIB around Haiphong. I have never seen a MiG. I have done and have seen and have experienced the following.

I have been to Kep Airfield, the Bac Ninh POL, Thai Nguyen, Phu Tho, Yen Bai, 'Thud Ridge' and throughout the valley around these areas many times. I have tried it 'high' and I have tried it 'in the weeds.' I have been hit and have watched them fire at me. I have seen a SAM launched at a flight of 'Thuds' and I have been so scared under fire that I once forgot to turn 'on' my cameras (perhaps it was the fascination of seeing muzzle flashes for the first time). I have tossed and turned in the night and gagged in the morning when I brushed my teeth. At times I have slept like a child. I have worried about myself and worried about the mission of others. I have seen men go to God and men go to booze. I have not seen a hero. I have seen men doing a given task because it was their profession. Maybe that is what makes a hero. I have seen a man for what he is and a war for what it brings and I now recognize that restful, peaceful sleep is one of the most precious things in the world. So, take a look at this and think: if it does nothing more that make a person think, it is worth writing. (Note: I write this extemporaneously; therefore there is some digression).

The single-ship concept for reconnaissance in both highly defended and undefended targets is the most profitable employment of aircrews and aircraft and offers the following advantages:

1. Maneuverability, without wingman consideration.
2. High-speed, low-level terrain-masking.
3. Weather penetration anytime.
4. Minimum radio transmissions.
5. Maximum speed employment.
6. Minimum enemy target development.
7. Maximum use of fuel, i.e., wingman will normally use more fuel than leader.
8. A chance to be alone in a decision and a plan.

The high-threat SAM will always, except in the most unique situation (i.e., movement of a SAM site to previously undefended area in order to surprise launch into known used flight paths), be located in highly defended areas. Therefore, consideration must be given to automatic weapons, 37, 57, 85, and 100mm anti-aircraft artillery, plus the SAM. High-altitude flying in a SAM area is out of the question. Although the probability of the enemy launching against a single ship is much less than their launching against a flight, you *can* expect a launch of up to three SAMs (minimum separation six seconds) at any time you fly above tree-top level.

How can you effectively acquire a target in a highly defended, high-threat SAM area? Flying at 4,600 to 8,000 feet, jinking, jinking heavily, until you're almost sick, works if you don't have to stay 'up' too long. If you have to be up longer than two minutes, this method is not satisfactory and the only way I think you can do it is 'in the weeds.' By 'in the weeds' I don't mean so low that flying becomes more dangerous than the enemy; I mean below the peaks in the mountains and about 50 feet in the flatlands. You fly 'in the weeds' except over major roads, railroads and rivers – at these points you 'pop up,' jinking to at least 4,600 feet, then descend, jinking, back to the weeds. About two minutes before reaching the defenses surrounding the target (always expect defenses around the targets we are presently flying) you hit the afterburners, pull the trigger for cameras and 'pop up,' jinking and looking. You keep all cameras going and continue to jink up to altitude for your target.

What altitude? Depends on the target. A bridge – don't go high and don't directly overfly it; an oblique gives all the information they need to know for pre- and post-strike. Remember, this is your most vulnerable position throughout the flight and the less time you are up at altitude the better your chances are. I suggest 6,000 to 8,000 feet for a bridge without ever overflying it, but rather cutting a turn inside the safest side, getting an oblique of the target, then running in the basic direction of the turn. Against POLs (petroleum, oils and lubricants storage areas), barracks, SAM sites, routes and area searches, the vertical is the only way you can get what is desired. Here again, however, the time that you remain in a position taking verticals is important. For pinpoints, offset the target, jink as you climb, jink as you level, overfly the target, roll wings level, hit the extra picture switch, jink and get out. What altitude? 8,000 to 10,000 – why go higher if you plan on going back down? Some think 15,000 is a good figure; maybe so, but its longer up and longer down and longer for them to be shooting at you. And don't think they aren't shooting – just look around, behind if its not in front, and you will see them walking up your tail, or where you have just been, or looked like you were going. They are shooting! So make your course unpredictable and your altitude undetectable. One thing to remember, no matter what altitude you think is best for your 'pop,' watch out for 12,000 feet. It's the 'roll in' altitude the Thuds use, and don't think that the enemy hasn't figured that out.

During the 'pop' you have got to think about missiles, so when you get a launch indication or see a SAM coming at you, your best maneuver is down. Unfortunately 'down' means into a higher concentration of guns, but the higher you are the longer the SAM can track you and the less your chances are of ducking it and ending up 'in the weeds' or behind a knoll to avoid others. You have to go down, and down does not mean a split 'S' (a split 'S' is just long enough in the 'roll over' to get a hit in your back). It means push the stick forward and keep your eye on the missile. You have to keep seeing it to avoid it. You have to force the SAM into a turn it cannot make. Remember, 'Gs' are relative to airspeed, and the SAM is going so fast it cannot out-turn you, even in the RF-101. SAMs can pull about 8 Gs, but that is not much of a turn radius when you're going Mach Two. The rest about missiles is best left to those who have actually had one launched at them. I have never seen one lauched at me, so I do not speak with authority.

Some more on 'down.' 'Down' means down to avoid the SAM but high enough, 4,600 feet, to avoid heavy fire concentration areas. It means down and direction changes. It means down and away to the hills, or in undefended areas to the weeds. Down means behind mountains. Down means not level, but down, jinking, using rudder and never zig-zagging, but zigging, zigging, zag, zig, then 'up' a bit, then down – unpredictable but eventually down. It means changing course from side to side, it means knowing where you are finally going to end up, full bore down.

Once you have acquired the target, it is get out and get home – keeping out of the hostile areas and 'on the deck.' Don't go after bonus targets. If you have had your cameras on all the way, from 'pop' to back in the weeds and you are in a heavily defended area, you will also have a lot of bonus targets without knowing it. You will also be able to see most of the AAA positions that fired at you – they are easy to spot, and their muzzle flashes and smoke are evident on the film. Even the Fansong radar pointing at you will be noticeable. The mission is fragged; so fly the frag – that is what you are there for.

What about hits? Hits must be expected and, strangely enough, small-arms hits in the aircraft are not usually felt. You will know it if a 37mm plus gets a good hit, and if you are hit, no matter what type hit, *go home!* You never know the damage it has caused, and going home is the only answer. Go home as expeditiously as possible and let everyone 'on our side' know you were hit, as it may develop into real trouble.

Regarding aircraft auxiliary equipment and the use of same while in a highly defended area. I feel that consideration must be given to the possibility that anything that transmits a signal can be used by the enemy to DF (direction find) your position; therefore the radio, tacan, radar altimeter and IFF (identification friend or foe) have to be considered. The tacan should be turned 'off' or put on 'receive' only. The radar altimeter is useful for the automatic camera function, if used, and transmits only directly down from the aircraft, so I keep it on. The UHF radio is manually set for SAR primary and placed on 'guard' – not all the time, but most of the time. The reason: if I want to talk, I want everyone to hear me because I'm in trouble. If I'm OK, I don't talk. At other times I set up the radio to have the strike frequency tuned in and listen to the fighters that I know are in the general area. By just listening I can tell how the air action and defenses are progressing. I always check for call signs and target locations of strikes going on while I am in the area. It is not SOP, but I turn my IFF to 'Stand by.' I don't want possible interrogation of my set – who knows, maybe they'll think I'm one of them! My cabin temp control is on 'defrost' and either 'dump' or just past the moisture point if circulation is desired. 'Dump' means no circulation, and it is unbearably hot in the cockpit at low-level, high speed. You can not go to cold in SEA because of the condensation you get in the cockpit. The 'D' ring 'zero delay' lanyard is not hooked up – it just means a ripped parachute if you bail-out low and fast. It is better to hope you have enough altitude left for a bail-out and a partial slow-down, rather than an immediate opening (a lost cause). I also recommend a clear visor on the helmet. It's for the time you lose part of the windshield, bail-out, or get dirt on your face on a negative G maneuver.

How about flying into a minimal SAM threat area? Well, in North

Vietnam any place can have SAMs. Even Route Package I can, so be alert for that one unit that can slip in and be ready for you tomorrow, when photos, etc, did not show up anything there today. In these areas, even up North close to Vinh, I recommend going medium and feeling out the situation. Feeling out the situation? Well, I have not mentioned the APR-25, -26 radar detector, mainly because, although it is a nice thing to have, if you believe everything it says you will never enter an area. The enemy 'spoofs' with his radar almost as much as he fires with it. What 'the machine' does do, though, is let you know when air-to-air is looking at you, when Firecan and/or Fansong are looking at you and when they are going into firing mode. It is a great machine for never letting you get complacent and it is great for keeping your mind on the business at hand. It is great for feeling out an area, and its greatest asset? It is a great jink-maker. When it talks, I jink!

When entering North Vietnam, Laos, or any other place that has little SAM threat, I go medium altitude and feel out the area for the target. When flying medium in the minimal SAM areas, one should keep in mind the weapons one faces and their maximum effective altitudes, i.e. automatic weapons = 4,600 feet, 37mm = 5,600 feet, 57mm = 19,700 feet, 85mm plus = 27,500 feet. The most lethal altitude is somewhere between 100 and 4,600 feet. With this in mind, I think a good altitude for photos is 15,000 feet, and 8,000 feet for feeling out the area. Now 8,000 feet does not mean 8,000 feet above the lowest land, but 8,000 feet above the highest land (other than rugged peaks). Entry from the land or sea is available, and the sea has the advantage in some respects but a marked disadvantage because the coast is defended in just about a straight line and you are expected from the coast. You are seen by radar for a long while and the weapons are easily pointed towards the sea. *But*, you are the safest over water, so feel out the area as you enter; if it feels safe, then continue in medium, 'dancing' into the area. Vary altitude and headings, but do not do the jinking you had to do in high-defense areas. If heavy jinking is required and there is a lot of activity, then you are wrong 'medium' and a 180-degree is the best answer. You have planned wrong for the situation this day and a new plan of attack is needed.

You should always have ready an alternate plan of attack, on the map, for a medium-altitude, heavy-jinking run to the target using terrain-masking, maneuverability and speed. Now, you get rid of the tanks, get your speed up and head in on your alternate course. I think the alternate course should be different from the one you attempted to use for the 'feel out' course. Why? Because the same things that just bothered you are going to still be there and you will be retracking a previous run. So make your approach from another direction, and not, this time, from the water. Come in from some terrain-masking and then up to 8,000 feet, jink in, get the cameras on early, get the target and jink out.

Say, about cameras – have them ready to turn on immediately after you take off. I think the climb check is a good time. You never know when you will overfly something significant, and setting up the cameras might be too late – so 'be prepared' always. Use the 'little lookers' and 'split verticals.' Try for the SV as prime, but have the 'little lookers' on too: they can save a mission and can be blown up and get all the information intelligence needs. The other cameras are not needed for missions other than the low with a 'pop,' so don't use them on the target run in a relatively safe area. Relatively safe I say – Route Package I or II, or Laos and western North Vietnam are relatively safe, and it is all relative. If you have to get a route or a somewhat long-winding strip, walk, bank and walk the aircraft down the route – the best way to get maximum turn in route-running is to turn 'off' the yaw damper. Vary altitude as you are walking down the road and watch the route in the viewfinder to be sure you have the coverage. If you miss a corner, don't go back and do 180s and 270s. Routes are defended, and though they may not be shooting, the defenses are there. Use the extra picture switch to the maximum, just before banking and just after banking – it ensures a frame each time you change heading

About flight-planning and scheduling. Schedules should be up the day before, showing general areas and designating the aircrews who will be going the next day. It is not necessary and is *not* the best idea to let the crew know the exact target he has tomorrow. If he knows he has a 'rougher than usual' target, it affects his rest and entire attitude the night before the mission. So I think it is best to let him know the Route Package he will be in tomorrow, but wait until he picks up the target folder to find out the rest. The schedule, once set, should not be changed under any circumstances short of an emergency. Let the ball fall where it may, but do not change the schedule. If an individual has a rough morning mission and gets a 'go,' fine. If he gets a 'cancel,' fine – then let him have a 'piece of cake' as an alternate, but don't put him on another rough target the same day. He is not mentally prepared to 'sweat out' another rough mission. Don't cancel him out completely either – make sure he gets an alternate, a 'piece of cake.'

The proper time to get your target folder and start the plan, I believe, is three hours before takeoff, not before and not later. I find that laying out the map and just looking is the best way to start. Have a cup of coffee and just look: look at the target, look at the high-threat SAM sites – just look. I sometimes just look for one half-hour; I digest the map and go to the relief map and digest the terrain. I watch others planning. Where are they going and how are they going in? What escape routes are they using? I watch and ask questions.

Important point to remember item – we in recce are individuals, flying single-seat, individual aircraft. We all have ideas, based on self-confidence, training, our experience and the experience of others. When we plan a route, we are all trying to accomplish the same end result.

Above: STATISTICS: Eddy O'Neil (far right) with six other RF-101 pilots. Gordon Page (far left) was killed in action on 7 March 1966; Jerry Prather (second from right) was killed in an RF-101 accident at Shaw AFB in 1967; and Wally Gustofson (second from left) was killed in a civilian flying accident circa 1980. (via Edward W. O'Neil, Jr)

When a recce pilot plans a mission, he alone is responsible for that plan and his life depends on the success of the plan. So never, never volunteer suggestions on how he should plan his flight. If he asks your opinion of his flight plan, tell him it is the best route you have ever seen. If you are asked for information, give it gladly, but do not be critical of anyone else's plan. Confidence in the mission is necessary and the reasoning behind his plan is not known to you, so look and ask questions, but do not volunteer information. One exception – something that happened to *you* over an area in his proposed flight.

It is in the Planning and Intelligence Room where you learn almost everything that keeps you current – and being current means day-to-day, hour-by-hour updating of all aspects of the war area in which you fly. You read the intelligence reports on yesterday's missions, you talk to everyone you can see about where they are going or where they have been. How did you go 'in'? What speed? Altitude? Everything! Any MiGs or SAMs? Everything! Watch the planning and you will see almost every way to get 'in' and 'out.' If you see a route that is not being used, ask why? There may be a good reason and, then again, you may have stumbled onto a new approach. Talk to 'Thud' drivers, F-4 drivers, anyone who flies into the target areas in other types of aircraft – you can learn from everyone who has been; and finally, you form do's and don'ts that become a part, a vital part, of your planning.

Now you are ready to start the process of how to get the fragged target. First, take your map and go read the frag for your mission, plot by colour the high-threat SAMs. Read the strike frags to find out who is going to be in the area and jot down who and where. *Before* you do any planning on the target 'run in,' look at the 1:50,000 maps that show gun positions in detail. You may find one side of your target relatively 'hot' and another 'cold.' This could determine your approach. Also, look at your map for marshy lands – guns do not sit well in the flat, flooded lands and it may be a good route to use 'in' or 'out.' Go to intelligence and take a look at previous photos of the area, and get as good an idea as possible of what the target and surrounding area look like.

Now, get things back into the planning room and pencil in your proposed route, check it out on the terrain map, look for good turn points and terrain you want to use for radar avoidance and checkpoints – get used to an almost braille use of the relief map.

A few words about checkpoints. Do not plan to fly over excellent checkpoints: plan routes offset to them. I think this is necessary all the time – you can use the same checkpoint over several times if you vary your offset each time, i.e., five miles north, three miles south, one minute past and three miles east etc. But don't overfly the obvious. If it looks like a good IP for you, it looks the same for the enemy.

Once the final decision is made on how you are going to get there, and how you are going to get out, draw the final lines with a black, easy-to-see marking pencil; make sure the marker you use is waterproof, as it rains here all the time and the lines smear when they are not waterproof. I use a 1:1,000,000 map for the route from takeoff to start point, then a 1:250,000 all the way to the target area. Draw your turns to coincide with the way you actually fly the bird. Don't draw 30-degree banks, you don't turn that way in combat. You use up to 90-degree banks and turn almost on a dime. I do nickel turns on a 1:250,000 in actual high-speed flight.

The planned exit should be based on the same principles as the entry. For the best planning it should not duplicate the entry; however, it often can and will be the same as the entry. Why? Because in utilizing the entry, you have selected a basically safe route – it holds, therefore, that unless there are MiGs anticipating an intercept on your 'out' track, the route, if offset slightly, should hold good for getting back. Offset slightly? You use the same 'in' line for your 'out' course, but you never get 'on course.' You knowingly stay off course from three to five miles, north or south or east or west of the line.

MiGs will be the major problem of the offset exit, so when you fly you'll have to exit rapidly: stay low – look behind and do not leave any space for someone to come in under and up your tail. You'll have to make the exit a 'dancing' course of turns to the right and left, looking behind, forward, up and into the sun. You're camouflaged, so you'll be hard to acquire, but when you 'pop' over defended areas and the target, you'll be a sitting duck if MiGs are there; and remember, they don't fly single-ship – there will be at least two of them. You'll have to plan on staying low and get to relatively undefended areas, at least 100 nautical miles from MiG bases, before you climb for the trip home.

Now look at the target, and if it is set up for a 'low with a pop' back off from the target and put a line for the 'pop' point. The 'pop' point and cameras 'on' are identical. Now put headings in bold print and arrows for direction. Put the headings all along the legs, so that they are constantly seen as the map is followed. Right under headings put airspeeds. For fuel conservation, I try to fly into the area up to my last 'IP for the run' at 480 knots. The speed from the IP to the target and back to the escape checkpoint is full military afterburners in the 'pop' and, if need be, on top and on the way down. Normally the afterburners are cut off on top of the pop. Figure 570 knots as a good speed at full bore with afterburners climbing on 'run in' – I know it is nine and one half and not nine or ten miles per minute, but it is what you will be traveling, so use it. The exit speed is 540 knots – some go back at 480 knots, but I find myself unable to pull the throttles back that much 'after the show.' I put down 540 knots, because that is what I end up flying. Keep 540 until the point in the escape where you climb, then it is climb and get home.

You have your lines, headings and airspeed. Now get a yellow or brown marker, and accentuate terrain features of the mountains and ridges you anticipate seeing – go to the relief map and you will see what you want in detail. Next, get a 1:500,000-feet map of the low-level area and look at the rivers it shows. If they show on a 1:500,000, you will see them on your low-level, so take a blue marker and increase the boldness of the river. Look for canals – they stand out and are easily seen, so mark them bold blue. Now get out your divider or speed tape and mark off the minutes on all legs according to speed. Set up a hackpoint every six to nine minutes and a final hack at the IP to the target. Put your time in one-half minutes on the final IP to target run and you are in business.

You want to be able, at any time a SAM or MiG alert is called, to identify that it is in your area. So, along the route put the route package and 'georef' (Geological Reference) sector designations on the map. I also put the code word for SAMs and MiGs – then there is not any fumbling or doubt about my situation if an alert is called. Also, put the RPs and georefs that are next to your area, with an arrow pointing to the direction of the area; then you will know if anything is close. Now that you have the flight planned, you sit down and memorize it. You memorize the headings and times. You memorize it from entry to exit. You spend all of your remaining time memorizing the flight plan; 020 degrees for three minutes, the Black River, 020 degrees for five minutes, the Red. You memorize it completely, then you fly it. Of primary importance is to *fly the plan*. If the plan cannot be followed on entry you should do a 180 and get out *immediately!* Entries must follow the plan. Exits can be modified to cope with changes in environment, but entries must follow the plan – so fly the plan.

What will the flight be like? Well, you won't have MiG cover, only under ideal conditions will you get a tanker, and elint will seldom be around; so you're on your own, fellow – really on your own! If you're lucky, you'll not be the last man of the day in the valley. Maybe some strikes will be going on; if they are, then expect some MiGs, but, lucky for you, most of the action will be on the 'Thuds,' so maybe you can slip in and out with little trouble. If you have to go in one or two hours after the strike, they'll be waiting for you, so remember, be prepared, you're not fooling anyone. When you 'pop' the guns will be manned and they'll look like strobe lights in a circle or, as one fellow put it, 'They're welding down there.' You'll see it, you'll see where the flak is bursting sometimes gray, and sometimes black with fireball centers. They're shooting at you, fella, and all the training and skill that you have acquired is directed towards this moment. So good luck! It's your turn in the barrel.

COCKTAILS OVER HANOI

10

CHINA

NORTH VIETNAM

THAILAND   LAOS

CAMBODIA

SOUTH VIETNAM

1. Da Nang   2. Vinh
3. A Shau Valley
4. Hanoi

*T*HE Grumman aircraft company is renowned for the quality of its products, such as the immortal Albatross amphibian, examples of which are still flying forty years after the prototype first took to the air. In more modern times they have produced the A-6 Intruder, an aircraft which launched the era of the fully integrated, computerized, all-weather attack and navigation system.

The Intruder first made an appearance in Vietnam in July 1965, when Attack Squadron VA-75, the 'Sunday Punchers', flew their A-6As off the deck of the aircraft carrier USS Independence, *to attack targets south of Hanoi. A year later the first Marine Corps Intruder squadron arrived, to be based ashore in South Vietnam. One of its pilots was Jesse Randall, and this is his story.*

I was with the A-6 program from the beginning of its conception and trained with the Navy at Oceana Naval Air Station with VA-42. We formed the first Marines A-6 squadron, VMA(AW)-242, at Cherry Point Marine Corps Air Station in North Carolina and took it to Vietnam at the end of 1966. I was on the advance party and had to set up the maintenance facility at Da Nang, while the squadron flew the airplanes from Cherry Point to California, to Hawaii, Johnsons Island, into the Philippines, Cubi Point and then across to Da Nang.

After we got established at Da Nang, we were constantly working on the problems inherent in all new types of advanced aircraft and had fifteen maintenance vans and 23 technical representatives from Grumman, Litton and other companies, continually striving to maintain the aircraft with full systems availability.

Our first missions were generally in the south, doing TPQ, visual bombing and a little bit of all-weather bombing. We hadn't started using offset bombing from a forward air controller's beacon yet, and we were not assigned missions north of the DMZ. Eventually we went to Route

Left: Jesse Randall preparing to board his A-6 Intruder for a mission out of Da Nang. (Jesse Randall)

Package I, just north of the DMZ, and were utilized against moving targets. The A-6 has a mechanism by which you can blank out your bombardier/navigator's radarscope other than moving targets. If the trucks or vehicles were moving at more than four knots, that blip would come up on the screen and we could lock on to the target and go in and bomb it. The inertial navigation system would allow us to plot our position and the computer would lock-on and compute the lead necessary to hit the target.

Our standard armament load was 28 500-pound bombs or sometimes 18 500-pound bombs and six 19-shot packs of 2.75-inch rockets, and we would select roughly three to six bombs for a moving target. This load was somewhat of a surprise to the Air Force, because at the time they were having problems getting bombs. We had plenty of them and we were going out with 28 and they were sending out their F-4s with only six.

Soon the Air Force began to recognize the capabilities of the A-6, and from then on we were tasked with missions deep into North Vietnam, usually in Route Package VI around Hanoi. We were given selected targets and would depart Da Nang, climb to altitude out over the water and then descend to low level for ingress to Route Packages V and VI. We would also go out over the mountains in Thailand and into North Vietnam through the Red River Valley. I will try to relate some of the things that we did.

We were normally briefed with an EA-6 pilot from VMCJ-1, because we didn't want to go into Route Package VI without some electronic countermeasures support. The EA-6 would stay at altitude 15 to 20 miles behind the A-6 flight and jam the radars trying to track us. When we first started flying North there was not much resistance, but when they learned about us they had many countermeasures. There were lots of SAMs, and to warn the towns that we were coming the North Vietnamese would signal across country with flashlights or lanterns. You could see a flash of light go right across the country from block to block into the town in front of us. Most of our missions were at night; out of the 386 missions during my year there, only eight were in the daytime.

When I first got there we were told that we would have to come in across the water at 700 feet or below. If you are not used to flying at such a low level, you found that whenever you made a turn you would rise up and couldn't keep the aircraft down. When they first told me that I would have to fly at that altitude, I said 'You must be nuts!', but by the end of the year we were all flying at 200 feet and treetop level, skimming everything we could to stay out of the SAM envelope. We learned that if you stayed below 2,000 feet, generally the SAMs could not track or lock-on to you. The whole process of survival was to be able to avoid any SAMs.

The A-6 is a two-man aircraft with a pilot and a bombardier/navigator. The bombardier/navigator controls the radar and sets the bombs, while the pilot flies the plane. You sit next to each other rather than fore and aft, and if the intercom is not working you can still communicate by taking your oxygen masks off and screaming to each other. You had to work as a team and we set up teams, and generally flew with the same person most of the time.

When we first arrived at Da Nang, most of our work was familiarization, where we would go out and fly close air support with a Forward Air Controller. They were unfamiliar with an A-6 and were totally shocked when they asked what ordnance we had on board and how much fuel we carried and were told that we had 28 500-pound bombs and could remain on station for three hours. Of course they thought that they could use us to drop one bomb at a time and hit 28 different targets as they wanted us to do visual close support just like the A-4s and F-4s. It took a long time to convince them that we were more accurate utilizing systems to allow us to lock-in on and destroy targets. Also, we did not want to do visual bombing, climbing to 8,000 feet and rolling in on 28 different targets.

When we could not maintain full systems in all the aircraft we would also fly a TPQ, which is a ground-controlled radar, and the TPQ controller would direct you across to a target. The verbal corrections were given in degrees such as 'Come left two degrees, stand by, stand by,' and then 'Mark, mark' when they wanted you to drop your bombs. Sometimes we would fly with five 2,000-pound bombs. I will never forget the day the controllers sighted enemy trucks in the open and Viet Cong running around and wanted us to utilize TPQ and drop all five bombs at once. When I came across the target and released all the bombs at once I almost bit through my tongue because of the G load on the aircraft when dropping 10,000 pounds in one go.

After training with the same pilots for three years prior to going to Vietnam, we got to know who was the best pilot for visual ordnance or for systems and we thought we knew who the real chargers and go-getters were. But attitudes changed when it came to actual combat: when we started going North, we found that some of the go-getters that we thought we wanted to be in combat with turned out to be guys that let you down. They would find any reason not to go North. Either the radar went down, the systems went down or something, and it was a real disappointment to see the reaction of some pilots compared to others. There were other pilots who always volunteered, who wanted the more dangerous hops, who always wanted to go to the deep North to down-town Hanoi where all the SAMs were. Their adrenalin would build up and they would go, even without VMCJ ECM support. Sometimes they would do foolish things, but it was enlightening to see that we didn't know who the real go-getters were until we experienced real combat.

When we first started flying up North, we tried different tactics of striking targets. I had a strike on the Vinh airfield one night and the

CO was taking the lead. We had an ECM aircraft and the CO was going to come in from the north and call a checkpoint at seven miles and I would come in two to three minutes behind him from the south. There was a big mountain near Vinh and the CO was going to come around it from the right side, the North, and I was coming around from the left side, the South. We were running in at 700 feet and at eight miles we would pull up to 1,800 feet to get above our own bomb blasts, drop our bombs and then get out of there. Well, the first time we did this the CO dropped his bombs and received no counterfire at all, but when I came along two to three minutes later the world lit up with 57mm AAA and four or five SAMs came up – it was really amazing. This taught us early on that single-ship missions were best, preferably at night.

There is one mission that I will never forget. It was around the time of Khe Sahn in 1967 and we had troops on the ground being overrun. The ground controllers called all the aircraft in that could possibly drop and we assumed that we would be using systems bombing, utilizing the beacon. The ground Forward Air Controller had a beacon that would identify his position on the radar screen and he would then tell us a heading and distance to the target from the beacon. The bombardier/navigator would then type this into the computer and the system would give you steering to the release point.

This time we were told 'There are sixteen of us and we are being overrun – do you have our beacon?' I came back with a 'Roger' and he said, 'Immediate! Drop on the beacon!' I said 'Clarify – drop on the beacon?' and he said 'Roger, we are being overrun – drop on the beacon!' When I came across the target, I dropped all 28 500-pounders, came around again and tried to talk to the ground. I said 'Check in controller, check in controller,' but there was no answer. I thought I had totally wiped out the unit.

I came back and I literally went to church after that and just prayed, because I thought I had wiped out sixteen guys. It wasn't until about two and half months later that I received a letter from an unknown controller thanking me. Yes I did kill some of my own Marines, but they were well dug in and my dropping the bombs directly on their position wiped out most of the Viet Cong and the twelve or thirteen survivors were able to withdraw safely.

It's amazing how your mind works, because you really only remember the goods things. We lost a couple of good guys, flying also at Vinh. I had a mission at the same time as Jim McGarvey, a hut mate and fellow Major. Jim was coming around the mountain at Vinh with his bombardier/navigator Jim Carlton and flew into the ground. They didn't come back that night and after taking aerial photographs of the area several days later that was the conclusion we came to. Flying that low was very hard and we lost several airplanes that way and a bunch of good guys.

I remember coming down the Red River Valley when Red Crown, the radar watch ship in the Gulf of Tonkin, called me up and said 'Wallnut

Hill, you have MiGs on your tail.' Swinging right and then left I could see them over my shoulder. Sure enough they were right behind me, so I dove for the ground and used terrain-clearance, flying as low as possible down through the valleys, and inadvertently went across the Chinese border. That was a 'no-no' because the Chinese MiGs and SAMs would be ready, and the Navy lost a couple of A-6s that way. Their crews never did return. However, by flying at tree-top level through the mountains and valleys we managed to escape – in fact one of them overflew me and I tried to pull up and knock the tail off the MiG, trying to be the first A-6 to claim a MiG kill! My bombardier/navigator, Charlie Dixon, was screaming at me 'No, no, let's go home!', so we did just that.

I was the first one to drop on the airfield at Haiphong and the fuel tanks to the southeast of the airfield. I ingressed over Thailand and was running in low when I was locked in by searchlights, and although I broke to the left and right I could not get out of the radar-controlled lights. What a scary feeling that was, particularly as they were shooting everything they had at me. There was nothing I could do, so I just carried on into the target, climbing to 1,800 feet to drop my bombs and then back down to tree-top level and out to the Gulf of Tonkin. I got away without a hit.

Another mission was in the vicinity of Hanoi. I came from the Thailand side and was crossing the Red River Valley when I got hit. The AAA round blew a hole in my wing so big that when I was on the ground I could stand up with my shoulders through it. The fuel was streaming out , my hydraulic pressure was dropping and when I tried to jettison my ordnance it would not fall away. I called Search and Rescue and advised them that I did not think I could make it to Udorn. Before I got half way to Udorn I was joined by the VMCJ-1 EA-6, so that at least someone would know where I went down, if I didn't make it and had to eject.

As I approached Udorn with the EA-6 close by and two Jolly Green helicopters in tow, I was sure I wasn't going to make it. Seven miles out the engine quit, but I was able to dead-stick it into Udorn, still carrying the 28 500-pounders. I couldn't believe it. We rolled out and I had to pump open the canopy by hand as we had no hydraulic pressure left. Charlie and I literally kissed the ground when we got out! We went to the Officers Club and the Air Force wouldn't allow us to buy a drink – everything was on the house. What a party that was! The Air Force was happy, because they still had a shortage of bombs and I had 28 on my airplane. I said 'Take them, they are all yours!'

One of the trademarks I had (most of the bombardier/navigators in the squadron got used to it eventually) was that following bomb release, I would pull the airplane up and do a big barrel roll and state 'Ho Chi Minh is a son of bitch!' It used to frighten the new guys who did not know what to expect, because we would pull up into the SAM envelope, but I never did have SAMs fired at me during a barrel roll.

When you see a SAM coming up at you, it looks like a telephone pole on fire. If you see it in time, you can dive into it, but at the levels we flew at, generally all you could do was break hard left or hard right. The ECM of the aircraft was good enough so that you always knew when there was one coming, but it was always frightening to have that bright light and a warbling sound coming into your headset and not knowing where the SAM was coming from. We would partially drop our flaps and yank the stick over and try to dive into the SAM to break its lock on us. Lowering the flaps would allow you to pull more Gs and make a harder break.

One of the few daylight missions that I flew occurred during Tet in 1968, when we had a three- or four-day ceasefire. Practically the whole squadron went to the 'O Club' to catch up on some drinking. We hadn't been there long when we were asked to fly, and I hadn't had much to drink so I said I would go. When we got airborne we were directed to the A Shau Valley where they had 40 or 50 trucks in the open. I was running in at approximately 2,000 or 3,000 feet and preparing to attack the trucks, when all of a sudden the sky started raining bombs. You could see the bombs falling all around us and apparently we had flown under an Arc Light strike. Above us were half a dozen B-52 bombers dropping their bombs. I could see bombs falling all around us and just closed my eyes and waited for a bomb to blow up our aircraft or go through our wing. Being in the middle of an Arc Light, with bombs blowing up all around you, is one of the most frightening things that can ever happen.

There was one thing that I will remember the most during my time in Vietnam. It happened when I was returning from a mission and was about 50 miles out from Da Nang. It was 0345 hours in the morning on 23 March 1967. All of a sudden Da Nang just lit up and there was this great, horrendous mushroom cloud and I was sure that Da Nang had had a nuclear hit. I proceeded on to Chu Lai, some 105 miles south of Da Nang, and could not figure out what had happened. I later found out that it was Fred Cone, a fellow A-6 pilot and hut mate and his bombardier/navigator Doug Wilson.

Fred had been cleared for takeoff and had sixteen 500-pound bombs and six 19-shot rocket packs on board. As he was cleared for takeoff, the Vietnamese ground controller also cleared a C-141 Starlifter cargo plane to cross the runway. As Fred began his takeoff roll the C-141 started to pull out onto the runway and when Fred saw this he veered to the right, but the port wing of the A-6 struck the nose of the C-141, flipped over onto its back and continued on down the runway.

Unfortunately the C-141 was carrying 72 cylinders of acetylene gas and the whole lot blew up, destroying the aircraft and killing the crew instantly, with the exception of the loadmaster who just made it out of the left troop door as the cargo compartment filled with flames. Fred Cone broke his knee in the crash and was pinned in the aircraft, but Doug Wilson found a hole in the canopy and crawled through and pulled him out. Fred was screaming that he wanted to go and try to help the crew of the C-141, but Doug held him back – there was nothing they could do. The A-6 was also burning and the fuel and ordnance started to cook off. They were lucky to escape with their lives.

We often lived as if there were no tomorrow and had narrow escapes on the ground as well as in the air. One day our flight surgeon, Bill Arndt, and I borrowed the CO's jeep to go to town for a steak. We had just passed the main gate when 'clunk,' something landed in the back of the jeep. We both realized at the same time that it was a hand grenade, thrown by one of the townspeople, and we leapt out of the jeep into the road. The jeep smashed into a tree, but the grenade didn't go off. It took a long time before we got that grenade, which was a dud, out of the jeep and carried on into town.

Da Nang was known as 'Rocket City' and the base was often mortared or rocketed, so we built revetments for the aircraft. They were made out of steel and filled with sand and the A-6 would just fit in the revetment with the wings folded. One day the squadron CO and the flight surgeon came back from Cubi Point in the Philippines, where we would go to wash our aircraft and take a couple of days R and R. He was extremely

Below: The morning of 23 March 1967, Da Nang Air Base. The wreckage of Fred Cone's A-6 with its tail-hook in the foreground and the tail of the C-141 in the distance. (US Air Force)

annoyed that there were no maintanence personnel available to take him through the refueling pits or direct him. The next thing we knew he had taxied into a revetment with the wings down and neatly removed two feet from each wingtip.

There was a minefield at one end of the runway and I remember one night a B-52 that had been hit made an emergency landing. He had lost flight control areas, was hit in the hydraulics and didn't have full braking power and couldn't stop. He went off the end of the runway and into the minefield and set the mines off, one after another. The plane was totally destroyed except for the tail section containing the tail gunner. He was just sitting there crying and they had to use a helicopter to get him out. It may have been a good idea to have a minefield at the end of the overrun, to keep the Viet Cong snipers away, but no one considered the result if an aircraft went off the end of the runway.

On my wedding anniversary, 14 April 1967, about a week before I was scheduled to go on R and R to meet my wife, I had a mission to go deep into Hanoi. On that night I had more SAMs fired at me than ever before. I think there were three or four on the way in and another half dozen on the way out. We dropped our bombs and got out of there, and I remember calling Red Crown to tell them in a high-pitched voice 'Feet wet! I mean – feet wet.' I was probably more scared that night than I have ever been. I had volunteered to fly the mission just before my R and R and it was my anniversary too: it seemed as if something was bound to happen to stop me making it back.

As we climbed out over the water my bombardier/navigator, Chuck Dixon, said, 'Well, what are you going to do tonight?' I said, 'Well, it's my anniversary, so I think I'll go back and have a Martini.' He reached down and brought out a big pitcher of iced Martinis, two glasses *and* the olives, and we drank Martinis all the way home from Hanoi.

THE WRECKING OF OLD 888

11

1. Pleiku
2. 15 Miles Inside Cambodia
3. Shot Down 15 Feb 67

O FFICIAL US Government records show that between 1962 and 1973 a total of 1,211 UH-1 aircraft were lost in combat in Vietnam. John B. Morgan was the pilot of one of these aircraft and was flying for the 4th Infantry Division Aviation Battalion at the time.

I was shot down on 15 February 1967. At that time my unit had been in-country about 40 days and operational only about two weeks. I was a WO-1, a Warrant Officer, flying as co-pilot for Major Charles A. Neal, the 1st Platoon Leader. Our mission that day was to reinforce a battalion of US infantry who were surrounded and under heavy fire by the NVA. Ours was the second attempt that day, the first having been unsuccessful due to the intensity of ground fire.

We were flying fifteen UH-1D slicks, organized in five 'Vs of three' in trail formation. Each V of three had about a 30-second interval as our landing zone was only large enough to accommodate three aircraft. We had picked up units of the 1st Battalion, 12th Infantry at a 'PZ' about ten miles south of the 'LZ'. Major Neal and I were flying the lead ship and had five Pathfinders aboard who would coordinate communications upon successful insertion.

The LZ was about 75 yards in diameter, surrounded by 60- to 80-foot trees and heavy brush. The American unit was dug in around the perimeter, leaving the center open and clear for landing helicopters. As we approached from west to east the artillery prep was shut off and the last round marked by smoke, as per SOP (standard operating procedure). At that time our two pairs of UH-1C helicopter gunship escorts started their race-track firing pattern and our door gunners were told to open fire. The gunships were firing 2.75-inch diameter folding fin air-to-ground rockets with nine-pound high-explosive warheads and quad flexible M-60s into the area surrounding the LZ.

Needless to say, this 22-year-old co-pilot in the lead ship, on his first 'hot' combat assault, was not the only one present with sweaty palms! As we started our deceleration and approach the noise was impressive. Machine guns and launching rockets could be heard 'second hand' through our helmet head sets, as the gunship drivers chattered over air to air VHF. Impacting rockets and our own door guns added to the din. All this didn't seem to impress the NVA, who were dug in and merely fired straight up as we passed overhead.

Another new sound added to the confusion – that of bullets passing through aluminium aircraft skin. One round came through the chin bubble an inch or so forward of my left foot. It passed through the radio console between Major Neal and myself, through his right calf, and ricocheted off his cyclic stick. The force of the bullet knocked his right foot off the right tail rotor pedal, which allowed his left foot to go forward to the mechanical stop on the left pedal. At this point I was just along for the ride, because the aircraft yawed hard left and hit the ground near the middle of the LZ, still moving at about 15 knots.

The toe of the right skid hit first, then the aircraft rolled 360 degrees to the right. As the main rotor blades contacted the ground the transmission and attaching parts departed – fortunately to the rear and not through the cockpit as is the case if the aircraft rolls to the left. I remember watching the landing zone and tree line do a beautiful slow roll to the tune of very loud crushing metal and wishing this would all come to a stop sometime soon. What was left of 'Old 888' came to rest upright in a cloud of red dust. Radio chatter from our wingmen and our crash convinced whoever was in charge to call a time out and the remainder of the ships aborted.

Our passengers had been deposited on the ground, some with injuries, as the aircraft rolled away from them. The door gunner on the right side was not as fortunate. He had been badly crushed and later that morning died of internal injuries without regaining consciousness. When the ship stopped moving I was out and into a good-sized foxhole about twenty yards away before I remembered my companions and guiltily returned to help free them from the wreckage. Major Neal was still strapped to his armored seat, struggling to free himself and obviously in a lot of pain. I unbuckled his seat belt and, with adrenalin shooting out my ears, dragged him by the shoulders to the foxhole I had found seconds earlier. His leg was attended by a medic who also did what he could for our door gunner.

As the noise of our departing brothers' helicopters faded, we settled down to wait in our now densely populated foxhole. M-16s could be heard returning what I quickly learned was the distinctive report of AK-47s made in the Soviet Union. On the other side of the LZ, no one bothered to expose himself long enough to shut down the engine of a wrecked H-23 Raven observation helicopter, which had crashed earlier that morning. What was left of its rotor blades flogged what remained of its fuselage and bubble, as its reliable Lycoming roared on and on.

An Air Force FAC appeared overhead in an O-1 Bird Dog. He coordinated with a pair of F-100 Super Sabres who did a mighty fine job of bringing napalm as close to the perimeter as I would care to have it. I could feel heat on my face as the canisters went off. Within three hours the first dust-off medevac Hueys had arrived. Major Neal was one of the first to go out – he got a ticket all the way home. I got a ride out with the rest of the crew – we were flying again next day.

After completing my year in-country I was posted to Germany. I was stationed at Ludwigsburg, which is just north of Stuttgart. I had my own little aviation section to provide the 3rd Support Brigade Commander with helicopter support. We had a CH-34C and in eight months I put in 350 hours, which isn't bad for a peacetime unit. However, the challenge soon wore off and I missed the special something that combat flying gave me. When people really need and really appreciate what you can do for them, life takes on a new meaning. It's an elixir which, once tasted, is tough to put down.

In any case I requested transfer to Vietnam. Some of my friends thought I had slipped a gear . . . perhaps I had. I was drinking too much and not at all happy. As it turned out, I may have made a good choice . . . I'm still alive and some of those same friends didn't make it back through their second tours. Shortly after I went back to Vietnam, the Department of the Army started ordering most of my flight school classmates back also. It seems there was a shortage of pilots in the pipeline and my class, as well as the one ahead and one behind, were called upon for a second trip, even though it may have been less than a year to ETS (estimated time in service).

My orders came back with Cobra transition and instructor pilots school en route. It didn't really excite me as they tried to extend my ETS by a year as a 'cost' of the school. I wrote the Pentagon and pointed out that the school was their idea and that I would attend only if my ETS remained August 1969. I got the school and kept the August 1969 ETS. I would have preferred to drive slicks again, but once you have a talent they use it.

Nha Trang was where I was supposed to go. It was a gravy assignment – villas by the sea, palm trees – but it was not to be. When I arrived at the replacement depot at Bien Hoa they were nice enough to give me a choice: 9th Infantry Division in the Parrot's Beak or the 4th Infantry at Pleiku. I said 'You can't do this to me . . . I have orders to Nha Trang!' They said, 'If you don't make a choice, we'll assign you.' I had just finished reading an article in the *Stars and Stripes* detailing how the 9th was currently getting its ass kicked, so I reasoned that since I already knew the Central Highlands, and how to best stay alive in that area of operations, I would be better off not jumping into a fire fight in unfamiliar territory. So I was back to the red dust at Pleiku in December 1968, during the dry northwest monsoon.

I went to the 4th Aviation Battalion, the very same one I had come in-country with in January 1967; B Company this time, the gunship company. They were in the process of turning in their Charlie model gunships for Cobras. It involved a round trip to Vung Tau to drop off the

'C' and pick up a brand new AH-1G. Vung Tau also happened to be an in-country R and R center. It is located on the tip of a spit of land which sticks out into the South China Sea, southeast of Saigon. It was rumored that the VC also R and R'd there, because there was never any trouble, at least while I was there. If you played your cards right you could always find something wrong with the ship you were picking up, and spend a day or two at the beach. There was a four-story building next door to the Pacific Hotel on which there was a roof-top Chinese restaurant. The food was great and you could almost forget there was a war going on.

I picked up Cobra 807 which was to be mine for the rest of the tour. Instead of flying direct, we went 'feet wet' up the coast to Qui Nhon, then west to my old stomping grounds. It was, in a strange way, like coming home. I moved into a hooch I had helped to build the first time around. The Division base camp was about a mile square and quite secure. It included, within its bunkered and wired perimeter, Hensel Army Airfield, named after the first of my brothers to die there. Several of the hooch maids who did day labor in the battalion area remembered me and were quite excited to see me. They were always friendly and hard-working. I've often wondered how they were treated after the spring of '75.

We would occasionally be rocketed during daylight hours. The big Soviet 122mms would zoom overhead and go off with a pretty good whoomp. Rarely would they do much more than make a few craters, but we would all hit the bunkers, including the hooch maids. They would chatter up a storm, just like a bunch of kids, then with the 'All clear' go back about their business. I hate to think they were working for the other side, but I suppose some were. Wonder if they got extra pay for working at ground zero?

Flying guns isn't as rewarding as slicks. Unless there was a combat assault to cover, we spent a lot of time on standby, either down at the operations shack on the airfield, or at the 2nd Brigade's forward HQ at a place they called 'The Oasis,' about twenty miles west. The aircraft were kept in revetments built of sandbags about chest high. All the time I was there they never suffered any hits from incoming. We worked in pairs – always. Two ships made up a gun team. We had four Cobra teams and four Loaches which were used for scouting. The company never did get rid of all the UH-1Cs while I was there. I believe we had two teams of C models up until the time I went home.

One of the Loaches had a people-sniffer device which would sample the air for combustion nuclei, such as camp fires and ammonia, as he flew low-level over a search area. That aircraft would be trailed within gun range by a Cobra. The second snake provided cover for the first and flew at sufficient height so its pilot could direct the people-sniffer using a topographical map. The other Loach stayed up high enough to provide radio relay to base camp in order to get permission to fire on targets.

When the people-sniffer operator got a reading he would transmit 'Mark' or 'Heavy mark.' The directing Cobra pilot would note the

Above: Bedecked with machine-gun ammunition, 40mm grenades and 2.75-inch rockets, John B. Morgan III helps rearm his Cobra. (John B. Morgan III)

location on his map. The sniffer Loach would be directed 'Left five degrees' or 'Right five degrees' to keep him on the grid line. When a search area had been covered thoroughly the heaviest concentrations were compensated for wind drift and permission to fire was requested. There were long-range reconnaissance patrols out there watching trails, so clearance had to be received. With clearance to fire we would roll in with flechette rockets and work over the area. Later an LRRP team would assess our work.

On one occasion I was acting as director on one of these missions when we happened to stray off our maps to the west. The area was about midway between Pleiku and Ban Me Thuot in an area of flat, brush-covered terrain. We hadn't found anything in our assigned search area and with ample time, fuel and curiosity I worked us west 'over the fence' into Cambodia. About fifteen miles in we started getting marks. The sniffer surprised a 'mountainyard-looking' individual who, rather than being cool, dove for cover. In the hunting business that's called 'fresh sign.' In a mile or so we got a very hot mark. There was a well-defined trail leading in from the north and out to the south, of what turned out to be a rest area on one of their infiltration routes.

There were numerous hooches on either side of a stream that made a distinctive meander which was later pointed out to the guys at G-2. The more we looked the more we saw, and the sniffer was going off the scale. When the low Loach started taking fire, we had to assume the natives were neither Cambodian nor friendly. They had made a grievous error.

As the Loach pointed out targets we worked them over. There were a lot and they were so confident of our respect of the border they hadn't bothered to dig bunkers. It was a turkey shoot. We went back across the line to rearm and refuel, came back and hit them again. By the time we had expended, word had spread to a gun team from Ban Me Thuot and like sharks in a feeding frenzy they went to work. A Loach took hits and went down; its crew, however, was rescued by his wing man, but the helicopter had to be destroyed by a team of F-100s using napalm.

We went back to Pleiku thinking it had been a pretty good day. Not so the General's staff. Our asses looked like hamburger when they finished. To this day I shake my head in disbelief. The handwriting was on the wall.

John survived the war that the politicians would not win and now flies crop-dusters in California. The author has a Christmas card from the Morgan family, showing John with his charming wife Sally and their equally good-looking teenage children, Matt and Jenny. If John has done the same as many pilots who flew in Vietnam, and has said little to his family about those days of war, they are wiser now. And this was only the half of it.

COMBAT AIRLIFT 12

1. Tan Son Nhut
2. Pleiku
3. Khe Sanh

*T*HERE *were many types of pilot in Vietnam. They chased MiG fighters over Hanoi in Phantoms, they hunted the Viet Cong in the South in helicopter gunships, and they all have a story to tell. Not much has been said, though, about the transport aircraft pilots, in particular those who flew the C-130 Hercules. A total of 34 C-130s were lost under combat conditions during the war, plus another dozen that were destroyed on the ground in air base attacks. Colonel Thomas Sumner flew the C-130 in Vietnam and could have become just another statistic. Luckily he did not, and in war luck is important.*

Prior to the Vietnam War I had not flown the C-130, but I was an experienced military aviator and had flown a tour of combat in the Second World War as a B-17 aircraft commander. I had been an experimental test pilot for a little over nine years, had accumulated about 8,500 hours of pilot experience and had operated about forty different aircraft, mostly bomber class, many transports and some trainers. I went through the C-130E training at Sewart AFB, Tennessee, in September and October 1966, which was followed by combat crew training at Pope AFB, North Carolina, in November and December 1966.

The Pacific Air Forces (PACAF) assigned the operating responsibility of Southeast Asia airlift missions to the 834th Airlift Division, which was located in Saigon. My organization, the 314th Tactical Airlift Wing (TAW) was one of three such wings whose primary role was logistical support of the tactical forces in Vietnam. The two other wings were located at Naha Air Base on Okinawa and at Mactan Air Base in the Philippine Islands. Our wing was equipped with the C-130E, the wing at Mactan had the C-130B and the one at Naha had C-130A models. The C-130E was the latest of the models and had the most load-carrying capability, the greatest range and more modern instrumentation.

Airlift bases in Vietnam were maintained at such locations at Tan Son Nhut in Saigon, Cam Ranh Bay, Nha Trang, Da Nang and Tuy Hoa. These were the major bases that were more or less permanently used during the war, but some others were also employed for special operations that might last for several weeks, such as Bien Hoa. From these airlift bases operations were conducted to support the Army, the Air Force and Marine Corps units at many locations in South Vietnam. These were airfields with names like Duc To, Phan Rang, Khe Sanh, Kham Duc etc. There were several hundred of these fields in South Vietnam: some were long, 10,000 feet of paved runway, and many were nothing more than an old dirt road, some as short as 2,300 feet. Some were all-weather airfields equipped with instrument landing systems, GCA or ILS, but most were strictly VFR operations for the final approaches. We were trained to make an airborne radar approach down to VFR conditions of about a 1,000-foot ceiling in order to land at such airfields.

In addition to normal, regular and routine resupply missions, we had on several occasions the assignments of moving very large Army units from one location to another. I recall one of these activities took place in about July 1967 when we moved the Army's Americal Division from a location near the Cambodian border to an area on the coast in the middle of South Vietnam. We moved everything the Division owned – troops, guns, vehicles, the entire organization. This was one of many missions I participated in that was generated to cope with enemy action that cropped up where it had not been before. We had a special task force of C-130Es composed of about 20 aircraft and about 50 crews. We flew missions around the clock, night and day, in any and all weather, and within about ten days we had moved the Division's several thousand troops and their equipment. The operation was performed without any major accidents or battle losses, although we had a fair amount of battle damage to several aircraft from small-arms fire and rocket attacks.

During the period I was in Vietnam, March 1967 to May 1968, the enemy did not possess any anti-aircraft weapons capable of firing much above 3,000 feet, with some minor exceptions of a few 37mm guns that could. Most of the battle damage we received came from small arms which were fired at aircraft in the landing or takeoff phase of flight. We would usually fly at altitudes higher than about 3,000 feet, avoid these weapons. Some missions did dictate flying very low, about 500 feet above the ground, but they were rare. The other source of attack would come from rockets and/or mortars placed near the airfields, as were the small arms, and the rockets would launch their projectiles while the C-130 was on the ground. Some airfields were continuously surrounded by the VC with these rockets and the arrival of a C-130 was frequently an invitation to a rocket attack.

I recall one particular attack that occurred at a base down in the Delta country. We had flown about five or six sorties from a base on the coast, Vung Tau, a small port city, hauling ammunition, mostly 500-pound bombs to be used by the South Vietnamese Air Force stationed at the Delta country base. The operation took all night long to complete. After each flight the load of ammunition would be offloaded onto a ramp area in the middle of the airfield, so by the end of the operation we had a very

Above: Lieutenant-Colonel Thomas Sumner (left, standing) and his C-130 crew. They were one of the two crews who flew the Bob Hope Troupe around the Southeast Asia theatre in December 1967. (Thomas Sumner)

large stack of bombs all neatly located in one place – and at that time the VC decided to hit the base with rockets. I believe they knew what we were doing and had waited until we had all the ammunition we were going to haul that evening in one place, so they could blow up the entire supply. If that was the case they had failed to train their rocket crew very well, because they hit all around the pile of bombs, but did not get any direct hits. During the attack my flight crew and the ground crew who had been offloading the aircraft found cover in a big ditch behind a huge pile of construction gravel and that gave us safety from the rocket fragments flying around. The only guy who had any problem was my flight engineer, who fell in a sewage ditch and came up smelling of anything but a rose. We hosed him off afterwards, and though he went home very wet he went home in one piece.

During my tour of duty there I estimate I experienced about twenty or thirty such rocket attacks on the ground, ranging in intensity from some so mild I slept through them, to others so intense I cannot to this day figure out how I escaped being hit. The attacks might occur at any place, the outlying airfields and the big home bases as well. Da Nang was such a major home base that it was the home to the special C-130s that were equipped as airborne battle stations, containing considerable communications gear and housing several officers and men whose job it was to direct the tactical air combat operations throughout the entire theater, including North Vietnam. During the Tet offensive of 1968 these attacks became so frequent and intense the special airborne battle-station of C-130s were moved to a base in Thailand that was safe from ground attack.

There was a base in the central part of South Vietnam, Pleiku, in what was known as the Highlands. This base was a major operating location for that part of the theater. It was hit many times by rockets and I happened to be there on about three of those attacks, one of which hit their ammunition dump – in fact hit it several times. I had just taxied out for takeoff; it was night and very dark when the attack started. The sky became very bright from the light created by the ammunition in the dump exploding – a very big fireworks display. The dump was not very far from the runway, so a lot of the debris from the explosions fell on the runway, making a takeoff run impossible. So we sat in the airplane and watched the show, wondering when we might get hit. We did not leave the airplane because there was no safe place to go at that end of the field. We were lucky, very lucky, as we were not hit by anything that night. When the attack stopped the ground crews at the airfield cleared the runway and we departed.

The hairiest experience I had regarding ground rocket attacks occurred at Khe Sanh during the Tet offensive. The North Vietnamese Army had completely surrounded the camp of Khe Sanh and air supply was the only way to bring the Marine Corps unit stationed there, together with some South Vietnamese, the supplies they needed, which were mostly food, ammunition and petrol. The runway was about 3,700 feet in length and was laid out on sloping ground, steep enough to require the takeoff to be always downhill and the landing in the opposite direction, uphill. Thus the North Vietnamese always knew where our touchdown point would be, where the liftoff point would be and, of course, where the offload location was. With this bit of intelligence they were able to aim their weapons accurately at these critical areas, which ensured you would be shot at and mostly likely hit during any missions to Khe Sanh. The only question was, to what degree?

The operation required that the C-130 spend minimum time on the ground. There was an offload ramp area located adjacent to the runway close by and at the end opposite from the touchdown end. The procedure was to turn off the runway after the landing roll out, taxi quickly to the ramp, drop the tailgate, unlock the pallets with their loads, keep the airplane moving so that the inertia caused the pallets to roll out of the cargo compartment onto the ramp, close the tailgate, continue to the departure end of the runway and take off. By following this procedure the time spent on the ground was only a few minutes, and we could usually get in and out before the enemy gunners could cause serious damage to the airplane, although we almost always got hit some place. They would shoot at us during flare out, during the offload and just as

Left: A C-130 Hercules comes under fire while preparing to take off from Khe Sanh. (US Air Force)

we lifted off, but since we were moving in these places the damage was lessened from being a sitting target.

I made about twenty trips into Khe Sanh during this period and was hit numerous times but got away with just minor battle damage each time. There was one trip, though, that I remember very well, because it was one in which I did not get one single hit but by all odds should have been blown to pieces. During the offload phase of the mission one of the cargo pallets became jammed in the guidance rails as it was rolling out of the cargo compartment. We had to stop the airplane to allow the loadmaster to work the pallet free. The jam was bad and our loadmaster was unable to quickly loosen it so we sat there with our engines running while he did his best to get the pallet moving again. After we had been stopped for about a minute the gunners began the rocket firing with considerable accuracy. To make matters worse one of the engines had a nacelle overheat light come on with full brilliance. Some warning systems in some airplanes are notorious for giving false warnings, but not that system in the C-130E – it was famous for its reliability to give true warnings.

A three-engine takeoff from that strip was impossible – not enough runway – and we did not want to get out of the airplane and become guests of the local Marine Corps. While the shelling was getting closer with huge chunks of debris flying all around us, my flight engineer and I discussed the overheat problem. The co-pilot almost shut it down by automatic reaction to the condition, but his training to follow my orders prevailed and he did not. The engineer and I figured out that the prop was still at a reverse-pitch angle, and even though the throttle was in a forward-pitch position this could happen if the prop control was slightly out of adjustment. The solution was simple: advance the throttle just a bit and put the prop in forward pitch, thus directing the airflow from front to rear instead of the other way around, which is the way the airflow is when the prop is in reverse pitch. If the prop is left in reverse pitch very long, the airflow through the engine nacelle is reduced to the point where the overheat light can be triggered on. The loadmaster finally got the pallet free and we moved forward to release the rest of the load, closed the tailgate, continued to taxi to the take-off position and proceeded to roll with the gunners shooting at us all this time.

We had been in the offload position, stopped, for about five minutes, drawing heavy rocket fire. They hit two helicopter revetments on the ramp next to our location and the debris went flying all around our aircraft. We could see direct hits being made on the ground near our proximity, and the explosions were very audible. The bottom line to the episode is they never touched us – not one single hole in the aircraft did we receive, which was just beyond my belief – so I guess that was our day to foil the odds.

YANKEE STATION 13

1. Yankee Station
2. Hanoi 3. Haiphong
4. Vinh

*T*HE first Navy strike of the 'Rolling Thunder' campaign took place on 18 March 1965, when aircraft from the carriers Coral Sea and Hancock bombed supply buildings at Phu Van and Vinh Son. By June, five aircraft carriers were on line at a geographical point in the Gulf of Tonkin designated 'Yankee Station'.

Throughout the duration of the war the aircraft carriers of Task Force 77, part of the US Seventh Fleet, flew strikes into North Vietnam and Laos. Between May 1965 and August 1966 another carrier was based off the coast of South Vietnam on 'Dixie Station'. From there, Navy aircraft flew missions in support of operations inside South Vietnam until sufficient air bases and squadrons were available to enable the Air Force and Marines to continue on their own. Dixie Station was also used as a warming-up area for newly arrived Carrier Air Wings. In the southern war zone the new pilots could 'get their feet wet', before venturing into the real world of AAA, SAMs and MiGs in the North.

The primary attack bomber employed by the Navy was the single-seat McDonnell Douglas A-4 Skyhawk. The 'Scooter', as it was often called, was armed with two 20mm cannon mounted in the wing roots and could carry up to 8,200 pounds of ordnance on its underwing and centreline pylons. The Navy and Marine Corps both used the A-4C, E and F models, the Navy sustaining the most losses with 196 Skyhawks lost in combat by the war's end.

One of the pilots who flew the Skyhawk from two different aircraft carriers on Yankee Station is John G. Kuchinski, now a Captain in the Naval Reserve. His experiences provide an insight into the war, as seen by the Navy pilots.

I entered flight training in October 1964 and received my wings on 9 June 1966. I spent five months undergoing A-4 RAG (Replacement Air Group) training with Navy Attack Squadron VA-125 at Leemore Naval Air Station in California and was then posted to VA-94 in time for its combat cruise aboard the USS *Hancock*. We were aboard the *Hancock* on Yankee Station from January to July 1967 and then on the USS *Bon Homme Richard* from February to September 1968.

Above: Commander Jack Wynn congratulates John Kuchinski (right) on his promotion to Lieutenant Junior Grade, while on the USS Hancock *on Yankee Station. (via John Kuchinski)*

On both cruises, the commanding officers were very strict. We were not allowed to descend below 3,000 feet above ground level to stay out of small-arms fire, and multiple runs on targets were forbidden. Minimum time 'over the beach' was the rule, and there was to be no 'hassling' over the ship with the other squadrons.

The COs wanted to bring everyone back, which they did. We lost only one aircraft on two cruises and he ran out of fuel trying to recover aboard *Hancock* in 'zero-zero' weather. Our sister squadron, VA-93, lost several aircraft and pilots on the *Hancock* cruise. Some losses were due to circumstances, but others were probably due to a looser airborne discipline.

One humorous incident occurred toward the end of the *Hancock* cruise. We were flying three Alpha strikes a day into North Vietnam, to the Hanoi-Haiphong-Nam Dinh area. There was a lot of tension in the squadron as we were nearing the end. The CO was trying to get the squadron ready for an Administration Material Inspection (ADMAT) that we were to receive once we got back to Leemore. So after one big strike we were all in the ready-room talking about the SAMs and flak, when the Executive Officer asked several of us to get our Divisional Officer notebooks and go over our ADMAT inspection items. This really seemed preposterous, given where we were and the fact that some of us might not make it back for the ADMAT. But we complied anyway. Later Lieutenant Junior Grade Bob Chernow, later an A-10 test pilot for Fairchild Republic, drew a cartoon on the ready-room blackboard of Snoopy, the 'Peanuts' cartoon character, peering out from barbed wire and with guard towers all around, saying 'I wonder how they're doing on the ADMAT.' The CO did not think it was funny and put Chernow 'in hack' – confined to his room – but it broke everyone else up.

When the *Hancock* cruise began, I was an ensign assigned to the Junior Officers' bunk room under the port catapault and shared the space with about twelve other pilots. On the line, bunkroom temperatures would get up to 110 degrees Fahrenheit as the space was not airconditioned. We all got a terrible case of heat rash, which made wearing flight suits uncomfortable. It was really ironic, living in such poor conditions and flying Alpha strikes every day. No one in the squadron or ship seemed to care much, however. When we went to the Catholic chaplain he got us permission to sleep on the flag bridge, an airconditioned space, using Army cots. *Hancock* also had little fresh water to spare. We had to go without showers, or take salt water showers, much of the time. The same was also true of the *Bon Homme Richard*.

Of the two cruises, the *Hancock*'s was the 'hairiest.' The first month was not bad because the weather up North was bad, so we went to South Vietnam and Laos on milk runs, usually dropping ordnance by radar through the clouds. After the weather cleared we went exclusively to North Vietnam. Since we had A-4Cs we would climb to 20–23,000 feet and then descend coming in to keep our speed up. The A-4C engine could not keep us, with a full bomb load and maneuvering at 350 knots plus, straight and level. We would roll in at 12–13,000 feet and be out by 3,000 feet AGL.

On Alpha strikes we'd go with twelve to sixteen A-4s in four-plane sections. There would be four to six F-8s overhead for fighter protection. Some of the A-4s would be flak-suppressors, going in first with rockets or cluster bombs to keep the AAA down. Also we'd have two A-4s with Shrike missiles separate from the strike group, who would work SAM-suppression. Most of the time it worked pretty well and you would see flak only in the target area. Sometimes there would be SAMs going in and coming out. They were usually easy to avoid if you saw them in time, because a hard turn into them usually caused them to overshoot. There were a few times when we would get caught in a crossfire and it was difficult to keep track of all the missiles. That's when you would lose somebody.

The A-4 was a pretty good aircraft for the time. It was small so the gunners could not see it rolling in and it was very maneuverable against SAMs. Also you could salvage a bad bombing run, sometimes caused by enemy fire. The drawback to the A-4C was the underpowered engine and the fact that we had to carry two 300-gallon drop tanks along with the bombs, usually four Mk. 82s.

Later versions of the A-4, like the A-4E, F and M really improved the utility of the aircraft: only one 400-gallon fuel tank on the centerline, more ordnance, better performance. Later A-4 engines in the J-52 series were of higher thrust, but emitted a smoke trail that aided AAA crews in picking up the aircraft. Adding smoke abatement systems cured the problem.

I went on lots of Alpha strikes while on *Hancock*. The most memorable were Hai Duong Bridge, Nam Dinh, Ninh Binh, Phu Ly railroad yard and Kien An and Kep airfields. We lost our Air Wing Commander at Kien An, our first big strike. I wasn't in his division, but I remember trying to evade SAMs in a crossfire from two or three different sites going in. His wingman, Doug Bailey, told me he got hit and turned to the beach, but was on fire and lost control of the aircraft and went in before reaching 'feet wet.'

One Alpha strike, later in the cruise, was to a coal pile near Haiphong. I didn't go on that one, but I remember a lot of pilots were fed up with the target planners, who risked men and aircraft on a worthless pile of coal when plenty of other real targets were available. The most spectacular secondary explosion I ever saw was at Ninh Binh. I was a flak-suppressor, and after I shot my rockets at a 37mm site I pulled off and turned toward the beach. Then the bombers began to make their bombing runs. As the first bombs hit, a tremendous explosion went up that seemed to encompass most of the town. Smoke and fire, all boiling and black, seemed to reach 3–4,000 feet. Back on the ship, we could still see the smoke from the flight deck. There must have been an enormous store of ammo and POL.

It was during the 'Bonnie Dick' cruise that President Johnson called a bombing halt north of the 19th Parallel. This meant we could strike targets only in the southern half of North Vietnam. All the major Alpha strike targets were now off limits. I remember this caused a wave of complacency to sweep over the over the Air Wing. Most pilots felt they

Left: Smoke, dust and mud boil skyward as Navy Skyhawks attack the Phuong Dinh railroad bridge in North Vietnam. (US Navy)

would make it back home, because they couldn't get shot down in the south. Several pilots took cameras aloft, both movie and still, to get shots of the their favorite flak site shooting, or of their bomb hits. This all came to a halt in our squadron when the CO, upon returning from a four-plane strike near Vinh, said something like 'There sure was a lot of flak out there today.' The Number Four man exclaimed, 'I didn't see any flak – I was too busy taking pictures!' The CO blew up, called the squadron together and forbade us from then on to take shots over the beach with personal cameras.

One day Lieutenant Commander Harv Eikel got shot down at a very hot spot called Vinh Son. Lieutenant Commander Floyd Probst and Lieutenant Mike Guenther coordinated the search and rescue effort. We first had trouble getting a helicopter, because the airborne SAR helo had just about exhausted his fuel and had to go back to the ship to refuel. Another helo was launched and headed in. The helo pilot was very nervous and had trouble following directions. Consequently, as we were escorting him, he flew over most of the hot areas. There was a lot of fire and we wondered how he could continue to fly through it. Finally he got to the area where the downed pilot was. Floyd Probst was trying to guide him in, but the helo pilot just got confused. Then the helo switched frequencies and we lost him. Meanwhile there was a tremendous flak barrage coming out of Vinh Son. All of the RESCAP A-4s flew right in front of the guns to draw fire away from the helo. The helo was still bumbling around when Eikel popped a smoke flare and the helo saw him. He was picked up OK and Probst told the helo to go west, to Nakhon Phanom and land, but the helo pilot insisted on flying back through all the flak. Somehow he made it.

My own 'hairiest' mission was a night road recce with Lieutenant Commander Hugh Lynch. The weather was bad, with lots of thunderstorms and clouds and very heavy turbulence. Hugh turned all his lights out, except for the tail light which I followed at three nautical miles, using air-to-air tacan. It was my job to follow him, and if he found something he would drop flares and we would both bomb it. As we went coast-in, around Vinh, a barrage of flak came up. It appeared they were aiming for Hugh by his jet noise and as the rounds got there I was flying by. Anyway, I got hit, but didn't realize it because of the turbulence and the concentration needed to follow his tail light. Finally he saw some lights and we dropped our ordnance and headed back to the ship.

Once 'feet wet' I joined and checked him over, then he checked me over and said I was OK. He took the lead back and I settled down on his wing in the clouds. Right away I saw my low fuel light. I checked my gas and, sure enough, I had only 500 pounds, whereas I should of had about 4,500 pounds. Hugh had just checked me over, so I thought I must not have transferred my drop tank fuel, but I checked it and it was empty. In my mind I was sure I had screwed up the switches and didn't transfer some fuel.

Above: *MIG kills painted on the island of USS* Bonnie Dick *in September 1968. (John Kuchinski)*

Anyway I 'fessed up and called for a tanker. I plugged the KA-3 with almost zero on the fuel gauge. He gave me about 4,000 pounds of fuel and I felt saved. We detached from the tanker and went over to the approach fix. Hugh started down first and I broke off to make another turn around the pattern before my approach. Then I saw that I had another low fuel light. I rechecked all the switches again and everything looked OK. Then I started down on the approach and called the ship again for a tanker as I was down to about 800 pounds. They asked me why I needed to tank again and I just gave them my fuel state.

I broke out of the clouds on the approach and picked up the KA-3 who gave me another 2,000 pounds. Then I flew it on down for the trap. When I trapped the Air Boss began to scream at me to turn off my fuel dump. I thought 'Oh no, you dumb sh**, you left the fuel dump on,' but I checked it and it was off. Then the Air Boss chewed me out for not reporting battle damage – I had a hole in my right wing! Anyway, I parked the airplane and there was Hugh Lynch all red-faced about not seeing the hole in my wing.

John retired from active duty in 1969 for a brief stint with Northwest Orient Airlines, but returned to the Navy again a few years later as a flight instructor. He later transferred to permanent status with the Naval Air Reserve and at the time of writing is currently working in the Pentagon for the Assistant Secretary of the Navy (Manpower and Reserve Affairs).

MARINE CRUSADER 14

1. Da Nang
2. Con Thien
3. Ejected into Sea

*I*N Vietnam, in accordance with Marine Corps doctrine, which dictates that the Corps provide all its own helicopter and fixed-wing support, the 3rd Marine Amphibious Force, who were responsible for all ground operations in the I Corps Tactical Zone, were supported by the 1st Marine Air Wing.

When a Marine ground unit found itself in need of air support, the request for help went through Marine rather than Air Force channels, to the 1st MAW Tactical Air Direction Center at Da Nang. If the request was urgent, a flight of aircraft on a pre-planned mission could be diverted to the area, or the TADC could launch standby aircraft from one of three 'hot pads'.

By 1967 there were ten Marine squadrons available in Vietnam for ground support. The aircraft usually selected for ground attack was the Douglas A-4E Skyhawk, which equipped four squadrons. Next came the McDonnell F-4B Phantom with four squadrons, followed by the Ling-Temco-Vought F-8E Crusader and the Grumman A-6A Intruder, with one squadron of each, based at Da Nang.

The Crusader was the only Marine aircraft in Vietnam configured to carry more than one 2,000-pound bomb, until the arrival of the Intruder. However, because the Marines believed the dual role of the F-4, plus its newer airframe and technology, lent itself better to the demands of Vietnam and to the image which the Corps wished to project vis-à-vis the Air Force and Navy, they began to phase out the Crusader and replace it with the F-4. Thus by 1967 there was only one F-8 squadron stationed in Vietnam.

When the Marines became involved in the war in 1965 their A-4 and F-4 aircraft were soon flying sorties out of Chu Lai and Da Nang, but the F-8, the mainstay of the fighter force, was not committed. The pilots in the F-8 community were very unhappy about that: they thought that they had a good weapons system and they wanted a piece of the action. After appealing to anybody and everybody, a staff study was done to consider the use of the Crusader in the ground attack role, with hardpoint modifications to the wings and the use of multiple ejector ranks.

Eventually the Marine Command relented and Marine Fighter Squadrons VMF (AW)-235 and -312 were sent to Vietnam, primarily in the ground support role. VMF (AW)-212 spent a tour on the aircraft carrier USS Oriskany on Yankee Station from late 1965 to early 1966. They saw a lot of action up North as both fighters and

Above: *Bruce Martin in his Marine Crusader. Note ejector seat handles above and behind his head. (Bruce Martin)*

bombers, and one of their pilots, shot down at Christmas 1965, was not released until Operation 'Homecoming' in early 1973. In August 1966, a fourth squadron, VMF(AW)-232, was sent from Hawaii to Japan and then on to Vietnam. One of its pilots was Bruce Martin, and this is his story.

When we found out we were going, the squadron roster was frozen, although we had the better part of a year before we were committed to actual combat operations. In that period we did a great amount of air-to-ground training in the F-8D and E, and in Vietnam the vast majority of our missions were ground support, although we also flew some fighter escort missions into Laos and up North. We had problems in that the Crusader was not designed for air-to-ground work. It had a lead computing gunsight and radar for air-to-air combat, so as far as bomb delivery was concerned we used the TLAR method – 'That Looks About Right.' You would pick a point on the gunsight and then place your target on that, allowing for drift and windage; people who had done it for a while became extremely accurate. The F-8 was a fine platform for rockets and strafing in any case, because they were flat-trajectory weapons.

The squadron was screened before going over, and we had a very capable and experienced group of pilots when we arrived in Vietnam.

The senior flight leaders, including myself, were sent over early to gain combat experience with VMF(AW)-235, the unit we were replacing at Da Nang. Generally the first couple of missions were quiet – maybe a little local radar bombing, usually in the daytime. However, my first mission was with the Commanding Officer of VMF(AW)-235 and we went on a night hop to Tchepone in Laos, one of the hottest places in town. Nobody even barked at us that time, but I was very impressed with the fact that I had even gone.

We relieved VMF(AW)-235 in November 1966, but by January 1967 around seventeen of our pilots had been transferred out of the squadron to various Group and Wing staff jobs. Many of the new pilots we received were short of F-8 experience, especially in air-to-ground delivery, and had to be trained on the job. This gave the airplane something of a bad name for a while amongst our customers, until the new pilots gained the necessary experience.

Our missions were usually flown in I Corps or the northern part of II Corps; sometimes we even got across to the Central Highlands, around Kontum and Dak To. The large majority of them were flown from the DMZ to south of Chu Lai. We also went into Laos on a regular basis and did an awful lot of work along the Ho Chi Minh Trail. We also flew two or three missions a day up North, hitting the area around Dong Hoi and Vinh and the lower Route Package One areas of North Vietnam. A favorite target was the gun emplacements around the Finger Lakes area, just across the Ben Hai River into North Vietnam.

We flew seven days a week, day and night. When we were on strip alert we were usually armed with eight 500-pound Snakeye finned bombs, plus our 20mm cannon. A second plane would often carry napalm and 5-inch Zuni rockets. The Snakeyes wore fins that would extend in flight and retard the bombs' descent, giving us time to get clear of the blast from the bomb if we were releasing at low altitude.

It was hard work operating out of Da Nang. When we first arrived we were living in open-side tents, with no airconditioning. The weather could be abominable, with lots of thunderstorms, heavy rain and low ceilings. If you flew at night, it was so hot in the daytime that it was difficult to sleep. We also had problems with our ground support equipment; there were never enough serviceable bomb loaders and our ordnance people often had to manhandle the 500-pound bombs onto the plane, by inserting pipes in the nose and tail where the fuses would go and muscle them on. In comparison, the Air Force on the other side of the base had airconditioned trailers, good equipment and a nice club. When General Seth McKee, one of the Air Force commanders, came to visit his son, who was a pilot in our squadron, he saw our living conditions and said, 'Boy, if my guys had to put up with these conditions they would quit!' In spite of this, the squadron morale was very good throughout the tour.

I had joined the squadron in the summer of 1964, had spent a lot of time in the Crusader and was comfortable in it. I felt pretty invulnerable as far as the missions we were flying were concerned. We were getting a lot of ground fire, but it was nothing compared to what the Navy and Air Force and our A-6s were facing up North in the Red River Valley, Hanoi and Haiphong area. Normally the worst we would see would be 37 and 57mm antiaircraft fire. Towards the end of our tour we were getting some SAM alerts down in the Route Package One area and around Khe Sanh, but I never saw one fired and, much to my dismay, I never saw a hostile aircraft.

The day that I was shot down started with a typical in-country mission for my wingman and I. Things started to go wrong when he had to abort on takeoff roll due to smoke in the cockpit. I continued the mission with my full load of eight 500-pound Snakeyes and contacted control to see if they had a single-plane mission for me. Normal SOP called for two aircraft on a mission, but exceptions were the rule, especially if we were operating below the DMZ.

Although Bruce did not know it at the time, that fateful day, 2 July 1967, was to end with one of the worst disasters experienced by the Marines in the whole Vietnam War.

The Tactical Area of Responsibility (TAOR) assigned to the 9th Marine Regiment was so large that the Regiment could not patrol any particular sector on a continuing basis. When the enemy realized that a sweep was in progress, they would melt away and then return when the Marines had moved on. In an attempt to counter this, it was decided to send A and B Companies of the 1st Battalion, 9th Marines into an area that had just been swept, in order to surprise the enemy as they moved back in. The area was just 1,200 metres east of the Marines strong point of Con Thien and a mere two miles south of the DMZ.

Operation 'Buffalo' began at 0800 hours on 2 July 1967 when both companies left night positions a mile east of Con Thien and began moving north. Company A was on the left and Company B moved along Route 561, an old eight- to ten-foot wide cart road, bordered by waist-high hedgerows.

By 0900 hours the Second Platoon of Company B had reached its first objective, a small crossroads 1,200 metres north of the cleared trace. As the Third Platoon and the command group moved up the trail, enemy snipers began to open fire. They moved off to the left to try to suppress the enemy fire, but ran into an even heavier concentration of fire and came to a halt.

Captain Sterling Coates, the commander of Company B, directed his Second Platoon to shift to the right to try to outflank the enemy position and at the same time ordered the First Platoon forward to provide rear security for the Company. The Second Platoon tried to move off the road but heavy fire forced it to remain where it was. By now the hidden enemy had opened fire from the front and both flanks, and mortar and artillery shells began to fall around B Company. They were caught in a well-prepared trap and, as the intensity of the onslaught increased, the number of casualties began to rise.

Company A had tripped two Claymore mines shortly after the sweep began and had to wait while medevac helicopters evacuated the casualties. As they tried to move east to join up with Company B they came under intense small-arms fire and soon had so many dead and wounded that they were unable to fight and move simultaneously.

In the meantime, Company B's position was deteriorating fast, as enemy artillery and mortar fire cut off the Second Platoon from the Third Platoon and the command group. The NVA troops then used flamethrowers to ignite the hedgerows on both sides of Captain Coates' unit, forcing the Marines out into the open. At the same time the enemy launched a ground assault and switched the artillery and mortar fire to the Third Platoon and the command group, killing Captain Coates, his radio operator, two platoon commanders and the artillery forward observer. The forward air controller attached to the unit, Captain Warren O. Keneipp Jr., until recently a VMF(AW)-232 pilot, took command of the company but soon lost radio contact with the platoons. Only the company executive officer, at the rear of the Second Platoon, managed to maintain radio contact with the Battalion CP, but the heavy enemy fire prevented him from influencing the situation.

Down the road, the First Platoon also took heavy punishment as it tried to push its way up to the lead elements of the company. North Vietnamese troops pressed against the flanks of the platoon, but the first air support had arrived and Staff Sergeant Leon Burns, the platoon commander, asked for napalm as close as 50 metres from their position. Burns recalls that 'some of it came in only 20 metres away, but I'm not complaining'. The air strikes gave the First Platoon the chance to reach what was left of the Second Platoon, and they quickly established a defence perimeter and started to treat the wounded.

As the reports of the action began to arrive at the 1st Battalion command post at Con Thien, the first assessment of the enemy strength was revised from a platoon, to a battalion and ultimately a multi-battalion force. The Marines were in deep trouble.

The battalion command post hastily threw together a scratch force of four tanks and a platoon from Company D and despatched them to the aid of Company B. Captain Henry Radcliffe led the small force down the cleared trace to the junction of Route 561, but as they turned north up the road they came under fire from an NVA unit that was trying to encircle Company B. As the tanks and helicopter gunships dispersed the enemy, Company C began to arrive by helicopter at an LZ secured by Radcliffe's Company D platoon. The enemy soon zeroed in on the LZ and the artillery barrage wounded eleven Marines.

Supported by the tanks, the lead elements of Company C pushed on down the road towards Company B. Half a mile up the road they came upon the First Platoon. When Radcliffe asked where was the rest of the company, Sergeant Burns replied, 'Sir, this is the company, or what is left of it'.

The relief force advanced further to try to recover the company's casualties and found the Third Platoon's position. The tanks laid down covering fire as the Marines set up a defence perimeter and began to bring in the dead and wounded. For Captain Gatlin Howell, the battalion intelligence officer accompanying the relief

*force, this was a daunting task; he had commanded the Third Platoon for eight
months.*

*The wounded were loaded onto the tanks and the relief force began a fighting
withdrawal under heavy enemy artillery fire. Two of the tanks hit mines, which
further slowed the withdrawal, and as they reached the LZ they came under
devastating artillery and mortar fire again. Many of the wounded were hit again
and litter bearers and corpsmen became casualties as well.*

*Company A had ground to a halt as the numbers of wounded increased.
One platoon managed to break through to join Radcliffe's relief force, but the
other two suddenly found themselves facing a ground assault by the enemy, as
they tried to set up an LZ for the medevac helicopters to evacuate the wounded.
The enemy advanced to within 50 metres of their position before small-arms and
artillery fire broke the attack, but Company A was to remain where it was until the
NVA withdrew later in the evening.*

*During the first few hours of the engagement, Marine aircraft flew 28 sorties
and dropped 90 tons of ordnance on the well-prepared enemy positions. One of
pilots involved was Bruce Martin. His story continues:*

When I asked control if they had any single-plane missions for me, they
replied that they had an emergency mission up near the DMZ and gave
me a briefing on the way there. I climbed to 15,000 feet and and flew up
the coast, turning inland for the last 14 miles to the target. It was a nice
hot summer day and as we were near the end of our tour I had borrowed
the Assistant Maintenance Officer's Nikon camera to take some shots for
us both. However, there was to be little chance to do that as the day's
mission turned out to be far from routine.

As I started to let down southeast of Dong Ha there was an F-4
coming off the target and he had been hit. I took some pictures of him
as he went by and then saw him go into the water. It turned out the pilot
was a friend of mine, Ray Pendagraff, and neither he nor his backseater
got out.

There was nothing I could do for the F-4, so I went on in and was told
to salvo all my ordnance in one go, as there was a lot of antiaircraft fire in
the area – 37 and 57mm and quad 50-caliber machine guns. I received a
target description and they told me to go off to the west and then come
back flying parallel to the Marines lines, from west to east.

I set up a ten-degree dive and crossed over the target at 250 feet and
450 knots, but as I released all eight bombs, everything in the cockpit lit
up and the aircraft bounced. The fire warning light came on immediately
and the utility hydraulic system failed. As I tried to pull up the Forward
Air Controller called me and told me that my bombs were 'right on.' I had
planned to come around again and go in for a strafing run, but when the
cockpit lit up I lost all interest in staying in the area.

In Vietnam we had been told that the enemy owned the land but
we owned the water, so if you were hit you should try and make it out
over the water before ejecting. When it became obvious that the airplane

Above and below: Navy pilot Lieutenant Jack Terhune from USS Coral Sea *shows how to perform an ejection after his Crusader's engine flamed out. He was picked up after only 80 seconds in the water. (US Navy)*

was holding together, I began to climb and head out to sea. I put out a 'Mayday' call and some A-4s with the callsign 'Miss Muffet' that were on their way in came alongside to escort me out of the area. The flight leader said, 'You have a very thin trail of smoke around your tail section, but I can't really see any big holes or anything.' So I continued to climb and asked him to tell me if it got any worse.

I got out to the water and turned south and began to think about getting the aircraft back, or at least maybe to Phu Bai where they had arresting gear on the runway. I called Red Crown, the destroyer that coordinates all the rescue efforts, on the Guard channel and as I was speaking to him I looked to my right and saw that the fellow in the A-4 was giving me a vigorous 'eject' signal. I looked at my instruments and saw that the exhaust gas temperature gauge was going up and heading toward the maximum reading. I looked in my mirror and there was a big cloud of black smoke behind me. Without further ado I reached up and pulled the face curtain to initiate the ejection sequence.

I felt the sensation of the aircraft falling away from me and then a lot of twisting and girating and then a terrific impact as the parachute opened. I looked around but couldn't see the airplane. I was later told that it had exploded about ten seconds after I ejected.

Since I was about six miles off the coast I reviewed what I had been told about water landings when I had jumped as FAC with the 173rd Airborne Brigade. I also recalled an article that I had seen in the National Geographic that talked about the population of sea snakes in the Tonkin Gulf and how they could raft up a quarter of a mile wide by about ten miles long. I thought that it hadn't been a very good day so far, and I really hoped I didn't land amongst those.

A number of people had been lost over the years in water landings, when they had become entangled in their parachute or shroud lines. As the parachute filled with water it had dragged them down. I was concerned about that and as I got lower I took off my oxygen mask and dropped it to gauge my height. It seemed like I still had a way to go before I hit the water. The usual procedure is to look at the horizon and wait until your feet touch the water and then release your chute and I knew that. However, I was not comfortable with that, so when it looked like I was about ten feet from the water I released the parachute and had about the longest two or three seconds of falling that anyone could imagine, because I was a little bit higher than I thought!

My lifejacket was already inflated, although the camera that I had tucked into it had, needless to say, disappeared. Once I got into the water I swam to my life raft, which had been stored in the seatpack and had come down ahead of me, inflated it and climbed in. I felt pretty good and decided to use all of the available survival aids, so I got out the signal mirror and was starting to unpack the salt water distillation kit, when I looked up, and hovering in front of me was an Air Force HH-53B Jolly Green helicopter.

They put a swimmer in the water, a pararescueman, and I got out of the raft and into the water as well, because the downdraft from the helicopter blades was blowing the raft away. The PJ put the horsecollar around me and they pulled me up into the helicopter.

When the PJ was back on board we headed for Da Nang and it was on the way there that I realized I had been hurt. I started to stiffen up and by the time I got back to the field I was hobbling around like a 90-year-old man. It was mostly cervical strain, later diagnosed as a compression fracture, and abrasions, but at least I didn't have any holes in me.

I asked the helicopter pilot how they had got to me so quickly and he said that they were out looking for the Phantom that had gone down and saw an F-8 going by with smoke pouring out of the ass end of it. They said 'That's a customer for sure' and just turned around and followed me.

I spent a night in the base hospital and had to wear a neck brace for about ten days, and then I went back flying again. Months later, back in the USA, I received a package in the mail. When I was shot down, I had been carrying an Air Force style plastic briefing book, with codes, pro-

Right: A US Air Force 'Jolly Green' Search and Rescue helicopter plucking a pilot from the sea. (US Air Force)

cedures, radio frequencies and other information in it. Apparently the charred book had been washed ashore and found by a Marine Recon Team, who saw my name in it and thoughtfully packaged it up and sent it back to me.

As a footnote, the Marines on the ground fought on until late in the afternoon when three companies of the Third Battalion were air-assaulted into position on the enemy left flank, causing them to break contact. It was too late for Company B though. Warren Keneipp Jr. the FAC attached to the commmand group, who took control of the Third Platoon when the other officers were killed, spoke to the Battalion Air Liaison Officer over the radio and said, 'I don't think I'll be talking to you again – we are being overrun'. He was later found staked out and beheaded by the NVA. Only 27 of the Company B Marines walked out of the action; 84 had been killed, 190 had been wounded and nine were listed as missing.

Twenty years later Bruce Martin still gets neck spasms from his ejection, but he is happy to have achieved 235 combat missions and returned home in one piece. He now resides in the Ogunquit, Maine area and still finds enough energy, like a true Marine, to run in an occasional marathon.

THE RESCUE OF PINTAIL 2

15

1. Udorn
2. Location of Pintail 2
3. Nakhon Phanom

JULY 2, 1967: the F-105 Thunderchiefs of the 44th Tactical Fighter Squadron had gone North again. A flight of four had just struck their target near Vinh, not far above the DMZ, and were conducting an armed reconnaissance mission on the way home. They had found some enemy gun positions and were strafing them. It was about 1635 hours and Captain Dale M. Pichard had begun his gun run. On the ground at Udorn Royal Thai Air Force Base the Sandy rescue flight of the 602nd Fighter Squadron (Commando) stood by as usual. Major Richard L. (Larry) Mehr takes up the story:

All four of us on Search and Rescue (SAR) alert at Udorn were fairly well convinced that we had gotten through the afternoon without a scramble. It was 1640 hours and, generally, if we made it that far we would make it through the next couple of hours and another alert period would be behind us. We were all wrong!

The single 57mm round hit the diving F-105 with a gentle thud. Within a few seconds the cockpit began to fill with smoke and the controls ceased to respond. Dale Pichard had no choice: he had to get out – now. Of all the places to bail out, he had picked one of the worst. He was about 20 miles north-east of the Mu Gia Pass, one of the main enemy supply routes from North Vietnam into the upper reaches of the Ho Chi Minh Trail in Laos.

When I hit the ground, I could hear gunshots all around me. I landed in a clear spot almost on a trail and knew I had to get away from my chute. It took me a few seconds to scramble out of the chute harness, grab the beeper radio and start running for the woods. I didn't run far – 50 yards maybe – when I realized that I had to hide, right then, or be captured. I lay down under some low bushes and almost stopped breathing.

My hiding spot was between two paths, and people were shouting and running along both of them. They trampled through the woods, coming within 20 feet of me. I just lay there in the underbrush feeling kind of exhausted. But the adrenalin was flowing so fast that it seemed everything was happening in slow motion. My pistol was still in its holster. I had decided that with so many people around it would be stupid to try to shoot my way out.

The 105s in my flight circled and strafed for a while, and I knew they would be picking out landmarks to give my position to the rescue force. Then they ran low on fuel and headed home. I lay perfectly still, hardly daring to breathe, for the better part of an hour. The North Vietnamese kept searching and shouting to each other and occasionally firing their weapons – I don't know at what – but they somehow didn't find me.

Pichard's flight members radioed his location to Crown, the HC-130P aircraft which coordinates search and rescue efforts, and they in turn immediately notified the HH-3E Jolly Green Giant rescue helicopters at Nakhon Phanom Royal Thai Air Force Base and their A-1 Sandy escorts at Udorn. Larry Mehr at Udorn continues the story:

'Scramble to the east!' At 1645 hours, that was the message we received over the squawk box in the alert trailer. I was lying on a cot trying to maintain interest in a paperback novel, and P. K. Kimminau was napping on another cot. We both hit the floor about the same time, each of us zipping flight suit pockets and combat boots as we moved to the door.

I was pulling alert under the callsign Sandy 7, normally the lead aircraft in the second two-ship element of four alert aircraft. Captain P. K. Kimminau, as my wingman, was assigned the Sandy 8 callsign. As we ran from the trailer toward our A-1E aircraft parked in the adjacent revetment, we were joined by Captain Jack Cochran, Sandy 5, and Captain Don Miles, Sandy 6. They had hastily abandoned their ping-pong game in the operations building when the alert was sounded.

In the frantic rush to get airborne, Jack Cochran had airplane trouble and was delayed. P. K. Kimminau and I had no difficulty during the start-up, taxi and arming procedures. The ground crews performed flawlessly, as they completed the arming process for the standard SAR load that consisted of six pods of 2.75-inch white phosphorus rockets, each pod with seven rockets; six 100-pound white phosphorous bombs; one 7.62mm gunpod with 1,500 rounds of ammunition; and the 20mm wing-mounted guns. In addition, each aircraft carried one 150 gallon external fuel tank on the right stub pylon and one 300 gallon external fuel tank on the centerline pylon.

Kimminau and I were airborne a few minutes before 1700 hours. Cochran and Miles were about three minutes behind us. As soon as Kimminau and I were safely airborne and our A-1Es were pointed to the east, I checked in with Crown Control, the Airborne Rescue Control Center. Since we were airborne first, Crown instructed us to act as the Low Lead element and then told Sandy 5 and 6 to rendezvous with the Jolly Green helicopters and escort them to the rescue scene.

The Jolly Greens were being launched from Nakhon Phanom Air Base about 110 miles east of Udorn. Typically, two of the Sandy aircraft would escort the helicopters into the rescue area and remain with them to suppress ground fire that might threaten the choppers. One of the two Jolly Green helicopters was generally designated by Crown Control to be 'Low Bird.' The Low Bird would be the one to make the rescue attempt, and the High Bird would remain in a relatively safe area as backup. Similarly, one of the Sandy aircraft would be designated as Low Lead by Crown Control.

The Sandy Low Lead would proceed immediately to the rescue area with his wingman. Upon arrival in the area, the lead Sandy pilot would assume responsibility as on-scene commander of the rescue forces. None of the rescue forces, including the Jolly Greens, were allowed into a rescue area, unless cleared by the on-scene commander. On the evening of 2 July 1967, I was designated Sandy Low Lead by Crown Control. Upon arrival in the area, I would be the on-scene commander.

As Kimminau and I headed east, Crown Control relayed the approximate position of the rescue effort. We were told that Pintail 2, an F-105, had been downed by ground fire. The other members of Pintail flight had sighted a good chute and a beeper signal. I used climb power on the old bird most of the way to the rescue area, since an A-1 at cruise power isn't the fastest machine in the sky. P. K. stuck right with me, and I'm sure that he winced a bit when I told him over our FM frequency that the site was approximately 20 miles east of the Mu Gia Pass, a rather tough area for an A-1.

En route to the area, we double-checked our VHF and UHF radios. I had learned on other rescue missions that radio chatter must be kept to a minimum, since we worked with all three radios during a rescue effort. Typically, the guy on the ground had only the UHF emergency frequency, but we used other UHF frequencies for contact with fighter support aircraft and with Crown Control. Also, we used VHF to communicate with Crown, with other Sandy aircraft and with the Jolly Greens. Finally, we used the FM frequencies as backup for working with the Jolly Greens, and as the primary frequency for communication between the Sandys. On occasion, the amount of chatter coming over the three radios became a hindrance, and we would have to call for radio silence, or momentarily turn down the volume on one or two of the sets.

We were vectored to the approximate location of Pintail 2 by the remaining members of his flight. It was almost 1800 hours by this time and knew we didn't have too much time left before full darkness. I told Sandy 8 to maintain a position well above me and to watch for ground fire, as I let down to about 500 feet above ground to begin the electronic and visual search. I could not make radio contact on Guard Channel with Pintail 2, but about 1845 hours I sighted what appeared to be part of a parachute. I flew over the chute several times trying to make certain that it was just that. I still had no radio contact with Pintail 2.

During this 40–50 minute period, Sandy 8 and I had received sporadic automatic weapons fire from the valleys to the east and to the west of the immediate area. The rescue scene was centered along a narrow ridgeline which extended between two heavily populated valleys with motorable roads and railroads running through each valley. There were numerous trails and footpaths along the ridge. The specific area was in rolling hills approximately 500 meters west of a main roadway.

Since the ground fire didn't appear to be too intense, nor too accurate, I decided to ignore it and concentrate on locating the pilot. In the meantime, Sandy 5 and 6 had escorted one Jolly Green helicopter into a relatively safe position about ten miles to the west of the area. The backup helicopter had to return to the base with a mechanical problem. Captain Gregory Etzel, the pilot of the other helicopter, was flying his first rescue mission, but he elected to remain on station without a backup to pick up his crew if they took a hit and went down.

At approximately 1900 hours, I still had no radio contact with Pintail 2 and I cleared Jolly Green 37 into position to look over the chute I had sighted. At about 1915, while making a pass over the chute, Jolly Green 37 made voice contact with Pintail 2. I instructed the other three Sandy aircraft to join with me in providing close escort – a weaving, moving figure-eight pattern above the helicopter – as Jolly Green 37 moved northward toward Pintail 2's apparent position.

As we approached the spot almost a mile north of the chute sighting, both valleys surrounding the ridgeline lit up with small-arms muzzle flashes and tracers from automatic weapons positions. I was too busy to count, but there appeared to be at least 100 small arms and eight to ten automatic weapons. Given the approaching darkness, each flash was quite noticeable. At the time, it was the heaviest concentration of ground fire that I had witnessed.

Shortly before this happened, Crown Control had instructed us to pull out of the area. As the on-scene commander, I had convinced Crown that we should attempt to pinpoint the pilot's position before leaving. But now the situation was getting appreciably worse. It was almost too dark to see the Jolly Green and the other Sandys, so I told Sandy 8 to hold an altitude 1,000 feet above the ground. Then I instructed Sandy 5 and 6 to maintain altitude separation above Sandy 8, and I attempted to stay with Jolly Green 37 who was right on the tree-tops. On our second move to the north, the ground fire seemed to get worse than before. So at about 1930 hours I recommended to Crown that we abandon the effort for the night and start again at first light. I instructed the Sandys and Jolly Green 37 to leave the area and to maintain altitude separation. I told Pintail 2 on Guard Channel to try to get to higher ground and that we would be back at first light in the morning.

On the ground, Pichard listened as the rescue force withdrew and the sound of their engines faded away. He stayed in the same spot and remained motionless until around midnight, when a breeze came up. It rustled the branches and made enough noise to cover his movements as he stretched his legs. Finally the North Vietnamese gave up looking for the night and left.

Pichard's wife had given birth to a little girl two weeks before and he had not yet seen her. He was determined to get out alive and began to look for a better position for the morning. It was going to be a long night. In the meantime, Larry Mehr and his fellow Sandy pilots had plans to make:

After landing back at Udorn, we discovered that none of the Sandys had been hit. The ground crews at Nakhon Phanom found one hit in the rotor blade on Jolly Green 37. All things considered, we had been fortunate to come out of the action as well we did. We had avoided a mid-air collision under difficult flying conditions and had received negligible battle damage to our dwindling fleet of A-1s. And, most importantly, we knew Pintail 2's location.

During debriefing, I recommended a well-supported effort for the rescue of Pintail 2 the following day. Specifically, I called for a minimum of five flights of two jet fighters each. Also, I recommended that each jet have a mixed ordnance load of general-purpose (GP) bombs and cluster bomb units (CBUs). I intended to direct the jet fighter strikes against the gun positions we had seen earlier.

During a telephone conversation with Colonel Jim Hartinger at the Seventh Air Force Tactical Air Control Center (TACC), I assured him that we had a good chance of getting Pintail 2 out of North Vietnam, if we were given adequate jet fighter support. Earlier, I had coordinated these thoughts with Jolly Green Operations and with the officers assigned to the TACC at Udorn. For the following morning, we arranged for departure times that would allow Sandy 1 and 2 (myself and Kimminau) to arrive in the area at first light – approximately 0515 hours. Sandy 3 and 4 (Cochran and Miles) were scheduled to escort the Jolly Greens and arrive on-scene at about 0600 hours. We hoped the 30–45 minutes would be sufficient to allow the jets, plus Kimminau and I, to suppress the ground fire before the arrival of the Jolly Greens.

It was close to 2300 hours by the time the debriefings and discussions about the mission were completed. The other three Sandy pilots and I gratefully headed for bed, knowing that we had a 0300-hours wake-up time. During our recap of the mission, we decided that Pintail 2 had only a slim chance of getting through the night without being captured.

During the briefing on 3 July, Kimminau, Cochran, Miles and I agreed as to where the heaviest ground fire had been sighted. My plan of action was to go after these positions first, then take on the others as we found them. We didn't know exactly how many jets we would have in support of the operation, but we hoped it would be sufficient. In anticipation of a lengthy operation, I had recommended that a KC-135 tanker aircraft be airborne for the jets to use for refueling. Then they could return to the area for strafing runs.

The weather in the rescue area was forecast to consist of clear skies with light winds out of the southwest. So I planned on using the white phosphorous (WP) bombs from each Sandy aircraft to lay down a smokescreen for the actual pick-up by the Jolly Green. Sandy 3 and 4 were to hold west of the rescue area with the Jolly Green. Given an effective smokescreen, we hoped the actual approach of the helicopters would be hidden from the guns located in the valley to the east.

It was still dark as we walked to the revetment to pre-flight our aircraft. En route, I was met by the Line Chief, who informed me that my aircraft was out of commission and none of the others could be ready for such an early departure. I couldn't believe it! Was the entire effort going down the tubes? I could understand his predicament though, since we were rapidly running out of aircraft due to combat losses and battle damage. Nevertheless, in a few carefully chosen words, I informed the Chief that he had fifteen minutes to find me a flyable airplane, even if it had to be one with a partial ordnance load. Apparently, he recognized the severity of the consequences I described to him. He returned in a few minutes with the number of a replacement aircraft that was being readied for my use. The pre-flight checks, ordnance arming and taxi/takeoff procedures were routine, although we lost a few minutes as a result of the aircraft change.

Right: Major Richard L. (Larry) Mehr (centre), with Captain Paul K. Kimminau (left) and Major Fred Gray (right). (Larry Mehr)

Some of our jet resources were already in the area when P. K. Kimminau and I arrived on the scene. One of the F-105 flights had already attacked a suspected gun emplacement with its GP bombs. I asked Crown Control to call off all of the fighters until we could again verify Pintail 2's position. The last thing we needed was an errant bomb or rocket ruining the entire operation by landing too close to the man on the ground. The rest of the jet resources arrived on their scheduled times on target (TOT). I instructed all aircraft to 'hold high and dry' to the west of the rescue area, as P. K. Kimminau and I began our low-altitude runs to determine the intensity of the ground fire and to precisely locate Pintail 2.

I established radio contact with Pintail 2 and flew over his suspected position several times at 100–300 feet above the ground. I had Sandy 2 maintain a position about 500–800 feet above my altitude as he watched for groundfire. On one of the passes Pintail 2 told me when I passed directly over him. Thus, I had him pinpointed within a radius of 20 meters. I did not detect heavy ground fire and I had not taken any noticeable hits as I trolled with the aircraft over his position. Accordingly, I then assumed the role of a Forward Air Controller and began to direct the jets in strikes against gun emplacements and other likely locations for enemy troops.

The first flight that I cleared in had the callsign Warhawk. It was a flight of four F-105s, each with six 500-pound GP bombs and five canisters of CBUs. I told them to 'hit my smoke' with the GP bombs, as I pulled up and checked the gun emplacement that I had just marked with one of the WP rockets I had on board. This particular emplacement was located in the northern sector of the valley, to the west of the ridgeline where Pintail 2 was hiding. I held a position to the east of the valley and told Warhawk to use a north-to-south approach to avoid the guns to the east. Each of the four Thuds dropped their ordnance precisely on target.

Next, it was Chicago flight with the same ordnance. Then came Dallas with 750-pound GP bombs and CBUs, followed by Omaha and Finch. Omaha had 24 500-pound bombs and Finch had 24 750-pound bombs. Before I cleared each flight in for its bomb run, I would select and describe the target, then roll-in for a marking pass with one of the 2.75-inch WP rockets. I left the setting on my gunsight at 65 mils depression, since I had not yet used any ordnance other than WP rockets. Every time I rolled in on a target, I would try to get the aircraft into a 45-degree dive angle, with the intention of pulling out no lower than 300 feet above the ground. For the most part, I would just get back to my roll-in altitude of about 2,000 feet, when the last jet would pull off the target and return to a holding pattern at altitude and to the west of the rescue scene. I had cleared Warhawk in at 0550 hours, Chicago at 0600, Dallas at 0608, Omaha at 0621 and Finch at 0637. We used the CBUs against suspected gun emplacements to the east of Pintail 2's ridgeline. On one of those passes, the CBUs triggered a sizable secondary explosion and fire in the target area, presumably from ammunition or fuel that was stored there.

As the jets depleted their heavy ordnance, I instructed them to refuel with the airborne tanker and to then return to the scene for strafing runs closer to Pintail 2's position. About this time, I noticed that my aircraft's fuel gauge was indicating much lower than it should have been. I assumed that I had taken a hit in the internal fuel cell. So, I directed Sandy 3 (Jack Cochran) to control the final strafing passes as I tried to conserve fuel by loitering to the northeast at about 3,000 feet. By this time, we had controlled 34 jet sorties, with each pilot hitting the targets with uncanny accuracy. I had flown jet fighters and controlled many other strikes. Unquestionably, these were the most accurate bombing and strafing passes that I had observed.

Following this, I told Sandy 3 and 4 to expend their rockets along some of the obvious trails leading to Pintail 2's position. I then had Sandy 2 escort the Jolly Greens into a position where they could observe the effort in relative safety. At this time, I decided we should carry out our plan to lay down a smokescreen with our WP bombs. So, I started a skip-bombing run to the north of Pintail 2's position, with the intention of Sandy 3 and 4 laying the southern leg of the V-shaped smokescreen. Each leg of the V was to be about 500 meters in length and we planned on using all eighteen of our WP bombs. However, I incorrectly set the intervalometer switch on my armament panel and managed to release only one bomb. Jack Cochran advised me of the mistake, and then he placed the northern leg of the screen and Don Miles laid down the southern leg.

At this time I relayed to Jolly Green 09, the Low Bird, the pressure altitude and temperature setting for the ridgeline area. I recommended an entry and exit route to Pintail 2's position, and asked Jolly Green 09 to observe my aircraft as I flew over the downed pilot's location. By now the smokescreen had formed somewhat of a canopy over the rescue area and visibility was pretty poor at tree-top level.

Jolly Green 09 acknowledged that he knew the pilot's position and began his low-altitude approach, jettisoning the chopper's external fuel tanks during the final 200 meters of the run-in. When the chopper was within 100 meters of the downed pilot's position, I instructed Pintail 2 to ignite one of the two smoke flares that he had in his possession. Pintail 2 responded with a flare that was readily apparent to Jolly Green 09 and the helicopter went into a hover over the downed pilot.

In the rear of the HH-3E the pararescueman, Sergeant Pighini, and flight engineer, Sergeant Robert Cotter, were busy. Because the downed pilot was not wounded the pararescueman did not need to go down with the hoist, so Pighini grabbed an M-16 and began to fire at some enemy troops coming over the hill, causing them to seek cover.

Above: Salvation for a downed pilot – an H-53 rescue helicopter comes in for a pick-up. (Ron Zegers)

From the moment a rescue helicopter goes into the hover, until the survivor is in the door, the flight engineer is the boss. Cotter guided the jungle penetrator at the end of the hoist down through the trees and watched as Pichard opened the petals and strapped himself in. Seventy-five feet above the ground Cotter told the pilot, Captain Greg Etzel, that he was ready to climb out, and as Pichard rose clear of the trees the Jolly Green started to climb out of the danger area. It was 0750 hours.

As a relieved Pintail 2 was pulled through the door of the helicopter, Larry Mehr led his Sandys down again.

While Jolly Green 09 was climbing to altitude on a westerly heading, I told Sandy 2 to follow me in strafing runs to the north of the helicopter's flight path. I told Sandy 3 and 4 to strafe to the South of the exit route. I didn't want a North Vietnamese gunner to raise his head at this point in the operation.

After determining that Jolly Green 09 was over the relatively safe terrain to the west, I relinquished control of the SAR forces to Sandy 3 and declared an emergency fuel situation. I advised Crown Control that

I had an indication of 300 pounds of fuel remaining and that I would attempt to recover at Nakhon Phanom (NKP). I made sure that Sandy 2 was away from my six o'clock position on my aircraft and then I jettisoned all of my external stores except the centerline fuel tank. I hoped that I had enough fuel to get me across the Mekong River and into NKP. Although the centerline tank had previously indicated empty, I switched back to it and managed to get another 2–3 minutes of running time. When the engine coughed and sputtered the next time, I switched back to the internal tank and I knew that the only fuel left was the amount in the internal tank. When that fuel gauge dropped to an indication of 'zero pounds,' P. K. Kimminau's presence on my wing was extremely reassuring.

About 30 miles east of NKP, I advised the ground radar controller of my predicament. I then asked him to vector me through the undercast so that when I broke into the clear I would have NKP at my 12 o'clock position for about three miles. The controller responded with excellent heading and distance guidance, allowing me to descend gradually during the last 20–30 miles. Kimminau and I broke through the undercast just east of the Mekong River with NKP immediately ahead. I called the tower from a wide, high, downwind leg and landed on the pierced steel planking that formed the taxiway (the runway was under construction). I noted my landing time of 0835 hours, exactly four hours after taking off at Udorn.

Sandy 3 and 4 escorted Jolly Green 09 to a safe recovery at NKP. Then Sandy 2, 3 and 4 recovered at Udorn without further incident. None of the other Sandy aircraft were hit during the operation. Jolly Green 09 did receive battle damage to one rotor blade, but fortunately it stayed together.

Upon inspection of my aircraft, it was determined that I had taken hits in the external centerline fuel tank and in the internal tank. I still have some of the fragments from the armor-piercing rounds that were recovered from the internal tank after it was removed and replaced. Jolly Green 09 recovered at NKP with Pintail 2 on board at about 0900 hours. Pintail 2 looked surprisingly well, considering what he had just gone through. He was returned to his home base that same day.

When I returned to Udorn later in the day and had a chance to get together with Kimminau, Cochran and Miles, we agreed to a man that nothing could be more self-satisfying than being involved in a successful rescue effort.

For their actions that day, Larry Mehr and Greg Etzel were both awarded the Air Force Cross, second only to the Medal of Honor.

By the end of July 1967, Larry Mehr had flown over 180 combat missions, 82 of them over North Vietnam. He then returned to the United States, having completed his obligatory tour of 80 missions over the North. During his tour, he was awarded the Air Force Cross, the Silver Star, the Distinguished Flying Cross with three oak leaf clusters and the Air Medal with eleven oak leaf clusters. He retired from the Air Force in 1972 after a career lasting twenty years and nine days.

Above: *Major Richard L. Mehr receiving the Air Force Cross and the Distinguished Flying Cross from Lieutenant-General John W. Carpenter. (US Army)*

BIG BIRDS AND LITTLE BIRDS

16

1. U-Tapao
2. Takhli
3. White Aerial Refuelling Track
4. Pleiku 5. Attopeu

*O*ne of the unsung stories of the air war over Vietnam is that of the airborne tanker crews. Between June 1964 and August 1973 the KC-135 tankers flew 194,687 refuelling sorties, provided 813,878 aerial refuellings and transferred a total of 1.4 billion gallons of fuel. To the thirsty fighters bound for downtown Hanoi the tankers were a lifeline that they came to depend on day after day. Many a tanker was credited with a 'save' when it rendezvoused with a fighter about to flame out due to lack of fuel.

Phil Gilbert was a tanker pilot in 1967 and, in common with many other pilots, was transferred to a different type of aircraft for a second tour of duty in Vietnam. In 1968 he became a Forward Air Controller and swapped his big bird for a little one, a Cessna O-2. His experiences give an insight into the life of the big-bird pilots, high above the clouds, and the little-bird pilots, dodging bullets down above the trees.

Whilst I have no credited saves from my days in the tanker business, unofficial and undocumented saves were not uncommon for all of us there. The proof of that is that, to my knowledge, no tanker crewman ever had to buy a drink in the officers' club at the fighter base at Takhli, Thailand, from where we often operated. The way we were looked upon by the fighter jocks was recognition enough for most of us.

There were many times when we offloaded considerably more fuel than was scheduled. This was not at all unusual when fighters coming off the target were disoriented from their scheduled tanker and had to grab the first tanker they came to. Frequently we seemed to be picking up fighters coming in from all directions, all desperate for fuel. We would end up offloading so much fuel that our fuel status would already be critical when we would arrive back at our home base at U-Tapao, Thailand, only to find that we'd have to hold due to a thunderstorm hanging right over the field or, if recovering at Takhli, that we might have to hold for a priority recovery of battle-damaged fighters.

We had one fighter, an F-105 I think, who flamed out as he approached us for fuel. As his plane tilted into a glide, his remaining fuel sloshed forward and he got an air start and zoomed up to make the hook-up, got enough fuel to get home and went on his way. This was a save, although it happened so fast there was nothing much to our credit other than we were there.

Perhaps I can take credit for a couple more saves if I may coin a new term – 'preemptive save,' a save that occurs before there is a need or even a situation requiring a save. After becoming one of the more experienced 'Young Tiger' crews, we were flying number three in a three-tanker cell. Both the lead tank and number two were on one of their first fighter refueling missions. Their only previous experience had been the B-52 'Arc Light' missions out of Guam or Okinawa. Offloading the prescribed fuel to the eight F-105s we each had was prolonged due to the necessity of dodging around the towering thunderstorms throughout the refueling area. During one of the cell's maneuvers around a thunderstorm, one of the frustrated fighter pilots suggested to the lead tanker that if we would all just continue straight and level they'd be able to get their fuel and still make their scheduled 'time on target,' which was so critical.

It was even more frustrating to all of us, because we could see that continuing on a straight course would take us into an area relatively clear of thunderstorms. The lead tanker replied that maintaining the refueling heading would take us out of the refueling area! Then, to top it off, the lead tanker suddenly announced that he had offloaded the scheduled amount of fuel and that was the end of refueling. The lead pilot said, 'We sure would like another thou' or so!' Tanker lead replied that only scheduled fuel would be offloaded and besides he, the lead, was at bingo fuel and would have to return to base.

Almost immediately the number two tanker said the same thing. I was so angry with the other two tankers that I broke formation protocol and discipline by announcing that any fighters who needed more fuel could drop back and get it from us, White Anchor 44. We immediately got six of the fighters from the lead and number two tankers who had already broken off and were climbing to 40,000 feet at a reduced speed to conserve fuel for their flight back to U-Tapao.

By maintaining the refueling heading, which took us out of Laotian airspace and into North Vietnamese, we quickly finished topping off our scheduled receivers and the six extra. As they broke off and formated for their attack, they each expressed their gratitude for topping them off. They then switched to the attack frequency and descended to the target area – Hanoi! I thought that the last thing they needed to worry about, as they dodged SAMs, triple-A and MiGs over Hanoi, was wishing they had been able to get that 1,200 pounds of fuel from their tankers.

I was ashamed to be associated with those two tankers, who went by the book as SAC had trained us to do, but in doing so had become what we called 'SACumcised.' As I, with the help of my excellent crew, had figured, we had no need to conserve fuel as the other two had done. We flew home at the briefed altitude and even picked up another two fighters who suddenly appeared. As we didn't have a coordinated radio frequency with them, we refueled them in radio silence, giving them each 2,000 pounds. We were still not quite at minimum fuel when we reached U-Tapao. I had words with that tanker flight leader at the O Club that night, even though he outranked me. In fact, only my six foot two, 210-pound navigator stepping between us prevented more than words being exchanged. I like to think that the lead and his number two crew were educated that day and evening and adjusted their thinking and attitude on future refuelings with fighters.

In recollection, it seems that my experiences as a FAC In Vietnam, though exciting at the time and memorable to me now, were not experiences ending with an exciting Hollywood finish that one reads about in books. They were, instead, finished because I was running low on fuel and was relieved by my replacement, or I was out of marking rockets and there was no more TACAIR available anyway, or weather conditions were deteriorating to a point where it was impossible to continue, or some other equally unglamorous reason. It just became time to go home, with seldom anything having been decided or accomplished for my efforts – probably the most typical situation in Vietnam for everyone there.

I served as a FAC with the 20th TASS while stationed at Pleiku in 1968. I flew out-of-country missions in Laos in an area of responsibility stretching from the southern corner of Laos down to the northern border of Cambodia. The area contained a number of highways; of primary

Right: Phil Gilbert, complete with flak vest, automatic rifle and survival equipment, prepares to fly another mission in his Little Bird FAC aircraft. (Phil Gilbert)

concern to us were the Highways 96, 110 and 16, the main routes in the area of the Ho Chi Minh Trail. For the second half of the year I flew as a FAC/Air Liaison Officer with the 21st TASS. These were in-country missions in an area of responsibility roughly from Dak To to the north, An Khe to the east, Ban Me Thuot on the south and the Cambodian border to the west.

One time I loaded the back seat of my O-2 with eight cases of beer and eight cases of soft drinks to fly out to our detachment of enlisted radio operators who lived full-time with the Army at The Oasis. The sixteen cases of beer and pop, a newly arrived pilot whom I was checking out, a full load of rockets and various other odds and ends we had on board put us very close to max allowable weight. I had planned to gently fly directly to The Oasis and unload the goodies, but as you might expect we got a call of 'troops in contact' while en route.

We ended up putting in a flight of four F-100s and four F-4s on a pretty hot target. It was very hard to try to show my student how to do all the maneuvering that was necessary to keep the fighters in sight and to keep jinking around so that the bad guys couldn't get a good shot at us. I had to be gentle, but with each maneuver I really feared that the wings would come off. They didn't, and eventually our airmen at The Oasis were happy to be resupplied.

In the spring of '68, overflight of Cambodia was strictly off-limits. However, while flying an out-of-country mission for the 20th TASS I had no choice but to do so. I took a few hits checking out a supply storage area that I had discovered just east of Attopeu, Laos, along a river near Highway 16. The large dose of automatic small-arms fire punctured, among other things, the main fuel tank in my right wing. At that point I was at the farthest range of my patrol and had used most of my fuel.

I wasn't immediately aware that the tank had been punctured and the remaining fuel in that tank was rapidly draining overboard. After a few minutes, I discovered that tank to be nearly empty and switched both engines to the tank to use it up before it was all wasted. To reduce weight I made one more pass at the supply dump and fired all fourteen of my rockets into where the firing had come from. I then called my home base at Pleiku to tell them my problem and that I would fly directly from my present position to Pleiku, which was also the nearest friendly runway to me.

I didn't announce over the radio that I would have to overfly Cambodia to do so, but they got the message. So did an Australian B-57 bomber with the call sign of 'Magpie.' Although he remained at altitude he sighted me and escorted me home for the hour-long flight. The rear engine began to run rough and I had to shut it down. This saved a little fuel, but looking down at the very remote, rugged terrain of Cambodia I wasn't comfortable with only one engine and kept thinking that I would sure be a tiny speck in that wilderness if I had to go down. I had a parachute, but decided I

Above: Phil Gilbert flying his 0-2 Forward Air Controller observation aircraft, armed only with smoke marking rockets. (Phil Gilbert)

would go for a crash landing in the trees if it came to that and started making plans with that in mind. As each remaining tank went dry, I'd go back and suck some more out of each of the four. Rescue efforts were not needed, as I made a straight-in, downwind landing at Pleiku. The front engine died before I had pulled off the runway. It was sure comforting to have Magpie encouraging me as I chugged along!

I got into a very personal war with a single truck which I spotted moving down 'the trail' just before dawn. It was unusual to see any truck in daylight and I could hardly believe my eyes. I called for TACAIR but none was available, especially for just one truck, so I decided to get it myself. I made my first attack and my rocket hit just a couple of feet in front of the truck. The truck speeded up, and as I came around to line up for another shot I received a very heavy burst of antiaircraft fire from some trees a little south of where I was maneuvering. I made a second attack and this time my rocket was a little short, but very close – so close that the truck stopped and I was happy to see the driver hop out and run up the hill into the trees. (We had heard some propaganda that the drivers were sometimes chained to their trucks so that they couldn't abandon them when attacked.)

I didn't want to kill anyone, but I sure wanted to get that truck. Each time I pulled off my rocket attack, that antiaircraft gun would get off a few close shots at me. This time, instead of seeing little fireballs coming at me, I could see the muzzle flashes in the trees, smoke hanging over the trees, and flak. I soon figured that the gun crew only got a clear shot at me for just a moment, because there was a ridge and a curve in the road which obscured me part of the time. I arranged my maneuvering so as to keep low enough to expose myself as little as possible, but I was determined to get that truck.

I made about three more rocket runs: each time I'd get shot at and each time my rocket was so close, but not a hit. The trouble with these white phosphorous marking rockets was that although they would burn almost anything and burn extremely hot, you had to hit the target – a foot one way or the other wouldn't do it. Had I had high-explosive rockets I would have burned him easily with the shots I had already made. It was so frustrating that I pulled up and away out of range of the gun and dug out my gunnery manual to check that I was doing everything correct. I was, so I went back to the truck which was waiting patiently for me right where I had left it.

I visualized the driver sitting up in the trees having a smoke, watching and laughing at my persistent attempts. I lined up with perfect airspeed, dive angle, rocket release point, everything, and the rockets would still hit a foot away from the truck. When my relief arrived, I fired my thirteenth rocket, pulled up and headed out as if I was on my way home. I then made a quick turn, dove right into the gun position and fired my fourteenth and last rocket to show my relief where the gun was. I then went home, very frustrated, my visions of having a truck with a red star painted on the side of my plane fading as I fired my last rocket.

My buddies back at the base tried to console me, saying that it was best that I missed because the truck probably was carrying children and nuns from an orphanage. My relief had no better luck, although he gave up after about five shots. The truck moved under the trees soon after he gave up, but checked a little later. The truck driver probably learned that the safest place for him to stay was in the driver's seat! At least the gun crew missed as well.

IF YOU FLY LOW-LEVEL DOWN A TRAIL, YOU WILL DIE

17

1. Chu Lai
2. Tam Ky

WHEN the 1st Cavalry Division (Airmobile) deployed to Vietnam from the United States in 1965, they brought with them the Army's first aerial reconnaissance squadron, the 1st Squadron/9th Cavalry. Flying scout helicopters and gunships, the 'First of the Ninth' was tasked with finding the enemy for the Division, and this they did very well indeed.

Whether a scout or a gunship pilot, there were certain rules that had to be observed when seeking or encountering the enemy. Most of the rules had been written in blood, by the experiences of the early pilots who learned as they went along. To get yourself killed or wounded by failing to follow the rules was foolish; to get someone else killed or wounded by your mistakes was inexcusable.

Douglas W. Nelms arrived in Vietnam in August 1967 and was assigned to the First of the Ninth at LZ Two-Bits in the Bong Son Plains. In October they moved to Chu Lai to work with the Americal Division, and on 6 November, whilst operating in the area of Tam Ky, Doug Nelms found out for himself what can happen when you fly with someone who ignores the rules. Doug recalls the incident:

Armed helicopter reconnaissance combat missions tend to fall into two categories – those you remember and those you don't. The ones you remember were generally because someone was doing his best to kill you, which was only fair since you were doing your best to kill him. The sound of bullets smashing through the airframe, or the disintegration of a plexiglass chin bubble and eruption of the radio console into smoke and sparks from a 50-caliber round remains forever etched in the brain, although the memory of the killing and the deaths of men under your guns often becomes blurred or totally blocked out.

The majority of missions for a gunship pilot, however, fell into the latter category – the easily forgettable missions of searching for an enemy who wasn't there. The only memories are colours – the solid green jungle canopy or the brown sandpits along the painfully blue South China Sea.

Left: Flying with B Troop, 1st Squadron, 9th Cavalry, Doug Nelm's gunship was armed with two M134 miniguns and two XM-158 seven-shot rocket clusters. (Doug Nelms)

Each mission lasted an hour, probably so that helicopter pilots could more easily compute their Air Medals: twenty-five missions equaled twenty-five combat hours, which equaled one Air Medal.

We carried 800 pounds of fuel and figured that ten minutes of flying burned 100 pounds. The manual had a nice graph for figuring the exact fuel burn for the weight of the payload, but since we always flew over max gross weight we didn't bother with the charts. We just flew one hour, then went home with our twenty minutes of reserve fuel and logged one combat hour, one combat mission, one twenty-fifth of an Air Medal.

That had pretty much been the story on the insertion mission in the Tam Ky Valley, just inland from Chu Lai – an easy and easily forgettable mission. For an hour we flew gunship cover for an insertion of infantry into a clearing at the top of some unnamed hill. We circled the Landing Zone, spraying the tree-line with machine gun fire as the unarmed slicks came in and flared, then dropped their nose and took off. The soldiers on board the slicks literally stood on the helicopters' skids as they approached the ground, one hand holding their weapons, the other holding onto the helicopter. During that one brief moment between when the tail was down for the landing and when the nose was dropped for the liftoff, the eight or ten soldiers would jump, firing as they hit. The helicopters rarely even touched the ground.

The insertion had been cold – no enemy fire, no enemy sighted. The only casualty was a trooper who landed in a hole and broke his leg. After fifty minutes of circling the area, firing up all our ammunition and generally costing the American taxpayer incredibly large sums of money, we called for a replacement gunship. When he came into sight, we departed back out the Tam Ky pass, flying low-level down the narrow jungle trail that was the only link between the coast and the valley.

Now, the first thing they tell a young helicopter pilot when he enters Vietnam is 'Do not, under any circumstances, fly low-level down a trail or a river. If you do fly low-level down a trail or a river, you will die. You will deserve to die because the stupid do not deserve to live.'

This fact did not particularly bother me because I was flying as co-pilot with our Executive Officer, Major Burroughs. I assumed he knew what he was doing. Having been 'in country' only three months, I was green as grass and assumed I was the one who was wrong for being concerned about flying low-level down this trail. What I had not been told was that some pilots' philosophy was that the best way to find the enemy was to get him to shoot at you, and that Major Burroughs had been shot down three times already and had lost about six co-pilots, either killed or wounded. These are the sort of things one needs to know.

With yet one more forgettable mission completed, albeit yet another ten minutes back to base camp, I swung the gunsight back up to the ceiling, latched it in place and reached down to the console to switch the guns from 'hot' to 'standby.' The weapons system had three positions: 'hot' when ready to fire; 'standby,' which kept the system on but deactivated the guns; and 'off,' which totally shut down the system, requiring an approximately thirty-second warm-up period before the guns could be fired again. Whenever a gunship was in the air, its weapons system was always on, but put on 'standby' inbound to the refueling or rearming areas.

On a Huey gunship, the pilot, or aircraft commander, in the right seat fires the rockets, which are fixed. He aims these by simply aiming the helicopter. The co-pilot sits in the left seat and is in charge of the mini-guns, two gatling-gun type systems that fire through six rapidly rotating barrels at a rate of two thousand rounds a minute each. He aims these two weapons by using a gunsight that pivots from the ceiling of the aircraft. A series of boxes projects a circle of light onto a glass plate, which is turned by use of a pistol grip. Turning the pistol grip right, left, up or down turns the guns, and when the circle of light is over the target, you fire. In theory you should then hit the target. This actually rarely happened since the system was developed under clinically perfect conditions, working every time. Under combat conditions the system generally lasted a few weeks before becoming totally inaccurate. It did, however, provide a general aiming point and from there you could wing it.

I had swung the gunsight back up to the roof of the cockpit, locked it into place, pushed back the armor plate just a bit so I could prop my left elbow on the window and put the mind half on watching the countryside and half on fantasy. Being in a combat zone even for three months makes you think of a lot of things you don't have any more, most of which couldn't be discussed at a church social.

Just as we flew over a thick cluster of bushes the half of my mind watching the countryside spotted someone jump up and dash towards a copse of trees. I stepped on the floor microphone with my foot, yelling something about a guy with a rifle running, then reached down and flipped the weapons system switch to 'hot.' I was reaching up for the gunsight when the helicopter went into a sharp left bank, throwing me against the armor plate, hitting right on the point of my left shoulder.

The shoulder instantly became simultaneously numb and acutely painful. I again tried to reach for the gunsight with my right hand and realized that my left arm was draped across it, with both hands in my lap. Ignoring the pain in my left shoulder, I forced it off my right arm and again tried to reach for the gunsight. I still couldn't move my right arm. It had gone to sleep. It was numb, with the tingling sensation that comes with the arm going to sleep, like leaving your arm over your girl's shoulder for the entire movie.

The helicopter was banked sharply toward what I found out later was an enemy machine gun nest, both door gunners were firing their machine guns full blast, we were taking fire in a major combat action and my arm had gone to sleep! I felt damned stupid. Then I noticed the small black hole in the middle of my right sleeve, just below the shoulder. Just a small, black round hole. Hadn't been there before. For what seemed like ages I just sat there and studied that hole.

I could still hear the guns firing, but they just didn't seem as important as that hole. For some reason, that hole had suddenly become the single most important thing in my life, and I really have no idea how long I sat there studying that hole before it sunk in that I'd been wounded. Once I figured it out, which really probably didn't take more than a few seconds, it began to hurt like hell.

I managed to step down on the floor mike to tell the Major that I'd been wounded and realized that I couldn't hear anything through the headset in the flight helmet. My first thought was that I'd also been hit in the head and was deaf. Then I realized I could still hear the guns firing. The radios must have been shot out. No, the radios looked fine and, besides, I could see the Major talking into his mouthpiece – I just couldn't hear him. It wasn't until I was in the hospital that I learned that the bullet had ricocheted off the right armor plate, entered my arm just above the elbow, ripped its way up the bone, exited just below the shoulder, then passed just behind my head and cut the helmet cord to the radios.

With a heroic effort, or at least what I thought was one at the time, I reached across with my left hand and grabbed the Major's arm, pointing to the hole in my sleeve. He looked, gasped and immediately broke off the action. It seemed to me that his expression of dismay was awfully exaggerated – it was just a little black hole. What he could see, and what I could not, was the hole at the bottom where the bullet had gone in and where the blood was pouring out. He put the helicopter into an extreme nose low position, pulling every knot of speed as we screamed just above the tree-tops towards the emergency field hospital. Which was just fine by me.

The trip seemed to take forever, although probably not more than a few minutes. I alternated between acute pain in my arm and a great nausea which swelled over me. First the arm would hurt, then the nausea would start low in the bowels and build up to a great crescendo as it moved up through my body, while I prayed that I would not throw up. The nausea would sweep over me, then pass, and the pain of the wound would dominate. Then the whole sequence would repeat itself.

Then I remembered: not three nights before I had been helping the crew chief clean the guns, when he pointed out that he'd rearranged the first aid kit. The Army, in its infinite wisdom, had put the tourniquet on the bottom of the kit. The crew chief knew from experience that the tourniquet was always needed first, so he put it on top. I remembered that.

The first aid kit was snapped to the side of the aircraft just behind my left shoulder. With great effort, I reached back with my left hand, pulled it down, set it in my lap and unzipped it. The tourniquet was right there, sitting on top, just as I remembered.

I pulled it out and used my teeth to rip off the paper wrapping, then just sat there, staring at it. I'd forgotten why I wanted it. I'd even forgotten what it was. The mind had gone numb. I had no idea why I was holding this thing in my hand. I do remember the crew chief reaching forward over the console and taking the tourniquet out of my hand, then pressing it on my arm just above the elbow. I tried to tell him that the·bullet hole was higher, just below the shoulder, but of course I couldn't talk to anybody. My umbilical cord to the outside world had been severed. I just didn't know it.

But it didn't matter, I didn't care. I didn't care about anything except the pain. I have no idea how much blood I lost and at the time did not even realize that I was losing any. I did notice that my pants' leg was totally soaked with something, but it didn't occur to me what it might be. I simply didn't care.

Unlike the MASH Units of Korea, made famous by the popular TV show, the emergency medical units in Vietnam were simply large tents set up in a secure area close to the area of combat. Each tent was a hospital unto itself, designed to patch the casualty up enough to get him to a permanent surgical hospital at a major base.

Even as the helicopter was touching down on the helipad, the medics were opening the door, pulling me out and putting me on a stretcher. I remember telling them over and over that it was no problem. I could walk. I would have been lucky just to be able to stand. Luckily, they ignored my protestations and carried me into the tent.

Next came shots – hundreds, thousands of shots. Maybe five or six. Without ceremony my 45 pistol was taken off, my chest protector removed and my shirt literally cut off my back. Doctors and corpsmen swarmed over me, shoving needles and tubes into my good left arm, while someone did something to my right arm – I never was sure just what. At one point someone with a cross on his lapel came over and started talking to me. I have no idea what he asked, or what I answered, but I remember thinking that if he started talking Latin I was going to be seriously concerned.

Within minutes they had the entire arm totally wrapped in bandages, with only the thumb sticking out. The left arm still had a tube plugged in constantly feeding me plasma; at least, I assumed that. One of the shots I'd received had made the entire episode just funny beyond belief and I kept saying something about changing the oil. They just smiled a lot and ignored me, all the time working on that right arm.

From the operating table I went back onto a stretcher and directly into another helicopter for the flight to the surgical hospital at Chu Lai.

On the flight back I kept staring at my thumb, then I realized that I could move it. Its scary being wounded – you never really know how bad it is at first and all sorts of fears haunt you. But when I realized the simple fact of being able to move my thumb, I knew it was all right. If you're wounded in the upper arm and you can move your thumb, it has to be all right.

From the helipad at Chu Lai I was carried into the waiting area of the surgical hospital. I was left on a stretcher, which was simply placed between two saw horses. The kid on a stretcher just beside me couldn't have been more than eighteen or nineteen. I noticed his leg was bandaged and asked if he'd been shot. He said he'd been on an insertion and just as he was jumping out the helicopter he made the mistake of looking up at a gunship that was spraying the tree-line, hadn't watched where he was jumping, went into a hole and broke his leg. I said I'd been shot and left it at that. On the other side of me was a wounded North Vietnamese soldier. I never did find out how he got there. Didn't want to ask.

Within a few minutes two medics came over and took off my boots and socks, then started cutting off my pants. Now at this point I was nude from the waist up, with the exception of my right arm, which was covered with bandages. These guys were making me nude from the waist down. A polite query determined that I was soon to go into surgery and my germ-laden clothes had to go.

I must have fallen asleep, because I suddenly looked up and there was a nurse standing over me. A female nurse. Now I'd only been in Vietnam for three months, but my association with women during that period had been nil. Nothing. None. At this point I realized that except for my bandaged area, I was totally nude. It was also at this point that the nurse leaned over and said, 'Is there anything you need?' Fortunately, I was very young and naive at that point in my life. If I'd given her the answer then that I would now, I'd still be locked away. However, with the tremendous loss of blood, I probably wouldn't have been able to follow through anyway.

Within an hour I was in surgery, with the doctors doing whatever it is they do while you lie asleep under their knives. This was followed by five days of recovery at the surgical hospital at Chu Lai, then to the evacuation hospital at Qui Nhon for another four days of recovery.

Less than two weeks after being wounded, I was on an Air Force C-141 en route to Japan and the 249th General Hospital for just over three months of recovery and physical therapy – and maybe just a touch of debauchery. But that's another story.

THE UNEXPECTED FAC MISSION

18

1. Hue Citadel Airport

*W*HEN Major Robert C Mikesh heard that the 8th and 13th Bomb Squadrons had been ordered to deploy from Clark Air Base in the Philippines to Vietnam, he could hardly contain his disappointment. He had been flying the Martin B-57 Canberra since 1955 and now, on 5 August 1964, the 8th Bomb Squadron was going to war without him.

The decision had been taken the previous evening by the President and his advisers in Washington, following the infamous Tonkin Gulf Incident. The reasons were of little consequence to Major Mikesh; he was stuck in Japan on a staff assignment and when his posting to Vietnam finally came up, it was as a Forward Air Controller rather than a bomber pilot.

Under the rules of engagement used in South-East Asia, ordnance could not be expended in South Vietnam and certain areas of Laos without a FAC to control the strike. It was the responsibility of the FAC in his slow, low-flying plane to locate the target, identify it to the attack aircraft and ensure that they dropped their ordnance in the correct place.

From the very start of the war the usual mount for the FAC had been the ageing, single-engined Cessna O-1 Bird Dog. It was in use in each of the four Corps Tactical Zones, but there were problems associated with its use in I Corps, in the northernmost part of South Vietnam. The terrain was rugged and mountainous and an engine failure usually meant certain death for the crew. A new aircraft, preferably one with two engines, was needed, but due to the length of time required to design and build one for the military, the Department of Defense decided to acquire a civilian model already in production.

The Cessna Aircraft Company put forward their Model 337 Super Skymaster, which had two engines mounted fore and aft of the cockpit. The main drawback to the civilian version was the side-by-side seating. Usually the FAC flew on his own and would need to be able to look down both sides of his aircraft. In an effort to improve the visibility, transparent fuselage and door panels were installed. Other changes included heavier skin for the wings, external pylons for the marker rocket tubes and a gunsight.

The first Cessna O-2A was delivered to the 20th Tactical Air Support Squadron at Da Nang on 2 July 1967, and although the pilots missed the visibility of the Bird Dog they were extremely pleased with the increased performance and ease of

145

control. There was the odd problem now and then that needed rectifying, and on 13 October 1967 Major Mikesh was asked to carry out a functional check-flight on an O-2A which had just had a tachometer replaced. His day as a Forward Air Controller in northern I Corps had begun with the usual early-morning visual reconnaissance over Thua Thien Province, to see what may have changed overnight as a result of enemy encroachment. After lunch there was a pre-planned air strike in the distant hills, west of Hue, where there was a suspected Viet Cong supply point. Finishing these two missions normally ended a typical day, often repeated seven days a week.

The war usually quietened down as the afternoon heat built up and Major Mikesh was grateful for the chance to get in the air again to cool off. He continues:

It was late afternoon when the airplane was ready, and I left the gravel runway inside the walled city of Hue at 1630 hours on what could have been an uneventful fifteen- or twenty-minute flight. Checking in with 'Big Control', our 'Victor' Direct Air Support Center for this northern sector, I gave them my time-off and intentions, as was the normal procedure. The usual unconcerned 'Roger' came back. I went on about my business in checking the airplane over, drinking in the refreshing air and at the same time observing the beautiful landscape that was taking on a deeper green as the late afternoon sun sank lower on the horizon.

The tranquility of the flight was suddenly pierced by the voice of a desperate radio operator calling for assistance. Using the callsign

'Mongoose,' he was transmitting in the blind for any 'Big' aircraft, our FAC callsign, to respond. I recognized the 'Mongoose' callsign as a Marine reconnaissance squad north of Hue and overheard 'Big One-Seven' answer. The Marines were under intense enemy fire and needed immediate air support. However, Big One-Seven had already been on visual reconnaissance for three hours and reported that he was on his way home and could not help due to lack of fuel. He had heard my report-in after takeoff and asked if I could help out. I had only a partial load of fuel and only seven smoke marking rockets, left over from the previous mission. I could do very little, but no one else was in the air.

I copied the coordinates of the Marine's position and headed to the general area. The Marines were established in a lookout position on a high ridge, where they could visually monitor enemy activities in the surrounding area. Apparently the VC were getting tired of having the Marines report on their ground movements and calling in air and artillery strikes against them. They decided to take the Marine's position and eliminate them. Judging by the continually rising pitch of my ground contact's voice, the situation was getting desperate.

As I proceeded toward the coordinates, I called Big Control and asked for air support aircraft, hoping to have fighters on station by the time I got to the Marines' position. This would waste no time in directing an air strike on to the target. So far, things were going routinely. Big Control gave me the callsign of a flight of F-4s and the frequency on which to call them. I made contact, but only to learn that they were heading north, to provide air cover for one of their comrades who had gone down north of the DMZ. I called Big Control for another set of fighters and was told that a flight would be at hand shortly.

By now I was passing across the top of the ridge where the Marines were in trouble. They confirmed that they saw me and let off a smoke flare to mark their position. The VC were on the north slope, but I could see little action at first. They hid themselves among the small growth along the bank as soon as they heard my engines. Their gunfire on the Marine position continued, and the controller said that they were now within grenade-throwing distance. Something had to be done right now.

The second set of fighters came on to my frequency, but just then they too were diverted to the north to provide air cover for the recovery of the downed pilot. The situation below was critical and would end within moments without immediate air support. Big Control recognized this urgency, but the only air available was the ground alert aircraft at Da Nang. They were to be scrambled immediately but by the time they might arrive the battle could be over.

There was no alternative now but to make attack passes on the advancing VC, even though this was just a lightly armed FAC airplane. Perhaps this would be enough to pin the enemy down until air support arrived. I rolled in and lined up in a dive on the area of the north slope where I was told the VC were located. I fired off one smoke rocket and watched it hit the ground as I banked away and pulled off. The Marine radio operator reported with excitement that my hit was 'right on!' Little damage can be caused by smoke rockets because they have little explosive impact, but when fired at you it can be concerning. The splattering of burning white phosphorous which causes the marking smoke is dangerous enough. The ground controller gave me corrections for the next attack and I rolled in and fired one more rocket. This could not continue for long, for now I was down to only five rockets and there was still no sign of fighter support. The sun was dropping fast and the Marines would not have a chance after dark.

The next pass was dry, trying to conserve what rockets I had left, yet making an attempt to slow the advance of the enemy. This seemed to cause them to keep their heads down, since they held their shelter for the possibility that I might fire off a rocket at them on each pass. As the shadow deepened, I was aware for the first time that the VC were firing at me with hand-held weapons as I made each pass. It was like flash cameras at half time in a football stadium. I was looking right at their muzzle flashes as I bore in on them at low level with each dive – and me without my flak vest, a 'must' item of personal equipment on any FAC mission. But this was only to be a simple functional flight check!

Now I was having to make two dry passes for every time I let off a rocket. As each one hit into an enemy position I was cheered on by the

Marine radio operator. This was probably more for his morale, for smoke rockets are not going to stop an enemy for long and the Viet Cong knew it. But it had slowed them, and although my seven rockets were now gone I was not going to let the enemy know that. I kept making random direction passes and jinking during each dive, in an effort to avoid being hit by their ground fire. Normally the enemy would not shoot at a FAC for fear of revealing their positions, but this was an exception.

To my surprise and great relief, a flight of Marine A-4 Skyhawks came on station and reported in, much sooner then the expected Air Force Phantoms. I described the location of the ridgeline to them and they immediately located it and spotted the remains of the smoke that lingered along the slope of the rise. With this recognition I cleared them to drop their bombs under the top of the ridge. Their 500-pounders hit their mark and brought a favourable response from the radioman. He reported that they all had their hearing impaired by the nearby blasts, but 'Keep 'em comin'!'

After the Skyhawks' second pass, a line of Hueys came into view and were snaking from the south side of the ridge to the the Marines' position. I was off to the side and away from the attack line of the A-4s as they prepared for another pass. This put me in a good position to watch with fascination the rapid extraction of the Marines as it took place. With the Skyhawks laying their ordnance on three sides of the area around the Marines, the first Huey made its approach. The helicopter hardly paused, with its skids not even touching the ground, as the Marines jumped on board and were whisked away. The second and those that followed did the same until all were safely off the ridge. It was all over in seconds and they were now on their way to the Marble Mountain Marine base, without the loss of a man.

It was nearly dark by now, yet there was enough light to still identify features on the ground. The Skyhawks continued the attack until their ordnance was expended, then headed for home. By now, I had bade them farewell, for I was very low on fuel after this forty-minute bout with the Viet Cong. The enemy had successfully neutralized the lookout post by having caused the Marines to leave, but now they were at the mercy of the 500-pounders from above.

Returning to my base with not enough fuel left to go elsewhere, I made my first, and thankfully my last, night landing at the Hue Citadel Airport, gliding across the protective wall that encircled this ancient city, over the moat and on to the 2,400-foot gravel runway that had no lights. With this, I had had enough for one day.

For his courageous work that day, Major Robert C. Mikesh was awarded the Distinguished Flying Cross. The official citation read, in part, 'The outstanding heroism and selfless devotion to duty displayed by Major Mikesh reflect great credit upon himself and the United States Air Force'.

GUESS YOU'RE ON FIRE

19

1. Da Nang
2. Demon 12 Shot Down

IN May 1961 President John F. Kennedy sent his Vice-President, Lyndon B. Johnson, to South Vietnam to discuss the escalating Viet Cong insurgency with President Diem. As a result of the discussions the amount of United States military aid was increased: more aircraft were to be supplied, the Army was to be expanded, and additional training centres would be set up. One of the centres was a joint American/South Vietnamese Combat Development and Test Centre, tasked with learning and improving counter-insurgency techniques and tactics.

One of the first ideas put forward by the new centre involved the use of aerial defoliants, to reduce jungle cover along major highways, where the Viet Cong frequently ambushed government convoys. The idea grew within months into Operation 'Ranch Hand' and the first Fairchild C-123 Provider transport aircraft, fitted with the MC-1 Hourglass spray system, arrived at Tan Son Nhut Air Base in January 1962. It is interesting to note that this was a full 30 months before the infamous Gulf of Tonkin incident and over three years before the arrival of the first American combat troops.

Over the years the programme expanded, and by the time it was halted in 1971, following concern about the side effects of the chemicals on humans, 41 per cent of the mangrove forests in South Vietnam had been affected, together with 19 per cent of the upland forests and 8 per cent of all cultivated land. Eleven of the nineteen million gallons of chemicals used were of the type known as 'Agent Orange'. Thousands of Vietnam veterans have subsequently filed disability claims against the US Government, alleging damage to their health caused by Agent Orange.

The political, legal, moral and ecological aspects notwithstanding, the defoliation programme seemed a good idea at the time and the first flight took place on 13 January 1962. Three weeks later, on 2 February 1962, one of the Ranch Hand C-123s became the first Air Force aircraft to be lost over South Vietnam when it crashed, killing the crew of three. Although the cause of the crash was never determined, from that time onwards the Thirteenth Air Force requested fighter escort for all future defoliation missions.

Five years later, whilst flying escort for one of the defoliation flights, Major Jake I. Sorensen and his back-seater, First Lieutenant John C. 'Mike' Aarni, discovered

that fighter escorts are just as likely to be hit by anti-aircraft fire as the aircraft they
are escorting. Jake begins the story of that eventful day.

On 31 December 1967 Mike and I were scheduled to fly armed escort in support of a C-123 Ranch Hand defoliation mission in the area of the Demilitarized Zone (DMZ). We were flying an F-4C Phantom from the 390th Tactical Fighter Squadron, 366th Tactical Fighter Wing, stationed at Da Nang Air Base and using the callsign 'Demon 12.'

We had arisen at about 0400 hours for intelligence, weather and tactical briefing at 0500 hours. Weather in the DMZ was characterized by low fog and stratus, so the sortie was delayed until an alternate mission could be found. At about 0700 the mission was changed to an infiltration route leading from Cambodia into the western edge of South Vietnam, along a rather shallow valley leading toward a small outpost called Dak To. The C-123 aircraft takeoff was about an hour prior to our takeoff, and a rendezvous was made with the flight of three about 0815 hours.

Mike and I were in the number two position of our flight of two F-4Cs, being led by Major Whitey Miller. Whitey had been shot down three days prior to this mission in the southern area of North Vietnam, known as Route Package One. He had managed to get to the sea where he and his backseater bailed out. Whitey was rescued by a destroyer and a Navy helicopter picked up Sam Martin, his backseater. However, while unhooking from the rescue sling he lost his balance, fell out of the door and into the sea, and was tragically lost before the pararescueman could get to him.

We joined the C-123s and escorted them during their spray run by making high-speed passes along each side of the formation. This seemed to have the effect of keeping the Goomers' heads down as these heavily shot up C-123s could attest. Having experienced no hostile fire during the defoliant run, the C-123s departed the area for home base. We, on the other hand, were called by an airborne Forward Air Controller, advised that he had an Army Company under attack and wanted to know if we would be so kind as to drop our weapons on their attackers. Replying in the affirmative, we proceeded into an orbit near the target area while the Forward Air Controller coordinated with the ground troops. When the FAC was sure of the target he marked the area with a white phosphorous rocket and cleared us to attack.

Whitey commenced the attack, dropping two of his six 750-pound bombs on his first pass. I had six pods of rockets, a gatling gun pod on the belly and four Sparrow missiles. On our first pass, I put in two pods of rockets. Since we were on target and saturating the immediate vicinity, Whitey dropped his remaining four 750-pounders on the next pass. I, in turn, fired all four remaining pods of rockets.

I was just starting the pull-up off the target when I felt a 'thunk' in the belly of the aircraft. Immediately the left engine fire warning light

illuminated, and as I started to retard the throttle the engine flamed out
and the right engine fire warning light came on. I was now established
in a right climbing turn, exiting the area and intending to head toward
Dak To.

During the pull-up I called Whitey, told him I had one engine flamed
out and the other indicated on fire and asked him if I was in fact on fire.
His reply was, 'Are you in afterburner?' When I said 'No,' he said 'Guess
you're on fire.' I was now at about 5,500 feet, headed toward Dak To which
was about twenty miles east of our position. Somewhere before we got
turned around, I told Mike to stay with the aircraft as long as possible
to get out of the target area.

I remember during the pull-up also trying to find the jettison button,
but I'll be damned if I could find it. I suppose that with all the lights
flashing and other goings on, the distractions were responsible. However,
if you could visualize sitting in a chair with your left arm extended, point
your finger three inches to the left behind the throttle quadrant and you
couldn't miss it; it was big and red and plainly visible. During the next
minute or so we prepared to eject, I think.

A couple of stirring events occurred: suddenly one of the four Sparrow
missiles fired, and a moment or two later another fired but did not release,
accelerating us about another 100 knots and giving us an additional 1,000
feet of altitude. Then the gatling gun started cooking off rounds. About
that time Whitey called to say that we were trailing flame about 300 feet
behind the aircraft and he thought we ought to get out.

Considering that we had one engine out, were low on fuel, and that
remaining was doing an unprogrammed burn, and the fact that about
this time the aircraft started bucking erratically, I told Mike to eject. When
his ejection seat fired and the canopy left the aircraft, the electrical system
went completely dead. I grabbed the handle between my legs and pulled.
The Martin-Baker seat worked as advertised. I tumbled once, which threw
my helmet off. It was now sometime around 0900 hours.

*In the back seat, Mike Aarni had felt the impact on the underside of the aircraft
as they came off the target and recalls that it felt as though they had been hit by
a sledge-hammer about five feet behind his seat. At the time they were heading
in the direction of Cambodia and Mike was relieved when Jake managed to turn
the aircraft around. However, the relief was short-lived as the situation worsened
and the cockpit filled with smoke. Mike asked Jake if he should eject and was
told 'We've lost the hydraulics – go!'. Mike continues his story:*

I had Jake's camera in the back with me and had been filming the
Ranch Hand mission earlier. I wanted to take it with me, but decided
to concentrate on the task in hand. At this time the adrenalin started
pumping and, recalling the problems other guys had had when ejecting,
I was determined to do it right. I set the camera down, ripped off my

clipboard and assumed the correct position. I reached down between my legs, grabbed the ejector seat handle and pulled. This was in the days prior to the 12-G rocket seat, when they had a 17-G ballistic charge to throw the seat clear of the aircraft. This type of seat caused back problems for a number of guys, myself included, due to the high impact through your back when the charge goes off, but it was better than the alternative.

As the charge went off and blew me up the rails and out of the aircraft all went black for a moment. My parachute opened automatically and I felt myself tumbling as the risers untangled themselves. As I descended my first thought was to let someone know that I was still alive. One of my friends had gone into captivity after bailing out and it took a year before anyone knew he was alive. I pulled out my survival radio and told Whitey 'Demon 12 Bravo, I'm in the chute and OK,' and had time to exchange a few more words with my flight leader before the ground began to rush up at me.

As I stowed my radio I noticed that I was heading for a small clearing in the jungle and tried to decide when to release my seat kit. You could pull a handle and let the kit fall away on a 25-foot long line, but it needed to be judged correctly or it would foul up in the trees. I decided to keep the kit with me, despite having heard in the past about a guy who did the same and broke his legs on landing. I did as I had been taught and looked at the horizon, not the ground, and when I thought I was about to hit, I pulled down on the risers. I hit the ground like a ton of bricks, but didn't break anything. I quickly got my seat kit and parachute off and dived into the nearest bushes, where I lay listening for any sound of the enemy but only hearing the birds and my own heart pounding.

Meanwhile Jake, who had ejected seconds after Mike, was on his way down too:

After my chute opened and I stabilized, I looked behind me to see if Mike was OK. I saw he was descending about a mile away, but his head was down and I was instantly concerned that he was injured. I hollered at him to no avail, realizing eventually that he had his helmet on and couldn't hear me. I then saw his head move and arms move and figured that he was OK. I also saw all the junk that was coming down with us – canopies, maps, papers etc. I had the instant thought that we were really junking up the area. Before I turned to look for Mike, I watched the flaming Phantom as it nosed over and crashed about three miles ahead of me. Then I began to concentrate on the descent.

It was a virtually clear sky with probably 60 miles' visibility, and it was very quiet and peaceful during the descent. The thought actually went through my mind that maybe sky-diving (practice bleeding as we called it) could be fun. As I started nearing the ground, however, I began to worry about getting caught up in some 200-foot trees that I was drifting toward (F–4C chutes are not steerable). It then became clear that I would land in a bushy area. At that point I released my survival pack which dropped about 30 feet and has the effect of lessening the impact shock. I than started to oscillate back and forth. As I approached the ground I said to myself, 'Look at the distant horizon; try to time yourself to hit just as you reach the height of the oscillation.' It worked just great: my heels touched the brush, I flipped over backwards and landed on my head. Actually my shoulders caught most of the impact and the ten-foot or so fall through the brush may have dampened the impact. At any rate, I was stunned for a few moments. I then disconnected my parachute which was spread out on the brush above me, got out my radio and called Lead and asked if they had heard from Mike. He said Mike was OK, and that they were out of gas and going home and would see us there.

It is interesting to note, at this point, that in our intelligence briefings it was considered best to be shot down in North Vietnam near a large city if possible, because if you were going to be captured these people were supposed to be the most disciplined and were not likely to kill you or let you expire from abject neglect. Also, in the area we were in, there were no friendlies per se. The Viet Cong and North Vietnamese controlled most of the area's inhabitants, so any indigenous personnel should be considered less than friendly. Consequently, I pulled out my pistol and was determined to shoot any individual that appeared threatening to me if I should be discovered. I couldn't get Mike on the radio, probably because of the dense brush. However, shortly the Forward Air Controller called and said he had a medevac helicopter on the way to pick us up. He advised me that Mike had landed in a clearing about a mile from me and would I please head in his direction. Since I could only see straight up because of the brush, he flew over my chute in the direction he wanted me to go. Soon I heard the helicopter as it made about three circular passes to see if he could draw any enemy fire and then set down next to Mike.

In the meantime Mike had emerged from cover and spread his parachute in the clearing to mark his position for the helicopter. It landed within minutes, and a much relieved Mike Aarni scrambled aboard.

They asked me if I wanted to get out and pick up the rest of my gear, but I thought 'Hell, no, they can have it.' Then, as we waited for Jake to make his way to us, I decided that I didn't want to leave them anything. I persuaded the door gunner to accompany me with his machine gun, and as we stowed my parachute in the helicopter Jake burst into the clearing, out of breath and with his .38 in his hand

Sorensen recalls his journey through the jungle:

I had struggled through the brush at Mach 2, and when I got under the 200-foot trees that I was worried about landing in, the brush cleared out and I was able to quicken my pace to Mach 4. When I broke into the clearing where the chopper was, the door gunner in his side door had his machine gun trained on me . . . I was hollering and waving my arms and was glad as hell he didn't have an itchy trigger finger. Mike was already on board with all his gear. The pilot asked me if I wanted to go back and get mine. I told him 'No!', and 'Lets get the f*** out of here!'

En route to Dak To the crew told us that they had seen us get hit, and since there was no place for them to set down in the battle area they decided to follow us, knowing we weren't going very far. Twenty minutes or so later we landed at Dak To, where an Army Battalion was stationed. They had gone through a rather heavy pitched battle with the North Vietnamese/Viet Cong several months earlier and there still seemed to be a great deal of activity in the area. We were ushered into an underground bunkered command post, where the duty officer gave us a can of soda pop and told us that the commander would be down shortly. He also told us that one of the Green Beret posts was monitoring enemy communications and it seemed that the local VC commander had promised the North Vietnamese Regimental commander a captured pilot before the year's end . . . and that they were still in the field looking for us.

Shortly thereafter a full Colonel named Tex Johnson, whose callsign was Cherokee (because he was a Cherokee Indian graduate of West Point), introduced himself and asked if we would like to go on a local inspection tour with him. He said the troops didn't get to see aviators very often and would like our company. I said 'OK' as a matter of courtesy, thinking we were going to walk outside around the local fortifications and be done with it, while we waited for transportation to Pleiku and then back to Da Nang. The Colonel then asked if we had any weapons. When I replied that we had our 38-caliber pistols, the Colonel said to the First Sergeant to issue us a couple of M-16s and we were to launch in twenty minutes! He then turned away and walked out of the bunker. I asked the duty officer where the hell we were going and he replied that they had captured a hill about thirty miles from there and had some heavy casualties and that an engineering company was preparing the top of the hill to receive helicopter-delivered artillery pieces later that day. We then took off in a chopper and landed in a bomb crater on top of a 4,000-foot hill. Broken clouds obscured the surrounding area, the wind was blowing rather briskly and it was cold as hell in lightweight flying suits.

As we got off the chopper and climbed out of the bomb crater the Colonel went off to talk to the company commander. I began talking to a rather battle-weary looking older Sergeant and asked him what was going on. He said that they had a number of casualties from booby traps coming up the hill and had chased the VC down the other side, pointing down the valley far below. Apparently they had only taken the hill about two hours ago! The company was digging trenches, cutting down trees with chain saws and wiring up stumps with primer cord to clear the area. About that time a great '*boom*' went off. Thinking we were under mortar attack, I jumped down in the bomb crater we had landed in. As I looked up the Sergeant was laughing and said, 'Bet you haven't heard that before, have you?' He proceeded to tell us that that was some of our boys dropping bombs on the VC below. Because of the wind and cloud cover and noise of the chain saws etc., we couldn't initially hear the aircraft, but then we saw two F-100s and two A-1s unload on the valley below.

After about two hours the helicopter returned and we boarded and flew back to Dak To. On arrival we were informed that a chopper was

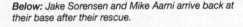

Below: Jake Sorensen and Mike Aarni arrive back at their base after their rescue.

waiting to take us to Pleiku, where a C-47 from Saigon would pick us up and take us back to Da Nang. At Pleiku we visited the local flight surgeon who looked us over and gave us a bottle of Old Methusela and a bottle of brandy. We went to the local chow hall, had some lunch and then went to flight operations where the C-47 had just landed.

Upon our return to Da Nang we commenced to open and sample the spirits the flight surgeon had given us. I must remark that Old Methusela is smooth and gets the job done very nicely. On landing at Da Nang the whole squadron was there to greet us, as well as the Ranch Hand crews that thought they were responsible for our having been shot down, by some strange manner of rationale. Anyhow, we were met with the customary bottles of champagne, and the Ranch Hand crew gave Mike a 40-ounce bottle of Scotch and myself a bottle of V.O. After the revelry we went to the flight surgeon's office to have our spines X-rayed. From there we went to the DOOM club (Da Nang Officers Open Mess), rang the bell at the Stag Bar, which meant that we bought the drinks and went through the traditional ritual of sticking our heads in the ceiling paddle fan for having screwed-up and gotten shot down. At about eight-thirty or nine we paid the bar bill of several hundred dollars, as the place was packed with Army, Air Force and civilian something or others and at 25 cents a drink that was a lot of booze. We then left the Stag Bar and, as guests of the Ranch Hands, were treated to a steak dinner and watched some Korean dancers put on a floor show as we ushered in the New Year 1968. In our case it was a very happy and memorable New Year.

Mike's last recollection of that night was of pouring his Four Roses whisky into his glass of Martini. He awoke the next morning to the sound of the squadron commander pounding on his door and, with apologies, asking him to stand alert as everyone else had gone out on operations. An hour later he sat in a new Phantom on the hot pad, waiting to go to war again. His head hurt.

Both men completed their tours of duty with the 'Gunfighters' and returned home safely. Jake was assigned to the Training Command as an instructor and Staff Officer, then returned to the war as a Liaison Officer to the Commander of the Seventh Fleet and spent another year aboard the Flag Ship in the Gulf of Tonkin. When he retired to Arizona in 1973 he worked real estate until 1985, when he accepted a position as a B-1B bomber project manager at Palmdale in California.

By the end of Mike's tour of duty he had flown 161 combat missions, 100 over North Vietnam and the balance over Southern Laos and South Vietnam. When interviewed by the author he was still in the Air Force as a full Colonel and serving as the Third Air Force Assistant Director of Operations in England. He still gets trouble occasionally with his back, but he is more than happy considering the alternatives. Every New Year's Eve both Jake and Mike toast each other's health and good fortune and think back to that eventful day when they diced with death and won.

RAPID FIRE AND THE 20 BLACK WIDOWS

1. Tay Ninh

*F*ROM August 1967 onwards, the mission of strategic and tactical reconnaissance in the II and III Corps Tactical Zones was the responsibility of Special Forces Provisional Detachment B-36. Organized by Major James G. Gritz as Project 'Rapid Fire' and located at Long Hai, B-36 comprised two A-detachment Mobile Guerrilla Force units, twenty Army long-range patrol personnel, two Cambodian Mike Force companies and one camp security company.

Project Rapid Fire reconnaissance teams would be inserted by helicopter in designated areas, to seek out the enemy and report on their movements. Usually a number of simulated insertions would be made, to try to confuse any enemy observers. Helicopter gunships would stand by in case of trouble and an Air Force FAC would usually be on call nearby. B-36 also had its own quick-reaction companies back at base, to be despatched immediately if a team were compromised and needed reinforcements. Usually the recon teams were inserted and extracted without problems, but on occasion all hell would let loose. One such occasion is described in an after-action report written by one of the helicopters unit supporting Project Rapid Fire.

On the morning of 4 January 1968, the 188th Assault Helicopter Company was involved in operations in support of Special Forces Detachment B-36. Nine 'Black Widow' aircraft were assigned to Tay Ninh East to assist B-36 in counter-insurgency operations over a thirty-day period. On that day B-36 had planned to insert two ambush patrols in the vicinity of coordinates XT113965 (LZ Rosie) and XT088881 (LZ Nora). The Black Widow ships lifted off at 0620 hours from Tay Ninh East, with a full load of troops, and proceeded to the two areas that had been designated for troop insertions. The objective of the mission was to attempt to acquire prisoners and documents.

First light found the Black Widow ships approaching the indicated LZs. Two aircraft inserted their troops into LZ Rosie and two others inserted their troops into LZ Nora. After completing the insertion, the flight returned to Tay Ninh for refueling and then proceeded to Trai Be to stand by for further instructions.

The ground troops in LZ Nora became engaged in fierce and heavy fighting with an enemy force of unknown size. They found themselves surrounded, and the ground commander radioed for an immediate emergency insertion of reinforcements. Two Black Widow aircraft returned to Tay Ninh East and picked up the needed additional troops, while the rest of the flight proceeded to the embattled LZ. The three Black Widow gunships began assisting the ground troops, making numerous gun runs, and two aircraft orbited the area waiting to pick up wounded personnel. Still another Black Widow aircraft, the command and control ship, orbited overhead the hard-hit patrol, directing and coordinating the other Black Widow ships. The two aircraft containing reinforcements arrived at LZ Nora and inserted their troops, then returned to Trai Be with the rest of the Black Widow flight until the area could be secured.

While shut down at Trai Be, the two aircraft that had inserted troops into the LZ related to the rest of the flight that they had received small-arms fire from the south side of the LZ. A radio message from the ground commander in LZ Nora requested two ships to extract several critically wounded men, and aircraft numbers 205 and 122 responded to the ground commander's request. The crews of the two aircraft were: 205 – Aircraft Commander WO Richard C. Rhodes, Pilot WO Kjell T. Tollefsen, Crew Chief PFC John I. Charlebois and Door Gunner SP4 John H. Newcomer; 122 – Aircraft Commander Captain Gerald W. Doht, Pilot WO George M. Jones, Crew Chief SP4 Tim M. Wingerd and Door Gunner SP4 Robert E. Matthess. Captain Doht was a new platoon leader and, as senior aircraft commander, WO Jones was giving him his aircraft commander's checkout ride.

Both aircraft commanders had considered the fact that the enemy fire had been received from the southern side of the LZ, and Captain Doht requested gunship suppression on the suspected enemy positions. The door gunners on the two slicks were also instructed to suppress the suspected area on departure. While approaching the LZ and while sitting on the ground on-loading casualties, both aircraft received a constant barrage of small-arms fire. When all casualties were aboard, both ships came to a hover, did a pedal turn and attempted to depart the LZ.

Aircraft number 205 received several hits and the aircraft commander radioed that he was going down with partial power. Aircraft number 122 followed the aircraft down and saw it hit the ground and roll onto its right side. Without hesitation, Captain Doht and Warrant Officer Jones landed their aircraft near the downed aircraft and deployed all able-bodied men aboard their ship to set up a perimeter defense around the aircraft. While on the ground, Captain Doht's crew learned that Specialist Fourth Class Newcomer, the downed aircraft's gunner, had been pinned beneath the aircraft. Captain Doht and Warrant Officer Jones took immediate action in an attempt to free the trapped gunner. A rope was attached to the downed aircraft and aircraft 122 attempted to raise it enough to allow

Newcomer to be pulled from beneath the aircraft.

The rope broke and the first attempt was a failure. Another attempt was initiated, only this time two ropes were used. Specialists Fourth Class Wingerd and Matthess displayed extraordinary professionalism in guiding and directing the pilots while they were attempting to raise the downed aircraft. The attempt appeared to be successful until the pinned man began to experience great pain and the attempt had to be aborted. Both crews knew that the entire area was infested with NVA soldiers and yet, when ordered by command and control to leave the man beneath the aircraft, Specialist Charlebois asked for five more minutes in which to free Newcomer and was granted the time.

While the attempts to lift the aircraft were in progress, another aircraft had landed and left a man on the ground before taking off again. This man, Specialist Dennis M. Wolfe, had requested his pilot to let him stay on the ground and assist the others in the rescue effort. The men knew they must work quickly if they were to free the pinned man. The only hope was brute strength. Wolfe and Charlebois physically lifted the aircraft for WO Tollefsen, who had gotten inside the aircraft, and WO Rhodes to pull Newcomer from beneath the aircraft. The four men carried him to aircraft 122 and all those still on the ground boarded 122 and returned to the 45th Medical Evacuation Hospital in Tay Ninh West.

After refueling, Captain Doht and his crew returned to the scene of the operation and found that the area around the downed aircraft had been secured by additional troops and that all the troops in LZ Nora had been extracted. The command and control ship told Captain Doht to proceed to LZ Rosie, orbit and await further orders to extract the troops. The immediate area surrounding LZ Rosie was reported to be secure, although the unit had been in contact earlier, which prompted their extraction. The ground commander requested his men be extracted and the Black Widow aircraft were told to enter the pickup zone one at a time. Captain Doht and his crew were the first to enter the PZ. The approach was made to an area which, at some time during the morning, had burned. As the aircraft neared the ground, it became engulfed in ashes and went into IFR conditions. Skillfully, Warrant Officer Jones lowered the aircraft to the ground.

The ashes cleared and the friendly troops were approaching the aircraft, when, without warning, the aircraft came under heavy enemy ground fire and was struck in the left rear of the fuselage by an RPG round. Both pilots went into action immediately and attempted to get the ship off the ground, only to have the rpm bleed off to 4,000 before the ship was two feet in the air. The RPG round had caused the loss of all cyclic control and only through luck was the aircraft settled back on the ground without rolling over. Although already having sustained multiple shrapnel wounds from the RPG round, Specialist Wingerd jumped from his seat and proceeded to Captain Doht's door in an attempt to get the

Above: George Jones's UH-1 'Ragin Cajun' after being hit by by the RPG round. (George M. Jones)

Captain out of the ship. Just as Specialist Wingerd was about to open the door, another RPG round hit the left skid, one and one half feet aft of the forward cross tube. The explosion knocked Wingerd to the ground, seriously wounding him. Captain Doht, realizing the seriousness of the situation, quickly departed his seat, exited between the seats and instructed Specialist Matthess to dismount his machine gun and take up a defensive position outside the aircraft. Captain Doht then proceeded to make his way, still under heavy fire, to the friendly position some fifty feet away. [Captain Doht should have stayed with his crew. However he was ex-Special Forces and instinctively went to their aid. Author.]

Back at the aircraft WO Jones was attempting to get out of his door when an enemy weapon pinpointed him and began to fire. Bullets flew everywhere, six coming within a fraction of an inch of hitting WO Jones. Exiting between the seats and jumping out of the left cargo door, WO Jones directed his first thoughts to his critically wounded crew chief. He knelt next to Specialist Wingerd, protected only by the suppressive fire being provided by Specialist Matthess. Unable to move Wingerd, WO Jones relieved Matthess of his M-60 and instructed him to apply first aid to Wingerd. Although the entire area was still under heavy ground fire, Matthess made his way back to the ship from his machine gun position and, undaunted by the bullets spanking the ground all around him, climbed back on board the ship to retrieve a first aid kit.

Bullet after bullet whined by Specialist Matthess as he went to the side of his fallen comrade. Matthess proceeded to apply first aid until a Special Forces man came out to their position in the middle of the open PZ. The Special Forces man and WO Jones decided to provide suppressive fire while Matthess carried Wingerd to the friendly position. Picking Wingerd up was not an easy job for Matthess as Wingerd outweighed him by seventy pounds. Falling several times en route to the friendly position, Matthess continually returned to his feet and pushed onward, carrying

Wingerd to the safety of the tree-line. At that point the friendly force of twelve had four or five dead and six wounded.

After both members of his crew had made their way safely to the friendly position, WO Jones and the Special Forces soldier stopped their covering fire and dashed to the tree-line. As soon as he had made it to the tree-line, WO Jones went to check on Wingerd's condition and found Matthess in need of more bandages to check the bleeding. Going from man to man, up and down the tree-line, WO Jones found the needed bandages and returned to the wounded man.

Captain Doht, in the meantime, had returned to the area behind the aircraft to assist the other soldiers wounded by the RPG round and subsequent enemy fire. While aiding the wounded men, completely unprotected from enemy fire, Captain Doht received a bullet in the left side of his head. [During this time, WO Jones thought that they were about to be overrun and that he would not make it out. He wondered what his relatives back home were doing at that moment and figured out that they were probably having breakfast . . . Author.]

Back in the tree-line, WO Jones manned his M-60 and helped Matthess to comfort and apply first aid to Wingerd until several 'Robin Hood' aircraft arrived with reinforcements. Shortly thereafter a medevac aircraft arrived and WO Jones and Matthess carried Wingerd to the aircraft, searching unsuccessfully for Captain Doht on the way. Another medevac aircraft arrived and the two men helped to carry the other wounded to the ship. The area was still very 'hot' so both men took up defensive positions until more reinforcements were inserted into the area. A Robin Hood aircraft then landed and picked up both WO Jones and Specialist Matthess and took them to Katum, where WO Jones learned that Captain Doht was still alive. The valorous actions of the crews brought about the accomplishment of the evacuation of the pinned gunner and all casualties.

The foregoing after-action report was to be submitted with a recommendation for several medals for the participants, but owing to operational requirements it was not submitted in time and nothing came of it. Warrant Officer George Jones survived the rest of his year in combat and is now the Senior Rotary Wing Captain of the Colgate Palmolive Company in New Jersey. He has in his possession the mangled back end of one of the RPGs which hit his aircraft, removed from the wreck after its recovery by CH-47 to Cu Chi.

Left: The strain of combat shows on the face of Spec 4 Robert Matthess, photographed in the LZ prior to the arrival of reinforcements. (via George M. Jones).

THE FIASCO AT KHAM DUC

21

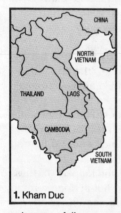

1. Kham Duc

*F*OLLOWING the loss of Lang Vei in February 1968, the only remaining Special Forces border camp in I Corps was that at Kham Duc. Located ten miles from the Laotian border on the extreme western fringe of Quang Tin Province, the camp served as a base for allied reconnaissance teams and a training site for Vietnamese Civilian Irregular Defence Group troops. The first Special Forces A-detachment had moved into Kham Duc in September 1963 and found the outpost to be an ideal border surveillance site. It was, however, a difficult place to supply.

The border region south-west of Da Nang was among the most rugged in Vietnam and was nearly uninhabited except for the Vietnamese military dependants, camp followers and merchants living across the airstrip in Kham Duc village. The camp, village and airstrip were all situated in a mile-wide bowl, surrounded by jungle and hills which rose abruptly to heights of over 2,000 feet.

Although C-130 crews had been using the 6,000 foot asphalt runway for years, they detested the difficult landings made dangerous by the weather and the terrain, with the Ngok Peng Bum ridge to the west and the high Ngok Pe Xar mountain looming over Kham Duc to the east. It became even more difficult in April 1968 when the C-130s began frequent landings to bring in American engineers and construction materials to improve the runway. The stacks of equipment piled beside the runway and the considerable amount of enemy fire from the nearby high ground did little to improve matters.

In the early hours of 10 May, the forward operating base of Ngok Tavak, built around an old French fort five miles from Kham Duc, was attacked by a battalion of NVA troops. The outpost was defended by a 113-man Vietnamese Mobile Strike Force Company, together with eight Special Forces and three Australian advisers and 33 Marine artillerymen. They managed to hold out until noon, when the survivors were forced to abandon the fort and evade the enemy through the jungle, until they were extracted by helicopter during the evening.

At the same time that the attack on Ngok Tavak began, the camp at Kham Duc was blasted by heavy mortar and recoilless-rifle fire. This continued throughout the day as the 1st VC Regiment of the 2nd NVA Division moved into positions encircling the camp. At first light C-130s began to arrive with reinforcements from the Americal Division and, despite the communist shells falling on the runway, 900 Americans and 600 Vietnamese troops had arrived by nightfall.

As the enemy ground attack began during the early-morning darkness of 12 May, General Westmoreland reviewed the situation and determined that the camp lacked the importance and defensibility of Khe Sanh. He directed that the camp be abandoned and the defenders evacuated by air, despite the strong enemy presence.

By 1000 hours, three of the camp outposts were in enemy hands and company-size NVA assaults were taking place against three sides of the main perimeter. Army and Marine helicopters managed to extract some of the troops, but a Chinook was shot down, blocking the runway until engineers managed to drag it clear. A C-130 landed immediately and civilians, streaming from ditches alongside the runway, quickly filled the aircraft. As the pilot, Lieutenant Colonel Daryl D. Cole, began the take-off run down the cratered and shrapnel-littered strip, exploding mortar shells bracketed the aircraft and burst one of the tyres. Cole aborted the take-off and unloaded the passengers while the crew worked frantically to remove the ruined tyre.

Around 1100 hours Major Ray D. Shelton brought his C-123 in, and took 70 people on board, including 44 American engineers. Despite heavy automatic-weapons fire and a dozen mortar detonations near his ship, Shelton took off safely. He was soon followed by Cole's C-130, which took off with fuel streaming from holes in the wings. His only passengers now were three members of an Air Force combat control team, whose radio equipment had been destroyed. Cole landed on a foamed runway at Cam Ranh Bay and was later awarded the Mackay Trophy for 1968 for his efforts.

Heavy ground fire led to the orbiting C-130 command and control ship post-poning any further evacuation attempts for the time being. At noon a massive NVA attack was launched against the main compound, but was stopped by ground support aircraft hurling napalm, cluster bomb units and 750-pound bombs into the final wire barriers. By the middle of the afternoon only 145 persons had been evacuated by the one C-123 and fifteen helicopter sorties. A dozen more transports were orbiting nearby, waiting their turn to go in, and, with time running out, another attempt was made at 1525 hours.

Major Bernard L. Bucher made a steep approach from the south in his C-130 and landed despite numerous hits. More than a hundred panicking civilian dependants crowded aboard and Bucher began his take-off run. He chose to take off towards the north, either unaware of, or disregarding, the concentration of enemy forces in that direction. As the aircraft cleared the northern boundary it was struck by enemy tracer fire, crashed and burned with no survivors. The Vietnamese troops amongst the Kham Duc defenders were, needless to say, shattered, having just watched their families die. It was not the first time, nor would it be the last, that the fighting performance of Vietnamese troops would be adversely affected by their concern over the presence of their dependants on the battlefield.

Landing behind Bucher was a C-130E flown by Lieutenant Colonel William Boyd Jr., who made an initial go-around just before touch-down. He loaded another hundred people aboard and took off to the south, banking after lift-off so that the aircraft would be masked by the rolling terrain. Boyd landed his Hercules

safely at Chu Lai, despite numerous bullet holes and a smoke-filled interior. For this flight he was awarded the Air Force Cross.

Lieutenant Colonel John R. Delmore flew in next, spiralling down from directly overhead. As he neared the ground, bullets tore through the ship and, with all hydraulics gone and almost out of control, the Hercules smashed into the runway. The wrecked aircraft came to rest at the side of the strip and the fortunate crew scrambled out unhurt. They found some shelter and were soon picked up by a Marine helicopter.

The loss of two aircraft in a matter of minutes did nothing to inspire confidence in the remaining transport crews orbiting above. However, three more C-130s made it in and withdrew the last defenders. This final evacuation was made possible by close-in air strikes, with fighters laying a barrage down along both sides of the runway during the run in and while the transports loaded. Lieutenant Colonel Wallace crossed the field at right angles in his C-130E, and made a 270-degree turn at maximum rate of descent with power off and gear down. Touching down, he made a maximum-effort stop and was immediately swamped by a hundred panicking Vietnamese. The loadmaster had to rescue a woman and a baby trampled in the rush, as the civilians and the last few Americans dashed aboard. Wallace took off to the south and safety, just as a helicopter swooped down to take the Special Forces command group out of the camp.

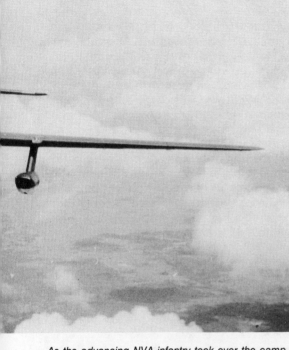

Left: A jet-equipped C-123K Provider in flight over South Vietnam. Joe Jackson was flying a C-123K when he pulled off his daring rescue of the combat control team at Kham Duc. (US Air Force)

As the advancing NVA infantry took over the camp, a near-tragedy occured. A C-130 flown by Lieutenant Colonel Jay Van Cleef was inexplicably instructed by the airborne control centre to land the three-man combat control team which had already had been evacuated earlier in the day. Van Cleef protested that the camp was almost completely evacuated, but the control centre insisted that the team be returned and left.

Obediently Van Cleef landed his aircraft, and the three controllers ran from the ship towards the burning camp. He waited patiently for another two minutes for passengers expecting to be evacuated, and when none appeared he slammed the throttles open and took off. He duly notified the control ship that they had taken off empty, and was shocked to hear the control ship then report to General McLaughlin that the evacuation of Kham Duc was complete. His crew immediately and vehemently disabused the commander and pointed out that the camp was not evacuated, because they had, as ordered, just deposited a combat control team in the camp. There was a moment of stunned radio silence as the reality sank in: Kham Duc was now in enemy hands – except for three American combat controllers.

Meanwhile, Major John W. Gallagher Jr. and the other two controllers took shelter in a culvert next to the runway and started firing at the enemy in the camp with their M-16 rifles. The command post asked a C-123 to try to pick the men up, *but as the aircraft touched down it came under fire from all directions. The pilot, Lieutenant Colonel Alfred J. Jeannotte Jr., could not see the team anywhere and jammed the throttles forward for take-off. Just before lift-off the crew spotted the three men, but it was now too late to stop. The C-123 took to the air and, low on fuel, turned for home. Jeannotte later received the Air Force Cross for his actions.*

Technical Sergeant Mort Freedman described how he, Major Gallagher and Sergeant Jim Lundie reacted when the last Provider took off, leaving the three-man team behind. 'The pilot saw no one left on the ground, so he took off. We figured no one would come back and we had two choices: either be taken prisoner, or fight it out. There was no doubt about it. We had eleven magazines among us and were going to take as many of them with us as we could'.

The C-123 behind Jeannotte was being flown by Lieutenant Colonel Joe M. Jackson and Major Jesse W. Campbell. They had left Da Nang earlier in the day to haul some cargo, while Jackson went through the bi-annual check flight that is mandatory for all Air Force fliers. They had been recalled and sent to Kham Duc, arriving as the command ship requested that they make another pick-up attempt. Jesse Campbell radioed, 'Roger. Going in'.

Joe Jackson had been a fighter pilot for twenty years before being assigned to transport duty. He had flown 107 missions in Korea and had won the Distinguished Flying Cross. He knew that the enemy gunners would expect him to follow the same flight path as the other cargo planes and decided to call upon his fighter-pilot experience and try a new tactic. At 9,000 feet, and rapidly approaching the landing area, he pointed the nose down in a steep dive. Side-slipping for maximum descent, and with power back and landing gear and flaps full down, the Provider dropped like a rock. Jackson recalls: 'The book said you didn't fly transports this way, but the guy who wrote the book had never been shot at. I had two problems, the second stemming from the first. One was to avoid reaching "blow up" speed, where the flaps, which were in full down position for the dive, are blown back up to neutral. If this happened, we would pick up even more speed, leading to problem two – the danger of overshooting the runway'.

Jackson pulled back on the control column and broke the Provider's descent just above the tree-tops, a quarter of a mile from the end of the runway. He barely had time to set up a landing attitude as the aircraft settled towards the threshold. The debris-strewn runway looked like an obstacle course, with a burning helicopter blocking the way a mere 2,200 feet from the touch-down point. Jackson knew that he would have to stop in a hurry, but decided against using the reverse thrust. Reversing the engines would automatically shut off the two jets that would be needed for a minimum-run take-off. He stood on the brakes and skidded to a halt just before reaching the gutted helicopter.

The three controllers scrambled from the ditch and dived into the aircraft as the surprised enemy gunners opened fire. At the front of the aircraft Major Campbell spotted a 122mm rocket shell coming towards them, and both pilots watched in horror as it hit the ground just 25 feet in front of the nose. Luck was still on their side, however, and the deadly projectile did not explode. Jackson taxied around the shell and rammed the throttles to the firewall. 'We hadn't been out of that

Above: President Lyndon B. Johnson presents the
Medal of Honor to Lieutenant-Colonel Joe M. Jackson at
the White House on 16 January 1969. (US Air Force)

spot ten seconds when mortars started dropping directly on it', he remembers.
'That was a real thriller. I figured they just got zeroed in on us, and that the time
of flight of the mortar shells was about ten seconds longer than the time we sat
there taking the men aboard'. Within seconds they were in the air again and one
of the combat team recalled, 'We were dead, and all of a sudden we were alive!'

General McLaughlin, who had witnessed the event from overhead, approved
nominations for the Medal of Honor for both pilots, who landed safely back at
Da Nang to discover that their C-123 had not even taken one hit! In January
1969 Colonel Jackson received the Medal of Honor in a ceremony at the White
House; Major Campbell received the Air Force Cross, and the rest of the crew
were awarded Silver Stars.

Following the evacuation, air strikes demolished the rest of the camp. Out of
the 1,800 military and civilians involved, 259 were lost, over half of these in the
crash of Major Bucher's C-130. The US Army lost 25 men and two Chinooks, and
two Marine CH-46s and two C-130s were destroyed. The battle had resulted in
a total North Vietnamese victory, for the last Special Forces border surveillance
camp on the north-western frontier of South Vietnam had been destroyed.

AN ODE TO MULESKINNER

22

1. Nui Ba Den Mountain
2. Cu Chi

*T*HE summit of the 3,235-foot-high Nui Ba Den mountain, known to the Vietnamese as the Black Virgin Mountain, was an ideal place to put an observation and radio relay post. The mountain dominated the landscape in that part of the III Corps Tactical Zone and was virtually inaccessible from the ground. However, it was in the notorious Viet Cong stronghold of War Zone C and, despite the difficulties involved, the Viet Cong would get round to attacking the outpost sooner or later.

In the meantime the troops had to be fed, and the resupply mission fell to the CH-47 Chinooks of the 242nd Assault Support Helicopter Company, the 'Muleskinners'. One of their pilots was Lieutenant Gary B. Roush, who had been assigned to the Muleskinners at their base at Cu Chi in May 1968. During his tour of duty he would complete 942 combat flight-hours, resulting in over 3,000 landings in terrain that varied from 100-foot-deep holes cut in the jungle to ships at sea.

I held the record for hauling the most people – ninety-seven, not counting chickens, dogs and pigs – and hauling the most cargo in the shortest amount of time – 80 tons, including five 105mm artillery pieces with ammunition and the crew's personal gear in twenty sorties in 63 minutes. On combat assaults carrying Vietnamese we could haul 60 to 70, but Americans were heavier so we could haul only 40 to 50. (The Chinook had 33 seat belts.) Most thought I had a charmed life, because at least twice my helicopter was completely surrounded by enemy tracers without taking a single hit and when bullets did hit my helicopter they never hit a person or critical component.

Aircraft maintenance was always a problem – during the year I had two engine failures in flight, lost one complete set of hydraulics, had a complete electrical system failure and had numerous minor failures. Any indication of a system failure was treated as an emergency, since some system failures would render the Chinook uncontrollable or cause it to disintegrate. During my tour one crew and passengers were killed when a single bolt failed in a transmission, causing the Chinook to disintegrate. One day while flying from 0630 hours to 2130 hours, I flew five different helicopters because of maintenance problems.

The Muleskinners formed a special relationship with the troops on the top of Nui Ba Den, so much so that their commander wrote them a poem:

An Ode to Muleskinner – Christmas 1968

Atop Nui Ba Den Mountain at thirty-two hundred feet,
The weather is wild and winds are real neat.
But daily we wait for your ship to arrive,
For without you Muleskinner we could not survive.

From Cu Chi each morning you take to the sky,
Vowing 'Curses on Dutcher' when you start to fly.
At Tay Ninh's 'Viking' you hook up the stuff,
Then on to the Mountain – that's when it gets rough.

The radios chatter and the voice that you hear,
Is Nui Ba Den Control bidding you cheer –
'Winds southwest no northeast, at ten no it's forty',
Then One-Six Delta asks, 'Hey, what's on this sortie?'

Is it Class One, or ammo, or diesel you bring?
So to avoid confusion we do our thing:
Pop smoke in three places – red, green and 'grape' –
Then watch you hover while our ground crew goes ape.

When the dust finally settles and we show you the place,
It's next to antennas in the smallest space.
But at these times we are sure you ask yourself why
A 'slick' or a Cobra you weren't destined to fly.

Now this holiday season is a time to insure
That we speak of good will and request you endure
The daily harassment we know we provoke:
Merry Christmas Muleskinner – this wish ain't a joke!

> Major Dutcher
> Commanding Officer, Nui Ba Den
> December 1968

Gary Roush recalls:

After receiving this poem, my hooch mate, Mike Ryan, tried to deliver a Christmas tree to Nui Ba Den Mountain that Christmas (21 December 1968), but was unable to pull a palm tree out of the ground at a fire base called Mole City. Mole City was set up just south of Tay Ninh on the Cambodian border, across from a known Viet Cong staging area. At this time the Americans were not allowed to go into Cambodia, so lightly defended fire bases were set up in vulnerable areas along the border to tempt the enemy to cross and fight. Attacking these fire bases proved to

Above: Gary Roush with his 'Muleskinner' Chinook. Try to imagine flying it up a mountainside in fog. (Gary B. Roush)

be devastating to the enemy because of our massive artillery and air support. Mole City got its name because of the earthen trenches, bunkers, and berms created with a small bulldozer flown in by a 'Superhook,' a Sikorsky CH-54 Tarhe.

The Muleskinners flew in most of the other materials and equipment and resupplied them daily. Mike figured a palm tree had shallow roots and would make a startling living Christmas tree on top of the 3,000-foot barren mountain, but even with the power of a Chinook the tree would not budge. A second attempt was scheduled for the next day with the assistance of a little C-4 plastic explosive, but Charlie attacked Mole City that night and the tree was destroyed. The Americans lost 21 dead and the Viet Cong several times that number. Although American positions were overrun during the night, their earthen defenses and superior firepower helped with their victory. Mike and I found them burning large piles of enemy bodies outside their perimeter the next day, when we flew in to resupply them and pull up the mountain's Christmas tree.

Flying to the mountain, which the Muleskinners did nearly every day since we were their primary means of resupply, never lacked excitement. If not having to dodge the clouds or radio antennas, it was hovering with a sling load at max gross weight while indicating 30 knots airspeed, with wind gusts to 50 knots, or remembering to carry a lighter load because of the high-density altitude.

At first light on 15 August 1968, while en route to routinely resupply the mountain, I noticed several miles out that they were 'socked in' with a low layer of clouds. I switched to their frequency on Fox Mike (FM radio) to confirm a weather delay in their resupply sorties. What I learned was that they had been overrun during the night and were desperate to get 22 wounded evacuated. The Viet Cong had taken advantage of the bad weather, knowing that the mountain top would not have close air support because of the conditions. Even the medevac Hueys had been unsuccessful in landing because of clouds.

The mountain-top commander was practically begging us to try to land. We were not normally asked to haul wounded since we were not properly equipped, but in this case being properly equipped meant being able to land. We made two attempts using IFR (Instrument Flight Rules) in the clouds, with the CO saying on the radio, 'We can hear you but do not have you in sight; keep on coming – you sound like you are on track.' As convincing as the CO tried to be, it definitely was not the same as Precision Approach Radar during flight school at Fort Rucker, Alabama.

After the second try in the clouds and feeling relieved we did not find 'the rocks in those clouds,' someone came up with the idea of hovering up the side of the mountain. The Chinook had plenty of power, especially considering we were empty. Fortunately we had not yet picked up our first sortie for the mountain from Tay Ninh. Also, after all the many past sorties to the mountain, I knew the terrain like the back of my hand. The only problem was, where was Charlie?

The Viet Cong had just recently broken contact after overrunning the outnumbered Americans. We rationalized that if our troops could not see us, neither could Charlie. Even though I had been shot at from this side of the mountain recently, the terrain was very steep and offered little concealment. After all, what self-respecting VC would expect a big lumbering helicopter to fly right over his head after a major attack. The element of surprise was on our side. So with all this rationale, to the base of the cloud layer we went, to hover IFR up the side of the mountain, hopefully aligned on the resupply pad and not their bank of antennas. After what seemed like hours with the pilot calling out obstacles, and the left door gunner watching for Charlie, the welcomed sight of the perimeter barbed wire, bunkers and finally the landing pad appeared. Needless to say, I was glad to have all four wheels safely on the ground. After a few seconds I started looking around.

The scene was like it had come out of a horror movie. In the swirling mist of the clouds I could just make out the outline of bodies and they were lying everywhere. The rotorwash from the Chinook was slowly clearing the area right around the landing pad, revealing the nightmare our troops must have experienced minutes before. Directly under my feet through the chin bubble was a gook with half of his head missing. Next to him was another grotesque figure of a Viet Cong and then the American dead and wounded neatly lying in a row on the edge of the resupply pad, giving us just enough room to land. The nearby uninjured troops who were on guard never took their eyes from the now-breached perimeter. This was not characteristic, since we were normally the center of attention, with everyone watching us perform our hovering feats.

Fortunately we could take all 22 of the wounded at once, because I certainly did not want to go through this again. But what about the departure? My memory recalled the antennas straight ahead, still covered by the clouds, and on both sides the bunkers with high RPG fences also in the clouds, so a vertical or 180-degree turn departure were the only two reasonable alternatives, other than hovering back down the side like we had come up.

I had one instructor during primary flight school at Fort Wolters, Texas, teach me how to do backward takeoffs, and my instrument instructor at Fort Rucker taught me 0/0 takeoffs under the hood. Doing one was crazy, but putting both together was suicide. A vertical takeoff was certainly possible, but how high did the clouds go and how would we avoid the mountains on the way down? The only logical procedure was a hovering 180-degree turn and then a 0/0 standard takeoff on the back course of a normal approach until we were sure to be clear of the mountain, then a standard instrument descent out of the clouds just like a VOR approach. Sounds simple, but how do you hover IFR in a tight LZ?

In order to get high enough to get all four wheels off the ground, the cockpit will be in the clouds and I will not be able to see the ground. No one thought to teach me how to hover IFR! But wait, I have made this turn hundreds of times in good weather, so with a little care and concentration on the instruments and the help of the other four pairs of eyes to stay over the landing pad it should work. There was no way I was going to stay on top of that mountain until the weather cleared.

The plan worked. Throughout the 180-degree hovering turn, at least one of the four other crew members had sight of the ground and gave me, in turn, the necessary directions to stay over the landing pad. Since the Chinook is so large and most loads in Vietnam were carried externally, out of sight of the pilots (the cargo hook was about 30 feet behind the cockpit), we were used to getting reliable hovering directions from the crew. I was not able to see the ground shortly after lifting the front wheels off the ground until we broke out of the clouds well away from the mountain. This marked my first and last 0/0 takeoff and landing in actual weather. There were other low-visibility landings due to monsoon rains, but no other below acceptable visibility takeoffs. After dropping off the wounded at the Tay Ninh Field Hospital, we went back for the KIAs but decided it was not worth the risk. Another Chinook picked them up after the weather cleared.

Because of limited space on top of the mountains, it was decided not to burn the Viet Cong bodies there, as was common practice. Instead they were put in a net to be hauled as an external load to a suitable burning site by a Chinook. Shortly after takeoff with the sling load of enemy bodies, the sling became disengaged from the cargo hook, dumping the contents over the adjoining smaller mountain. Since the Viet Cong owned that mountain they were given an unexpected chance to recover their dead.

GUNS AND SLICKS 23

1. Camp Bear Cat
2. Vinh Long 3. Phu Bai

*T*HE 240th Assault Helicopter Company was one of the many Army Aviation Companies to serve in Vietnam. It arrived in May 1967 and was assigned to Camp Bear Cat, in the III Corps area to the east of Saigon near Long Binh. In common with most other Assault Helicopter Companies, the 240th consisted of two lift platoons flying seven to ten UH-1 slicks and one gun platoon equipped with UH-1C gunships. The slicks were troop transport helicopters with the call-sign 'Grayhound' and the guns, armed with various combinations of rocket pods and machine guns were the 'Mad Dogs'.

The usual role of a gunship platoon was to escort the slick platoons during an aerial assault. They would accompany the troop transports to the target area, attack any enemy found in the Landing Zone (LZ) and provide fire support to the troops once on the ground. If the troops were lucky, the LZ might be 'cold' and their landing unopposed. However, as the war progressed, the Viet Cong and North Vietnamese Army units could often figure out the likely landing zones, and a cold LZ often turned hot, usually as the slicks flared over the landing zone and were committed to land.

Occasionally, an assault force would arrive to find that they had stirred up a hornet's nest and a major battle would ensue. One such conflict took place on 18 October 1968 when the Mad Dogs gun platoon were in support of an element of the Ninth Infantry Division near Vinh Long. The story is told by Terryl Morris, a Warrant Officer pilot with the Mad Dogs.

An infantry company had been conducting a routine sweep of a tree-line, when one of its members triggered a booby trap, causing a couple of casualties. A medevac helicopter was called to extract the wounded, but as it approached the pickup zone it was hit by a rocket-propelled grenade and crashed into the tree-line. A reaction force was scrambled and inserted further up the tree-line by our sister company, the 191st AHC 'Boomerangs.' Their mission was to provide a blocking force while the first infantry company went after the downed crew of the medevac.

As the first company approached the tree-line, it came under light fire from an estimated squad-size force of VC. It was decided to insert another infantry company on the opposite side of the tree-line to block all avenues of escape for the enemy force. Our mission was to provide one heavy fire team of three guns, to cover the insertion of the company by ten troop-carrying slicks from the 240th.

As I was piloting the number two ship, it was my responsibility to make all outside calls, the first of which was to contact the 191st to check on any problems they may have had on their insertion. The 191st lead gun, 'Bounty Hunter Lead,' reported that the LZ had been cold and that they had made several gun runs along the tree-line and had received no return fire. I passed this information along to the slick lead and the lead gunship. The slicks had already received artillery clearance, to ensure that they were not about to share their airspace with a salvo of shells, so there was nothing for me to do but sit back and relax, for what was sure to be another boring escort mission.

The sun was beginning to set as we approached the LZ, and we slid into position on the right side of the formation of slicks, as our lead gun and gun three moved into position on the left side of the formation. About two minutes out, lead and number three began to move out ahead of the slicks to start their gun runs, and I broke left and then right to pick up the number three slot for the initial attack. I was somewhat disappointed because my job was to follow the others until the slicks were down in the LZ, before I could do any shooting. Once the slicks were in the LZ we would then set up a racetrack pattern, with each gunship covering the one in front, and everyone would get to do some firing. I would fire our two mini-guns while Chief Warrant Officer Waggie would shoot the rockets.

A shadow had spread across the LZ and the tree-line had become very dark. There was a small finger of trees that projected into the LZ about two-thirds of the way up the LZ, and I heard the slick lead telling his flight to guide in on that point. The lead gun was about three hundred meters out in front of the flight and had started his run. Gun three was covering him and would begin his run as soon as lead broke to the right, across the front of the flight. About that time I heard the lead gun yell that he was taking fire. I looked for him and finally saw him heading out to the left, trailing a column of smoke and heading for a nearby rice paddy. I called to gun three, who replied that he had been hit and was going to try to reach Vinh Long.

The slicks were just touching down in the LZ and the sky was filled with green tracers. I could see mortar rounds impacting in the LZ around the slicks and I heard Grayhound lead yelling for covering fire on the tree-line to his front. The normal chatter on the radios was now a constant call for help from several slicks down in the LZ and from several that had made it out but were badly shot up and going down in the local area. A stream of tracers cut across the nose of our aircraft, then something flashed by that scared the hell out of me. It was a large white ball, quickly followed by several more in rapid succession; it was fifty-cal, the helicopter pilot's nightmare!

We began our run along the tree-line, directing a steady stream of mini-gun fire into the enemy positions. This must have really upset them, because they shifted their fire from the slicks to us. We completed the first run, and as we came around our two door gunners began to suppress the enemy positions with their M-60s to cover our break. My door gunners were the best there were: one in particular, Spec Four Ogdon, could cut the straps off a VC's sandals without breaking his skin. Ogdon was having a field day with so many targets to shoot at, taking out one after another. As we came around again all hell broke loose. I had spotted at least three fifty-cal positions, and we were only one gun, the other two having been shot down, leaving us with no one to cover our breaks. We made one more run, expending our rockets and most of the mini-gun ammo, trying to concentrate on the fifty-cal positions. I know we knocked out one for sure and stirred up another. I heard the grunts on FM calling for arty and possible air strikes on the enemy positions, and I heard that slicks from the Boomerangs were en route to insert more troops.

Bounty Hunter lead called, stating that he was about ten minutes out, so we decided to make another run to take some heat off the grunts and downed crew members in the LZ. We flew low-level along the length of the tree-line, while I hosed down everything I could with the mini-guns and Ogdon covered our tail as best he could with his door gun. Our pass brought a concentration of fire upon us, and you could feel and hear the bullets hitting the aircraft. I kept glancing at the console to see if any of the caution lights were on, indicating a hit in a vital area, but none ever came on. We expended our ammo just as the Bounty Hunters were arriving on station.

We returned to Vinh Long to assess our damage and, to our surprise, we had taken only a dozen or so hits, although one fifty-cal had hit the main rotor mast, which could have been a disaster. We lost four of the ten slicks in the LZ and all the remaining had been hit; some were pretty badly shot up. Both guns had gone down on the initial pass, with gun three attempting to reach Vinh Long; he didn't. The miracle is that, despite all the hits, only a couple of crew members were wounded and none killed. We found out later that there were two VC battalions and an NVA regimental headquarters in the tree-line, not a VC squad, and that they had four fifty-cal positions, several thirty-cal positions and a bunch of AK-47s and RPGs. The grunts pounded the area all night with arty, air and helicopter gunships. When they moved in the next day they found a sizable bunker complex and over a hundred bodies.

In April 1969 Terryl Morris was awarded the Distinguished Flying Cross for his actions that day. The citation read, in part: 'For heroism while participating in aerial flight evidenced by voluntary actions above and beyond the call of duty: Warrant Officer Morris distinguished himself by exceptionally valorous action while piloting a UH–1C gunship in support of the 9th Infantry Division north of Vinh Long'. Terryl survived his year with the Mad Dogs and returned to 'the world' and another posting.

In February 1971 the South Vietnamese Army launched Operation 'Lamson 719', a cross-border assault against the enemy sanctuaries in Laos. Unfortunately, the US Congress had forbidden the use of American ground troops in the operation, and heavy enemy resistance and bad weather caused the offensive to bog down. The one thing that the Americans could provide, however, was air support, and the helicopter gunships were particularly useful as the South Vietnamese troops began to withdraw in the middle of March. They paid a price for their effectiveness though, with over a hundred helicopters lost and hundreds more damaged. By this time the new AH-1G Cobra gunship had arrived and it was found to be able to absorb much more punishment than the older UH-1C gunship. Terryl Morris found himself able to testify to this fact, following a mission on 22 June 1971. He had returned to Vietnam for a second tour of duty and was now a Captain, flying the Cobra with D Company, 101st Aviation Battalion, the organic aviation unit of the 101st Airborne Division (Airmobile) out of Phu Bai.

We had been working with Command and Control North Special Forces operations in and along the Laotian border. One of the Special Forces teams had been observing an enemy unit for about a week. They had been working in a large field on the Laos side of the border and building what were suspected to be bunkers along the tree-line near

Below: MAD DOGS IN ACTION – two rockets from Terryl Morris's UH-1C gunship en route to Charlie in the tree-line. (Terryl Morris)

the field. Every morning, about 0700 hours, the NVA would come out of the trees, some going into the field to work and some going to work on the bunkers. There they would remain until about two or three in the afternoon, then go back into the jungle. They all wore NVA uniforms, so we assumed they were out of a base camp located in the jungle opposite the field. The field was bordered on one side by a river and on three of the other sides by high mountains. It was decided by CCN to conduct a raid to capture a prisoner or bring back some bodies to examine for documents, unit identification etc.

About 0600 hours the next morning we departed our base, taking a southern route which would bring us into the valley up the river from the south. The SF team observing from a nearby mountain peak informed us that the enemy soldiers were in the field at that time. At approximately five minutes out we went down on the river low-level and headed for the field to begin our initial attack. When we were about two minutes out the SF team leader informed us that the enemy had heard us coming and had moved to a long tree-line and trench in the center of the field. I was flying a Cobra with a 20mm cannon under the left wing, so I instructed my wing man to take the lead and put his rockets on the trench in the center of the field. We climbed to about 1,000 feet to begin our attack.

The first run did what I expected it would: as the lead fired his rockets and then broke away, the NVA in the trench scrambled out and ran for the tree-line. I caught them in the open field with the 20mm, killing a number on the first pass. The SF observer relayed a message to us from CCN, telling us to break off and rearm so that we could cover the assault team that was en route. This we did, calling at a nearby rearm point about midway to Da Nang, and then returned to the valley.

The bodies were still in the field when we returned, and we began to suppress the nearby tree-line. The slicks were about five minutes out with the Special Forces assault team on board. We made a couple of passes along the tree-line and, having received no return fire, we informed the slicks to come on in. The slicks landed, discharged their troops and departed the LZ. About that time things started popping. We received some small-arms fire from the tree-line and then a large force of NVA emerged and began to advance from the tree-line toward the 21-man team on the ground. As the US troops pulled back toward the other side of the field, they found that they were being funneled into a mine field. They had no choice but to stand in the open field and fight. They called for an immediate extraction.

The slick lead had seen what was going on and was about two minutes out on his way back in. We had been taking fire from positions all along the tree-line and I instructed my wingman to put his fire on those positions, while I tried to slow down the attacking force in the field with rockets and 20mm cannon fire. I had never seen several hundred men in

Above: *Terryl Morris with the AH-1G Cobra that he flew for 'D' Company, 101st Aviation Battalion, 101st Airborne Division, in 1971. (Terryl Morris)*

the open before, so I was in hog heaven. I wanted to make a long slow run, to take out as many as possible in one pass, so I slowed to about forty knots and opened up with the twenty. I was having a great time, the 20mm was tearing them to shreds, and I continued my run all the way to about thirty feet and then broke to the left over the river. The slicks had come in beside me and as I broke I heard the slick lead saying he had his troops and was on his way out; my wingman had picked them up and was covering their departure. As we climbed out of the valley we received several air bursts and a lot of small-arms fire, so we made one more pass, dumping our remaining ammo into the tree-line – a kinda goodbye note I guess. Then we pulled up alongside the slicks and escorted them back to Marble Mountain.

When we landed the Special Forces team was waiting for us and came running over to my aircraft, banging on the side and yelling and screaming. I thought that maybe we were on fire or something. As I got out of the Cobra the slick lead came up and stated that he wanted to shake my hand, like I was some kind of a hero or something. I then learned that as the lead slick had started his descent into the valley he had come under fire from a fifty-cal position on the cliff opposite the river; just then a Cobra pulled up alongside him and stayed in that position all the way to the ground, taking the hits aimed at the slick. I looked at my aircraft and just about died: the side was a mass of holes, some as large as my fist. The 20mm had been making so much noise and I was so excited I did not hear or know that I was taking hits, especially from a fifty-cal. Had I known that he was there I certainly would have been making other plans! They assumed that I knew the fifty-cal was taking on the slick and assumed that I had pulled in between the NVA gunner and the slick to save the flight lead. Being somewhat modest, I didn't say anything – I didn't want to ruin their excitement!

Three months later Captain Morris was awarded the Silver Star for his actions. He survived his second tour of duty and, as of this writing, is serving in Combat Developments, Test and Evaluation Division, at the US Army Infantry School with the rank of Major. He awards include the Silver Star, Bronze Star, four Distinguished Flying Crosses, four Purple Hearts, fifty-three Air Medals and several miscellaneous service awards.

PART THREE: WINDING DOWN THE WAR

On 1 November 1968 President Johnson ordered a halt to all bombing of North Vietnam. His peace-negotiating team in Paris believed that they were making progress and recommended relieving the pressure on Hanoi. Perhaps, with hindsight, they should have increased it instead. Four days later, as the North Vietnamese began to repair their roads and bridges, strengthen their anti-aircraft defences and increase the movement of troops and supplies to the South four-fold, Republican Richard M. Nixon defeated Democrat Hubert H. Humphrey and became the new President of the United States.

Although Nixon did not order the resumption of the 'Rolling Thunder' bombing campaign, he was a stronger President than Johnson and during his term of office he did authorize cross-border incursions into Cambodia and Laos, approve secret bombing raids into Cambodia and eventually, when all efforts at a negotiated peace had failed, order the mining of the North Vietnamese ports and the sending of B-52 bombers against Hanoi.

With the end of Rolling Thunder, there were now plenty of aircraft available to attack the Ho Chi Minh Trail infiltration route through Laos and Cambodia. Unfortunately, the North Vietnamese also had plenty of AAA weapons to spare now, and many were moved to protect the Trail. The first story in this chapter is told by an AC-130 gunship pilot, who fell foul of the improved defences but lived to tell the tale.

Back in South Vietnam, changes were afoot as word of the new Nixon adminis-tration's policy of 'Vietnamization' filtered down the chain of command. Although January 1969 saw the US forces in South Vietnam reach a peak of 365,000 Army personnel and 176,800 from other services, the new policy meant that American ground troops would start to take a back seat as the Army of the Republic of Vietnam took over the fight.

Most of the fighting now was against regular North Vietnamese Army troops, following the decimation of the Viet Cong during the Tet offensive. They were tough, well-trained and highly motivated, as the tales from the helicopter pilots in this chapter will attest.

In July 1969 the North Vietnamese released three American prisoners-of-war into the hands of an American anti-war group in Hanoi. At a press conference they revealed that which their own government had tried to keep quiet about for two years, that the prisoners-of-war were being beaten, tortured, placed in solitary confinement, provided with only minimal medical treatment and otherwise mistreated.

During the summer the first US troop withdrawals began, and in October, while the North Vietnamese continued to drag their feet at the peace talks, a quarter of a million anti-war protesters invaded Washington, DC. The war was being decided not in Vietnam, but on the streets of the United States.

In April 1970, President Nixon authorized a cross-border offensive against the enemy sanctuaries in Cambodia. Both ARVN and US troops were involved, supported by tactical aircraft, B-52s and helicopter gunships. It was a major setback to the North Vietnamese, but it provoked a serious backlash of public opinion in the United States. An anxious Senate passed the Cooper-Church Amendment, which prohibited the use of American ground troops in Cambodia or Laos after 30 June. The allied forces had no alternative but to withdraw, although the air strikes continued.

American troops and aircraft continued to pull out of South Vietnam and Thailand as more South Vietnamese Air Force squadrons were formed and the ARVN Divisions began to shoulder the war effort. Over the border in Laos, an enemy troop build-up led to a pre-emptive ground offensive by ARVN troops in February 1971. However, without the support of US ground troops, the offensive stalled and ended in a hasty retreat, despite the best efforts of US tactical aircraft and helicopter gunships. The operation did, however, buy Washington time to continue the programme of Vietnamization and delay the enemy offensive for another year.

All hell broke loose on 30 March 1972, when North Vietnam launched a conventional ground invasion of South Vietnam from bases in Laos and Cambodia and from North Vietnam across the DMZ into Quang Tri Province. By then, most of the American troops and aircraft had left, and a rapid series of squadron deployments to Thailand and South Vietnam was necessary before US air power managed to halt the enemy advances.

On 8 May 1972 President Nixon went on television to announce that he intended to cut off the flow of supplies that had for so long permitted Hanoi to continue the war in the South. The next day US aircraft began to drop mines into the waters of the North Vietnamese ports, and on 10 May, three and a half years after President Johnson called a halt to the Rolling Thunder campaign, full-scale bombing operations over North Vietnam were resumed. Within days, new 'smart' bombs were being used against dozens of bridges in the North and the skies over Hanoi were filled with dogfighting Phantoms and MiG-21s.

As the end of the year approached, Nixon finally lost patience with the enemy and sent the B-52s against Hanoi. In making such a momentous decision, the President clearly showed that he was made of the right stuff, and the bombing did indeed bring an end to the war; nevertheless, America was in too much of a hurry to get out.

When the peace agreement was signed on 27 January 1973, over 200,000 enemy troops were still in place in the South, and within two years the communists would take over the entire country. By the end of March 1973, 591 US *prisoners-of-war had been released by North Vietnam and had returned home to an ecstatic welcome. Nixon was feted as a hero who had brought the POWs home and ended the war. However, not everyone came home.*

A total of almost 2,500 men were still unaccounted for, mostly pilots and air crew. Whilst half this number are listed as killed in action, remains not returned, the rest are either prisoners-of-war or missing in action. None of the 560 men missing in Laos or the 82 missing in Cambodia was released at the end of the war, despite a good half of them being captured alive. Some POWs known to be held in North Vietnam never made it out.

As the Nixon administration became embroiled in the Watergate affair, the men known still to be held as prisoners-of-war, particularly in Laos, were forgotten and subsequently ignored by successive administrations. In an attempt to ensure that these brave men are not forgotten, their plight is discussed in detail in the last story of the chapter. This book, after all, is for them.

NIGHT OF THE SPECTRE

24

1. Ubon
2. Spectre Hit By AAA

*T*HE Lockheed AC-130 'Spectre' was the ultimate gunship. It was a far cry from the early Douglas AC-47 'Spooky' gunship, with its three 7.62mm gatling guns, and the Fairchild AC-119G 'Shadow' and AC-119K 'Stinger' gunships. The AC-119 gunships were a stop-gap replacement for the AC-47 as there were not enough spare C-130s around for conversion at the time, under the AC-130 Gunship 2 programme.

The AC-119G was armed with four 7.62mm minigun pods and used for the support of troops in contact with the enemy and for airbase defence. It was about 25 per cent more effective than the AC-47. The AC-119K, with its additional pair of underwing jet pods and improved armament in the shape of two 20mm cannon to supplement the four miniguns, was used exclusively in the truck-hunting role over the Ho Chi Minh Trail. The first AC-119G 'Shadow' squadron arrived in Vietnam in November 1968 and the first AC-119K 'Stinger' squadron a year later in November 1969. Between those dates, only four, and later six, AC-130 gunships were operating over the Trail, pending delivery of more advanced 'Spectres'.

The first AC-130 gunship had arrived in Vietnam for field trials in September 1967, and its success led to the decision to modify more of the type. However, the Air Force could not spare any of its C-130 fleet: they were all needed for airlift duties throughout South-East Asia. Seven early-model JC-130s were available though, and the first of these was converted to gunship configuration by June 1968; combat operations began with four aircraft in October 1968.

The AC-130 was armed with four 7.62mm minigun modules and four 20mm gatling cannon. Two of each were mounted forward of the main landing gear on the port (left) side of the aircraft and two each aft of the gear. In addition, a Night Observation Device (NOD) or Starlite Scope was carried – a sophisticated piece of equipment which enables the user to see targets on the ground by utilizing the available star- or moonlight. The NOD and a primitive infra-red sensor were fitted to the port side of the aircraft and a bread-board computer was also carried to co-ordinate all the variables involved in a side-firing weapons system. These early AC-130s were operated by the newly formed 16th Special Operations Squadron at Ubon Royal Thai Air Force Base, and the Commander of Spectre Crew Number One was Lieutenant Colonel William Schwehm.

Bill Schwehm's tour of duty began in September 1968 and lasted one year. During that time he served for a short period as squadron standardization pilot and operations officer, and for the last seven months of his tour was Assistant Deputy for Operations (Gunships) of the 8th Tactical Fighter Wing, the parent wing of the 16th SOS. He takes up his story:

The primary mission of the AC-130 gunship was night interdiction of the North Vietnamese supply lines from North to South Vietnam. The destruction of enemy trucks was our main objective; however, on a few occasions we did fly fire-support missions for friendly ground troops. During our year, my crew was credited with the destruction of 228 trucks and three anti-aircraft guns and the probable destruction of another 67 trucks and one helicopter. The latter was unconfirmed as the RF-4 reconnaissance plane could not find or get pictures of the wreckage. In all, we were hit five times by antiaircraft fire, with two crew members killed and three wounded. I was blessed with a good crew and what I consider to be the finest airplane ever built. Although the AC-130s we flew were the first C-130s built, they were sturdy and, modified as AC-130s, were state-of-the-art in weapons systems. I believe that the few AC-130 aircraft assigned to the 16th Special Ops Squadron contributed immeasurably to our efforts in Southeast Asia. We received

Below: Lieutenant-Colonel William J. Schwehm (left, standing) and his Spectre crew.

Right: A black AC-130 Spectre gunship in the revetments at Ubon in Thailand. (US Air Force)

little recognition and, when compared to other flying units, very little reward.

Most of my 126 combat missions and 583 combat hours were flown with my own crew, although during the first few months of my tour I flew with new aircrews during their qualification missions. These were the scary missions, since we were in a combat environment with inexperienced crews. This does not mean that I was all that experienced, because I was not. I was also new to combat, but when I flew with my own crew I was at the controls, instead of standing behind the pilot's seat while under very heavy and sometimes accurate antiaircraft fire. It makes a difference.

Our missions were flown at around 4,500 feet above the ground and at 145 knots. I was with the first group of four crews which formed the 16th SOS, and the most aircraft we had assigned during my tour was five. They were all early A models and had the four 20mm guns. We did a lot of local modification during our tour, because we were in the learning process. Together with Carl Cathy, the commander of the 497th Tactical Fighter Squadron, I drew up the procedure for the F-4 escort business. We flew with no external lights, so I had our maintenance people come up with a shielded rotating beacon for the top of our aircraft, so that the escort pilot could see us from above.

All of our missions were over Laos, since President Johnson's prohibition of North Vietnamese airspace was on at that time. This allowed the North Vietnamese to bring a good part of their antiaircraft artillery into Laos, which they did. It was not unusual to receive 300–500 rounds of AAA on one four-hour mission. We did encounter AAA rockets; however, I do not believe we got any radar-controlled SAMs. We did get radar-controlled gunfire, and half way through my tour we had the jamming equipment installed in our aircraft.

The night flights over the Ho Chi Minh Trail were always hazardous, even with F-4 escorts to take on the antiaircraft guns. Bill Schwehm's luck finally ran out on 24 May 1969 when his crippled Spectre was destroyed in a crash-landing at Ubon RTAFB. He might well have got away with the landing had the starboard undercarriage gear not failed him at a crucial moment. Ironically, the reason for the collapse was probably directly attributable to damage incurred on an earlier mission on 5 March 1969.

On that date they were flying a night reconnaissance mission over the supply trails leading to South Vietnam, when the aircraft was severely damaged by anti-aircraft fire. Colonel Schwehm had already destroyed one truck and was firing on another when the aircraft was struck in the centre aft fuselage by a 37mm anti-aircraft round. The bursting shell penetrated the aft sensor compartment and sent fragments hurtling through the starboard main gear well. Immediately after taking the hit, Colonel Schwehm moved his aircraft out of the target area, checked for injured crew members, and initiated a return to his home base.

On the way, battle damage assessment indicated that it might be difficult to lower the starboard main gear. Shell fragments had penetrated the bulkhead next to the gear, and Colonel Schwehm correctly assumed that it had been damaged. Upon arriving in the recovery base area, he ordered the landing gear handle to be placed in the down position. The nose and port main undercarriage extended, but the right main gear remained up. He then ordered his flight engineer to go to the rear compartment and attempt to lower the gear using the hand crank. The flight engineer made several attempts, using every method he knew, but without success.

When it appeared that the undercarriage could not be extended, Colonel Schwehm turned the control of the aircraft over to his co-pilot and proceeded to the rear to inspect the damage personally. He was prepared to make a wheels-up landing if necessary, but he knew that his aircraft could be severely damaged or completely destroyed in the attempt. Considering possible crew injuries and the *fact that the AC-130 gunship was an extremely limited and valuable resource to the war effort, he was determined to make every possible effort to avoid a crash-landing. With fuel running low, any action would have to be accomplished with decisiveness and depatch.*

Colonel Schwehm inspected the damage and immediately discovered that a fragment had penetrated the soundproofing on the landing gear bulkhead. Using a crash axe, he removed the thick fibreglass soundproofing which covered an inspection plate and saw that the bulkhead below the plate had been broken and pushed out toward the undercarriage jackscrew and track by the shell fragment. The bulkhead was jammed tightly against the jackscrew and was preventing the gear from extending. Using the crash axe and a large screwdriver, Schwehm prised the section of bulkhead away from the jackscrew while the flight engineer tried to crank the gear down. This procedure was successful and the gear extended and appeared to lock.

Colonel Schwehm returned to the cockpit and took control of the aircraft. He ordered the crew to assume their crash-landing positions and informed the crash recovery team that he was preparing to land. He then executed a perfect approach and, holding the aircraft off the runway until the last possible moment, made a perfect 'feather-light' touch-down. This time the relieved crew walked away from their brush with fate; the next time things would be different.

On 24 May, two and a half months later, Bill Schwehm prepared for yet another mission. The aircraft to be used was the same one, 64-1629, and the call-sign was 'Carter'. The pilot/navigator briefing was held at around 1600 hours and the crew briefing at about 1730. One of the things that they were told at the 1600 briefing was that intelligence had it that Russian advisers were known to be assisting the North Vietnamese gunners in an effort to get one of the gunships. Bill continues the story:

Takeoff was at 1800 hours as I remember and the weather was good. I don't remember there being a moon that night. There were thirteen members of crew on the mission: besides the two pilots, three navigator/sensor operators, flight engineer, illuminator operator and four weapons mechanics, we also had a student navigator and a photographer on board. The photographer was on board because at the time we were doing some experimentation with photography through a starlight scope, in an effort to confirm our truck kills. We arrived over our area, which was a section of road south of Tchepone, at about 1830 and we were called immediately by an Army Mohawk sensor aircraft and directed to a column of enemy trucks that they had found in the area. We located the trucks and had just rolled into our firing orbit when the illuminator operator, whose job it was to lie down at the edge of the rear ramp and call out the antiaircraft fire heading our way, shouted 'Ten rounds. Six o'clock. Accurate.'

I started to roll out, when we were hit. Four 37mm rounds went by on each side: one struck the right wing, inboard of number three engine, and the last hit the tail section, mortally wounding Staff Sergeant Troglen, the illuminator operator, and severing all hydraulic lines, control cables and electrical wires, rendering both rudder and elevator inoperative. I had started a turn back toward Thailand when the normal system hydraulic warning lights came on, followed immediately by the backup system lights. This of course caused the loss of the flight controls as well as the gear, flaps, nosewheel steering etc. The aircraft started into a turning descent to the right, and it appeared that this would soon become a spiral. I had no flight controls and no rudder or elevator trim, but I did have aileron trim. With the use of engine power and aileron trim I was able to attain straight and level flight; however, the aircraft was climbing. To correct the climb I braced the control column to full forward position and ordered all the crew members to the flight deck.

We had two crew members who had been wounded, one very seriously. Staff Sergeant Troglen had been at his station on the ramp when we took the hit in the tail and he received massive head injuries. The photographer had been hit in the leg. It was because of the wounded, and the fact that we were over Laos, that I decided to try and return to Thailand. We managed to get to within nineteen miles of Ubon, where I ordered all non-essential crew members to bail out. As the crew went to the rear troop door to bail out, the aircraft again became tail heavy and began to climb into a stall. At the same time one of the crew balked in the doorway, and it took a boot in the backside from one of the navigators to send him on his way. Remaining on board with me were the copilot Major Gerald Piehl, flight engineer Staff Sergeant Cecil Taylor and, unknown to me at the time, a navigator/sensor operator who had declined to bail out.

I had the flight engineer crank down the gear, and we set up for an emergency landing attempt at Ubon where the runway had been foamed. We flew our missions with ten degrees of flaps, so that was what we had. I managed to get lined up with the runway; however, it was nose-first and a very hard landing. As soon as I reduced the power, the aircraft's nose dropped hard on the runway. We had taken a bad hit on the aircraft about a month earlier and the right gear had been badly damaged. Only field repairs had been made on the gear, and about 2,000 feet down the runway the right gear failed and we veered to the right, despite the application of power to number three and four engines. As we left the runway the right wing struck the runway barrier cable house and sheared off with a big explosion and fire. We skidded along the dirt until we hit the second barrier reel assembly head-on and stopped. I told the copilot to get out and waited while he released his seat belt. We finally left, although by now my legs felt like rubber. The aircraft was almost totally engulfed in fire, but since we had lost the right wing that side of the aircraft was clear of flames. As we departed through the right forward escape hatch I saw my two crew members running away from the aircraft. However, when I joined the two that I thought were my copilot and flight engineer, I discovered that they were the copilot and one of the navigators, who had refused to jump and not informed me when I ordered the crew to bail out. My engineer was still on the aircraft and we would not find his body, along with Sergeant Troglen's, who had died of his head wounds while in flight, until the next day when the burned-out wreckage was examined. All of the crew members who had bailed out were rescued.

One of the fire trucks was burned with 629 when its engine failed and had to be abandoned. After that all the firefighting equipment was pulled back and the aircraft and Sergeant Taylor were left to burn. I was extremely disturbed about this and threatened bodily harm to the nonrated Lieutenant Colonel who was the fire marshall. The fact that the fire department was removed was also included in my report to the Seventh Air Force. The 8th Tac Fighter Wing had also lost an F-4 on a previous mission whilst using the Carter callsign. The callsign was never used again.

JON BOULLE AND THE PHROG PHLYERS 25

1. Quang Tri
2. Helicopter Valley

*F*INDING a Marine Corps helicopter pilot to discuss his experiences with the author was not an easy job. They are more elusive than Army helicopter pilots and, being Marines, are generally shy, retiring people, not given to discussing their exploits in public. However, perseverance brought the author into contact with Jon Boulle of Lockport, Ilinois, who agreed to tell of his year in Vietnam, on condition that 'You can edit it all you like, paraphrase it, but don't bend it. The facts are there on the paper. The memories are here in my head'. Unbent as requested, this is Jon Boulle's story, as told to the author:

Where to start? Where to start? I have never been able to say the things I'm going to tell you. There are two reasons: first, I was greatly embarrassed by them, and secondly, in this country, until recently, I was considered little better than a mass murderer. In fact, my wife doesn't know a lot of this. But I'll tell you and let you be the judge as to whether or not they are worth publishing.

Being a Marine is something special in this country as it is in yours. In fact a lot of the traditions we kept are directly descended from the Royal Marines, such as Mess Night, complete with bagpipes and a toast to the Queen (or King as it may be). To be a Marine pilot is to be the chosen of the chosen. This was my goal from the age of seven or eight. I decided that I would be a Marine pilot and land on an aircraft carrier just like *Victory at Sea*, a 1950s documentary on TV every Sunday.

I graduated from Penn State University (1968 National Champions in football) in 1967 and went to Quantico, Virginia, for Officer Candidate School. After eleven weeks (pilots spent an extra week due to the nature of the physicals we were required to take; the normal time was ten weeks) I was commissioned a Second Lieutenant and after three days' leave reported for flight school training at Pensacola, Florida. Here I 'went back to school' for eighteen months to learn the physics, weather, survival techniques and assorted and sundry things they taught us there. I received basic flight training, acrobatics, navigation (both radio and basic) and carrier flight ops in fixed-wing aircraft. I was then given basic and advanced helicopter training in all of the above disciplines all over again. After fourteen months I was assigned to a Marine unit, the Third Marine Air Wing based in Southern California. From this Wing I was assigned to HMMT-301 – Marine Medium Helicopter Training Squadron 301, based in Santa Ana, California – and here I was trained to fly the CH-46 Sea Knight. This bird was built by the Boeing-Vertol Division in Philadelphia and had been on the commercial market for a while.

A bit about the bird. It is a tandem-rotor, elongated banana, powered by a pair of General Electric turbine engines, producing approximately 1,500 shaft horsepower each. These in turn fed into a mix box, which combined the horsepower of both engines into a single shaft which fed the gearbox, which in turn drove the rear rotor. There is also a shaft from the gearbox running along the top of the cabin to the front gearbox, which fed the front shaft. The rotors counter-rotate, which keeps you from spinning like a top when power is applied to the shafts. The rotors are controlled by a complex mixture of hydroelectrical motors and actuators, which allow the pilot to control the whole damn mess and make it fly. We used to say that it really did not fly, we just did it with mirrors.

After being designated a '46 driver I was given two weeks off and then shipped to Vietnam. I arrived in-country in April of 1969 and my first reaction was to the heat and the smell. Now I'm just your typical white, Anglo-Saxon Protestant and not all equipped for this type of place, but, with a sense of adventure that had got me this far, I checked in with the First Marine Air Wing at Da Nang. I was told my squadron assignment and where the unit was located and that was it; no one told me how to get there! Someone pointed it out to me on a map but that was all. Three days later, I caught a ride on a C-130 going to Dong Ha which was only a few miles away. I arrived there late in the day, so I got a bed with a bunch of grunt (ground) officers.

The next morning I was awakened by a rocket attack that seemed like it lasted seconds or hours. I was thrilled and at the same time scared: this was the face of *war*! Organized mayhem, orchestrated to the epitome of destruction by its participants. On the way to the mess hall for breakfast, I witnessed what this was all about. The Boeing Technical Rep had had his head blown off by one of the rockets and what was left of him was lying in the street. The rockets had been fired from North Vietnam, only twelve miles north of Dong Ha. I was still in the 'new guy daze' and was not affected by the sight; my only thought was 'God what a mess.'

I got a ride in an open jeep ten miles south to Quang Tri where my new squadron was located. I checked in to HMM-161, the 'Phrog Phlyers' of Provisional Marine Air Group 39, First Air Wing, Republic of Vietnam. I was officially a participant.

I was given all my gear for living at the base and then went to the paraloft for my flight gear. Here I got my thirty-five-pound bullet bouncer, or chicken plate as the doggie pilots (Army pilots) called them. I then went to the armorer to get my weapon, which was supposed to be a 38-caliber Model 19 Smith and Wesson revolver. The armorer gave me one, but not any bullets. I asked for some bullets and he said that he was all out of .38s. I asked what bullets he had and he said that he had plenty of .45s. So I said OK, give me a 45-caliber automatic. He said he couldn't do that. I asked why, and he said that I was only authorized to carry a .38, not a .45, so all he could give me was a .38 pistol and .45 bullets. I just looked at this guy: the book *Catch-22* was written at Penn State by Joseph Heller, an English professor, and here I was caught in a Catch-22 situation and this wasn't any f***ing joke! I asked what I was supposed to do with an empty gun – throw it at them? He just turned and walked away. I took the damn gun and left. The next week, on an in-country training flight, I was able to buy 38-caliber bullets on the black market from a Vietnamese tycoon in Da Nang. I was beginning to learn what this was all about, and I did not like the look of things. This was not the war John Wayne had fought and won in the Pacific against the heathen yellow demons of the Rising Sun. This was a completely modern war where the combatants bought their own ammunition. This meant that only the rich guys would win.

Our mission in Vietnam was to support the ground units in various ways. Resupply was exactly what it sounded like. We would haul water, food, ammo and anything else out to the ground units wherever they were. This included ice cream in special containers, or a birthday cake for a General's son out in the bush. We even hauled nurses from the hospital ship back and forth to the General's compound for his pleasure, or whatever he had them for. We never asked, but these 'ladies' were usually quite drunk when we took them back out to the boat.

Medevac was probably the most important thing we did, and probably the most dangerous from our viewpoint. There were three categories eligible for medevac. The first was Emergency types: these guys required immediate medical attention to save their lives and were first priority under all circumstances. Nothing bumped these missions – these folks had to come out, and usually it was done under fire from small arms or mortars. This is the place where we got shot up usually and took many casualties. The NVA troops knew that the choppers would come, so they would set up something special for us and just wait. And we would oblige them and fly into their little trap.

The next category was Priority types. These were guys with bad wounds that needed medical treatment quickly, but would last up to six hours without it and still live. These missions were often mixed in with emergencies, so they got the same treatment. We then had a category called Routine, people unfit for combat either physically or mentally but in no danger. All enemy troops captured that were wounded were in this category, except for NVA officers. Enemy officers were always a

Above: Sea Knights from HMM-161 the 'Phrog Phlyers' landing Marines in a cold LZ. (Author's Collection)

priority medevac if they were wounded. The last category were the Permanent Routines, the dead. All Marine dead, except those completely blown apart, were brought home. Even bodies found after two weeks in the jungle were brought out. The Marines never left a dead colleague on the battlefield if they could find enough of him to bring back, and sometimes this wasn't much. To this day I can recall the smell of body bags and the smell of blood. If I get a whiff of that plastic they used for the body bags anywhere, it is as if I had taken a hard blow to the body. I have to get away from that odor at all costs.

One of my most vivid memories of flying medevac was the day I got an emergency call for two guys that had set off a 250-pound bomb that the VC had rigged as a booby trap. The lead man, a rather large black guy, had stepped on it and it had gone off, blowing him in half right at crotch level. The fragments had hit his buddy behind him in the chest. As I flew in I could see the black guy, spreadeagled in the LZ with his teeth clenched. As I landed I could hear him screaming over the noise of the rotors. He was still alive: why is anyone's guess, because his body from the waist down was nothing but hamburger, and that ended at his crotch. All that was below that was a red pulp on the ground. His buddy was still alive, despite having a hole in his chest that my crew chief could see his heart pumping through. Needless to say, neither of these guys made it, not because we didn't try, but because no one could suffer that kind of damage and still live.

The second story I can tell was not as graphic but it is rather pointed. One night, after we landed and parked the bird between the revetments, I was walking down the back ramp when I slipped and fell flat on my back. I got up with no damage done and went into the ready room for de-briefing and to fill out the after-action report (AAR). As I walked into the light, one of the guys asked in a rather shocked voice if I was OK. I said yeah, I felt fine, and then asked why he asked. He told me that my back was completely covered in blood and that it looked like I had been hit. What had happened was that there was so much blood on the floor of my bird that I slipped on it and was covered in some other guy's blood. I went to the O Club and got drunk (after I showered).

Recon inserts were not a choice mission to fly. This involved picking up a team of Force Recon guys, usually a team of six, and depositing them in some God-awful area way out in the jungle. These Force Recon guys are equivalent to the British Special Air Service and not to be confused with the Recon Battalion that is attached to every Division. These guys were hard dudes and did the vast majority of all the 'snooping and pooping' (as they called it) in Laos, the DMZ and all points north. These guys got me my nickname of 'Stump.'

The technique that we used when putting these people in place was to make several false landings all over the area and they would get out of the chopper at only one stop. This was to confuse NVA search parties and would give them a dozen locations in which to search for these six guys. As it happened, that day we were putting a team into the A Shau Valley, and the elephant grass was up to my rotors so I couldn't see the ground. I kept bouncing all over the place like a pogo stick, letting the team off at their chosen spot and then making a few more false landings just to keep things confusing for the NVA. When we got back to Phu Bai that night the tower called and said that I had something hanging from my bird. Upon landing I found that during my time in the A Shau I had driven three tree stumps through the belly and stub wings. When I had lifted off they had stuck in the plane and I pulled them out of the ground and carried them home with me. From then on I was called 'Stump.'

You brought up 'Helicopter Valley.' I guess that place is more famous than I thought. That little piece of real estate cost us a lot of people and a lot of helicopters. It was in my AO (Area of Operations), and we avoided it like the plague. It got its name mostly because of all the CH-34s that went down there, not '46s, although there were '46s there too. This valley was a shallow grove, rather than a sharp deep one that most of the others were. It ran basically east and west. East of it was the outpost of Con Thien, where the NVA tried to uproot a Marine outpost by every means possible. That's why Helicopter Valley became itself. The NVA tried to move troops toward Con Thien from that direction, so the powers that be decided to head them off at the pass and lift in blocking forces. The major problem was that the NVA were dug in on the ridges north and south, so anything flying into valley or, worse yet, trying to land in the valley, was immediately brought under a heavy crossfire. The result was a valley littered with wrecks of a variety of helicopters, mostly CH-34s with a sprinkling of everthing else. I have flown through Helicopter Valley after the NVA had withdrawn back across the DMZ, so I can't say what it was really like in there when it was 'hot,' but it was a damned unfriendly looking place anyway.

Lets talk about flying conditions. In the summer months, March through October, we were generally CAVU to the moon as we used to say (ceiling and visibility unlimited – crystal-clear days with nothing between you and the moon but clear air). However, the monsoon was another story. I was given a mission once out of Phu Bai to go to Da Nang and hook up there with the air support group people and fly resupply missions. My wingman and I took off in really terrible weather, with low clouds and heavy rain. We went IFR 25 feet in the air and never saw each other again from then until we landed at Marble Mountain in Da Nang. We radar-vectored out to sea, so we could avoid flying through the pass that was just north of Da Nang. After being sent out to An Hoi for our supply runs, I was diverted to pick up a medevac on top of a mountain that some bird Colonel thought would be good to occupy during the monsoon. The weather was so bad that no one else had been able to land to pick up the guy. My copilot was Major 'Cess' Poole (Lloyd was his real name), and he couldn't figure a way in, so I decided to try my way. I flew up to the mountainside right at tree-top level, slowed to 70 knots and began to hover up the side of the hill. I reached the crest at around 1,700 feet, completely fogbound, then turned and followed the ridgeline. I asked the grunts for smoke and they popped a yellow smoke for me. I flew until the fog turned yellow and eventually found the LZ and picked up the man. Now I had to get down. I knew that the mountain was steep, so all I really needed to do was get far enough north and let down, and I should end up just slightly southwest of An Hoi, although it would be bad-guy territory. I did it and I am writing this, so obviously I made some right choices that day. No medals for that piece of work. I didn't ask for one and that was fine. I did my job, I saved a life and I brought the bird home, but I personally felt that I flew one hell of a mission that day.

A friend of mine, Jerry Berry, probably flew the gutsiest mission I have ever heard of. I know all about it because I was on the awards board for the squadron then and got the after-action reports. He was to pick up some recon Marines in an area we called the Tennis Courts. His gunships had gone in to the LZ several times and had been shot out of the LZ each time; they couldn't neutralize it. Finally, Jerry tried it with the gunships flying close support to suppress fire. He did this three times, getting shot out of the landing zone each time, and was unable to get our guys out. By now the gunships were out of ammunition and suggested to Jerry that he forget it and wait for fixed wing support. The guys on the ground did not think they could wait since they were compromised (isn't that an innocuous word for having your titty in the wringer?). Jerry went in for them the fourth time, knowing his gunships couldn't support him. He took extremely heavy fire, but succeeded in getting the recon team out. I felt that this display of bravery was worth the Silver Star at least. It was clearly bravery in the face of the enemy. The Major, who will remain nameless although I remember I his name, wanted to award him a single-mission Air Medal. SAMs were a dime a dozen over there, so I felt that this was a slap in Jerry's face and said so. I was relieved on the spot of my duties pertaining to the awards board. Jerry, if you are reading this – man, I tried!

LETTERS FROM PLEIKU

26

1. Kontum
2. Mike O'Donnell Crash Site
3. Dak Seang 4. An Khe

*W*HEN the details of the US aircraft losses in South-East Asia were finally declassified on 31 December 1981, they revealed that the Army had lost a total of 4,321 helicopters between 1962 and 1973; 2,246 had been combat losses, and the remainder operational losses.

The job of an Army helicopter pilot or crew member was regarded as being one of such high risk that it came second only to that of a Special Forces or Long Range Reconnaissance Patrol member. By the end of the war, 926 helicopter pilots and 2,005 aircrew had been killed. Although their names can be found on The Wall in Washington, DC, the reason for their being there is generally known only to their families and friends.

The helicopter pilots in Vietnam could always be relied on to get the ammunition to a beleaguered company at night, to brave the strongest ground fire and the worst weather to pick up the wounded, and to continue making gun runs on the enemy after the last round had been fired, to support the troops in contact. Sometimes, whilst laying their life on the line for their comrades, they would pay the final price.

This story is told to honour the memory of a handful of those pilots and their crews: Mike O'Donnell, who was killed whilst attempting to rescue a Special Forces team from the jaws of death; Roger Miller, captured by the North Vietnamese whilst trying to save his wounded aircraft commander; and Ricky Davis, shot down by his own side. Their stories are told by James E. Lake, their friend, who flew with them and who will always remember them.

I arrived in-country on 3 May 1969. I was nineteen years old and a product of the Warrant Officer Candidate program. My first assignment was to the 170th Assault Helicopter Company in Pleiku. The 170th 'Bikinis' and two sister companies, the 119th 'Alligators' and the 189th 'Ghostriders' were stationed at Camp Holloway, along with the 361st 'Pink Panthers,' a Cobra outfit, and the 179th, a Chinook Company. All were members of the 52nd Combat Assault Battalion, part of the 1st Aviation Brigade. Like all the Assault Companies, the 170th was a Huey outfit. We had about twenty-five UH-1H slicks and eight or ten UH-1C gunships. Each aircraft had a crew of four – the aircraft commander (AC), the pilot (Peter Pilot), the crew chief and the door gunner.

We acted primarily as a resource for other units in the area. Each day mission requests would come down through our Operations from other units. In contrast to many of the units in the South, ours were often single-ship missions. Consequently, we rarely operated in the big formations characteristic of operations in the South. The area around Pleiku was covered with heavy jungle, interspersed with the occasional village and rice paddy. Our landing zones, LZs, were rarely large enough to accept more than one aircraft at a time. Often there were holes in the trees that required a hovering approach down through 200 feet of trees. Crew coordination and pilot techniques were critical since the aircraft were usually over gross weight and would rarely develop full power. An H model in good condition should be able to pull 50 pounds of torque before bleeding rpm. Ours would begin to bleed rpm at 35 pounds, because of wear and the accretion of dust and dirt in the compressor section. We performed resupply, medevac, combat assault and gun missions. We had enemy contact on daily basis.

In 1969 and 1970 the area around Pleiku was controlled by the NVA. When we had major enemy contact it was usually with them rather than the VC. We got shot at almost every day, though you could rarely see who shot at you. This was idle pot-shooting as opposed to the kind of fire we would take in a hot insert or extraction. Their usual technique was to rip off a clip of AK at you and then duck. Many times we would see the muzzle flashes and return fire, but you would never know if you hit anybody. Strangely enough, even with all the noise in a Huey, you could usually hear them shooting at you. Most of the time they didn't hit us, and when they did it was usually in the tailboom. Once you got accustomed to it, it was fun. We looked forward to getting shot at because it would break the monotony of sixteen-hour days, with an average of ten hours of flight time. Besides, it always made for good stories back at the club that night. Not that these idle pot-shots couldn't be hair-raising.

The first time I recall being shot at and taking hits was shortly after I arrived. I was flying as Peter Pilot for Keith Fish. This man was, as were all the ACs, a tyrant in the cockpit, and all of my attention was centered on trying to please him. I was a lot more worried about what he would say about my performance and abilities than anything that the NVA might dish out. We were on standby at Dak To when we were told to go medevac an ARVN (soldier of the Army of the Republic of Vietnam) that had been wounded. The unit with the wounded man was on the side of the mountain slope next to the runway at Dak To. There was no LZ, so we rigged with ropes to extract him from a high hover over the trees. Keith came to a hover at about 30 feet and the crew chief lowered the ropes to the ground. It took a few minutes to rig the wounded guy, and as the job was being finished an automatic weapon was fired at what sounded like very close range. Almost simultaneously the crew chief shouted that we were taking fire and were taking hits. Keith decided that it was time to leave, and he made a rapid departure. Unfortunately, in the heat of the moment, he forgot the fact that he had a wounded ARVN swinging on a McGuire rig 30 feet below the aircraft. This became painfully clear a moment later when the crew chief, a snide youth named McLarty, wryly informed him that he was dragging the wounded man through the trees. 'You're dragging the dink through the trees, Sir.' Keith snatched him up out of the trees, but I'm afraid it was far too late by then. I never checked on the condition of the wounded man, but I doubt that he made it. They killed the character with the AK a few minutes later. I guess he figured he'd give his all for the chance to shoot down a Huey. We counted over twenty holes in the airplane from the centersection to the tail. None were in a critical area, and no one was hit. A Huey can take a lot of punishment.

I made AC after three months and 300 hours, about average. So did the other pilots that arrived in-country with me. A Huey pilot's story really begins when he makes AC. Until then he is under the thumb of someone else and is allowed very few independent decisions and usually doesn't fly when the sh** hits the fan. Peter Pilot's job is to learn as fast and as well as possible. In a sense, you gain an identity when you become AC; that identity is your callsign. No one but the people in your unit know your name. Your identity to everyone in the AO (Area of Operations), including the NVA, was your callsign. Callsigns were handed down individually from AC to AC. If you made it to the end of your tour you gave your callsign to a new AC that you liked and had trained. If you didn't make it, your platoon leader made the assignment for you. If you were in the chain of command, your callsign went with your position. For instance, if you were the platoon leader of the second flight platoon – Red Flight – your callsign was Bikini Red. Mine was Bikini 24.

A few months after I made AC, the 170th was transferred to Kontum. This little town is along the Ia Drang River, some forty miles north of Pleiku. We took the place of another sister company, the 57th AHC Gladiators. Kontum was deep in the middle of Charlie's country. We never had much control over the area. In fact, the area to the north and east of Kontum was all freefire zone: in other words, anything or anybody was free game. The main mission of the 170th in Kontum was to support what was known as FOB-2 (Forward Observation Base 2). This was a classified long-term operation of the Special Operations Group (SOG) of the Special Forces that involved daily operations into Laos and Cambodia. This was before the invasion of either Cambodia or Laos, during the time when there were no American troops there.

SOG operated out of Kontum, but staged out of Dak To. Our mission was to take teams of six to ten men from Dak To and insert them deep into the forest on the other side of the fence. Dak To is located near the tri-border area, which made it easy for us to move south into Cambodia or north into Laos. The terrain is mountainous and covered with dense forest. We ran the mission with four slicks and four Cobras. We were usually supported by A-1Es – Spads from Da Nang that would come out and stay on station until we needed them. The mission was controlled by a Special Forces officer on board an Air Force O-2 FAC. In addition, we were assisted by the King Bees, an elite Vietnamese unit flying old ex-Marine H-34s. As opposed to most Vietnamese pilots, these guys were great. They were courageous and audacious and I was told that a guy had to have 2,000 hours to make AC with them. Like us, they sustained terrible losses on the FOB mission; as I recall, they were finally all lost or killed. There was very little interaction between ourselves and the King Bees, since they spoke poor English and we spoke practically no Vietnamese. We had great respect for them, however. I do not remember where their home base was since they only staged out of Dak To as we did.

We generally received our FOB mission briefing in the morning in Kontum. We then moved up to Dak To and refueled and then flew west to the border. Once across the border we could run into anything. Of the four slicks, two would be set up as insert birds and the other two as cover birds. The air mission commander, Red Lead, was the AC of the first insert bird. We configured our cover ships with 50-caliber door guns rather than M-60s. This gave us a bit of extra firepower and we needed all we could get. The job of the cover birds was to extract the crew and passengers of the insert birds if they were shot down. Most insert missions were into cold LZs. This was not always the case, however, since sometimes they either knew we were coming, or just happened to be in the LZ in force. After making the insertion we returned to Dak To and waited to extract the team we had just inserted or another team that got into trouble. Extractions were usually hot and often involved heavy ground fire from small arms, 37mm and 57mm AAA, fifty-cal, quad fifty-cals, RPGs, B-40s and missiles of a type that I couldn't identify at the time. It was on one of these missions that Mike O'Donnell was killed.

Mike arrived in-country a few months after I did and although he was a Captain and the platoon leader of the second platoon he was a junior AC. The AMC (Air Mission Commander) for FOB missions, Red Lead, was usually the senior AC, regardless of rank; that day, 24 March 1970, I was Red Lead. We had a team in contact about fourteen miles inside Cambodia. They had been in contact all night and had been running and ambushing, but the hunter team pursuing them was relentless and they were exhausted and couldn't continue to run much longer. I brought our extract birds out on station, but the team was not near an LZ and we were unable to extract them immediately. We waited in a high orbit over the area. We were in radio contact with the team and it was apparent that the situation was deteriorating. The team leader, a Lieutenant named Jerry Pool, was whispering over his radio that the NVA hunter team were right behind them. We had been on station for approximately 45 minutes. The team had not reached the LZ yet and I wanted to be ready when they got there, so I elected to take the extract birds back to Dak To for fuel. I told Mike, who was flying Red Three, to stay on station in case of emergency.

We returned to Dak To, quickly refueled, and returned to station. When we were about ten minutes from the site, Pool came over the FM and said that if he wasn't extracted right now they would never get out. What he actually told Mike was, 'If you don't come and get us right now you ain't got any balls at all.' Mike elected to do just that and began an approach to a small ravine just as we arrived on station. He came to a hover in the ravine and stated 'I'm down.' A moment later he said, 'I've got all eight, I'm coming out.' Those were the last words he ever spoke.

About a hundred meters from where he lifted off, something white streaked from the slope on the side of the ravine. It struck the aircraft and the aircraft exploded. Bodies were blown out the doors and fell into the jungle. There was a moment of stunned silence and the next words spoken came from one of the Cobras, Panther 13: 'I don't think a piece bigger than my head hit the ground.' A large secondary explosion followed with a yellow flash and a cloud of black smoke billowing from the jungle. Panther 13 made a second high-speed pass over the site. Two more white streaks passed just behind him and exploded on the other wall of the ravine.

I decided to go down myself and see if there was any way to get to the crash site. As I neared the ground, intense ground fire from the entire area greeted me with red and green tracers. I could not see the crash site since it was under heavy tree cover. There was no place to land and the ground fire was withering. I elected to return the extract team to Dak To before we lost more aircraft. I have never forgiven myself for leaving them. Mike was put in for the Congressional Medal of Honor, but the CMH is very political and it is rarely awarded when there isn't a lot of brass involved in an operation. He was posthumously awarded the Distinguished Flying Cross, the Air Medal, the Bronze Star and the Purple Heart. He was also promoted to Major.

We found the poems in his personal effects when they were inventoried. We thought he wrote them for his girlfriend, though he never said so. He talked of her often. Mike was a poet first and foremost, but he was also a talented guitar player and singer. He was especially good with Paul Simon's stuff, and whenever I hear Simon I think of Mike.

I call 15 April 1970 Black Monday. To me, every 15 April will be Black Monday. It started out routine. I was flying Red Lead on FOB with my good friend Bill McDonald flying Red Three. My Peter Pilot was Johnny Kemper, an ex-Special Forces E-6 turned Warrant Officer, who had two previous tours and nerves of steel. I often chose to fly FOB with Johnny, because he was as strong and reliable as anyone I ever met. About mid-morning we began to hear reports of some of our other birds in heavy action at Dak Seang. Dak Seang, a Special Forces camp, was about twenty miles north of Dak To in a valley surrounded by high mountains. It was all Charlie's country.

Above: The late Mike O'Donnell with the Slick that he flew with 170th Assault Helicopter Company 'Bikinis'. (via James E. Lake)

Our unit had made a combat assault, carrying ARVN troops to the top of a small hill just north of the camp. The second aircraft in the lift was flown by Al Barthelme and his Peter Pilot with just two weeks in-country, Roger Miller. In a tactic common to the NVA, they let the first aircraft land, drop its troops and depart the LZ. As soon as the second bird touched the ground they hit it with intense fire from all sides. It immediately crashed in the LZ. Al reportedly crawled through the chin bubble to exit the bird, but was then hit in the back and fell or was dragged into a bomb crater. Miller was unhurt, as was the door gunner and the crew chief. They were surrounded by NVA at a range of twenty meters in fortified positions. One by one the rest of our birds tried to get them off that hill. They were shot down like geese. By this time Bill and I had heard that it was Al down on the top of that hill and we launched for Dak Seang.

When we arrived, several hours had passed and King Six, the Air Force Big Wig in the sky, had called on the Air Force to do what the Army couldn't. Air Force salvation appeared in the guise of a pair of HH-3s, Jolly 27 and Jolly 29 accompanied by four A-1E Skyraiders, called 'Sandys.' After a prep of the LZ by some F-4s, Jolly 27 started his approach. He said, 'Jolly 27, about a quarter of a mile out; Jolly 27 taking fire; Jolly 27 taking heavy fire from 360 degrees; I'm having some hydraulic problems

. . . ' They crashed and burned in the trees. Jolly 29 didn't get that close. After getting his dose of ground fire he limped back to Pleiku.

By now Bill and I were sure that if we didn't do something Al would never get off that hill. We returned to Dak To and requested the assistance of what SOG called the Bright Light team. This was a combat emergency response team, consisting of select Special Forces people who would respond to an extreme situation. They were very tough, courageous, and they were often killed. The request was granted, and with the Bright Light team on Bill's airplane we returned to Dak Seang. Bill and Al were high school friends that had grown up together in St. Mary's County, Maryland. He would make the first approach and I would cover him.

Like Jolly 27, Bill started to receive heavy ground fire a quarter mile from the LZ. Undaunted, he pressed on and landed next to the downed crew. The ground fire was awesome. They were being fired upon at close range from 360 degrees. The door gunner and crew chief were firing back into the charging NVA soldiers, who were running within a few feet of the airplane. Tom Benne, Bill's Peter Pilot, was shot through both legs by a round that come through the armored seat. The door gunner and the crew chief from Al's bird leaped on and were both shot multiple times in the process. Miller jumped on and then jumped off again, saying that he was going back for Al. When Bill touched down he had 1,100 pounds of fuel. After 30 seconds on the ground he reported that he had 400 pounds left, everyone was hit and he was coming out. Soon after liftoff he lost pedal control. Fuel was pouring out of a huge hole in the fuel cells. He made a slow turn to the south and made an approach to the wire at Dak Seang. He landed just inside the wire. There were hundreds of NVA just outside the wire, less than a hundred meters away.

I began to take ground fire from the wire on my approach and touched down a few seconds after he did. As I landed in front of him, facing his aircraft, bodies were falling out of the doors. Both my door gunner and crew chief left their seats and rushed to Bill's airplane. Johnny unstrapped from the right seat and jumped out, running to help. The ground fire was continuous, and bullets were smashing through the windscreen and the instrument panel as they carried the wounded from Bill's bird to mine. Everyone except Bill had been shot, most of them several times, and blood was everywhere, I got them all aboard and lifted off. I thought we had gotten Al. I was wrong: he wasn't there. His body was recovered two weeks later, unidentifiable except for the green St. Mary's County tee-shirt he wore. Miller was captured by the NVA and I don't know what became of him. Both the door gunner and the crew chief lived; I don't remember their names, although I should. We lost a total of nine airframes and I don't remember how many people. Black Monday is not far away now, I'll remember it all over again then.

In one of Mike O'Donnell's poems is a reference to Ricky Davis. He was tall and slender and good-looking. I don't recall where he was from. Ricky joined our gun platoon, the Buccaneers. The poem read:

'I am breathing . . .
Taking back everything and more . . .
I have melted
From the sheets into the net above me
And back into the sheets.
I have watched the ground
Come to me
And I have crashed,
I have died
And I am alive . . .
My God, where has
Fast Ricky gone?'

26 Feb. 70

We were often given temporary duty lasting from a day to a few weeks in other areas outside our normal AO. Just after the first of the year we were given a mission to An Khe, the 1st Cav's infamous 'Golf Course.' We had both slicks and guns involved. One evening the gun team, a light fire team consisting of Brian Devaney in the lead bird and Ricky Davis on his wing, were returning from a mission. It was well after dark when they entered the traffic pattern, which was directly over the bunker line. Devaney ordered the team to 'come up safe' on weapons systems and Davis acknowledged. Devaney landed and, upon doing a pedal turn, noticed that Davis was not behind him. He called him on the radio, but got no response. He took off again and noticed a fire outside the bunker line. Upon closer inspection he found that it was Davis's Charlie model, enveloped in a raging fire. He flew back to the airfield, where he was told that the ground fire that had shot down Ricky Davis had come from the bunker line, our bunker line. We were enraged. Devaney was determined to go hot on the bunker line, but he couldn't be sure which bunker the fire had come from. He was going to destroy the entire bunker line, the entire base, but we stopped him. A few hours later we were ordered to leave An Khe and return to Kontum. We never found out what happened to the troops that shot down Ricky Davis. The bodies were later recovered from the crash site. They were burned into little black lumps.

Devaney tired of guns and a few months later he decided to try his hand at slicks. He was short by then, but never one to pass up a challenge. The day before he was scheduled to DEROS he decided he would fly FOB – a parting shot, sort of stick his finger in fate's eye. It wasn't really a hot extraction: they took only one round. It came through the left door, passed between the seat back and the sliding armor plate and shot Brian Devaney in the chest. He was in a hover and promptly crashed. The pilot who was with him told me that, after being pulled from the wreck, Brian took off his sunglasses, looked up at him and said, 'Oh f***.' Then he died. He went home the next day anyway.

We had another gun pilot named Rodger Hansen. His gun team got into some heavy action in the Plei Trap Valley late in '69. The Plei Trap was a very nasty place and Rodger was shot down in a bamboo thicket. He and the rest of the crew came through the crash OK, but they were surrounded by NVA and darkness was approaching. One of the slicks, flown by Bill McDonald, came in to get them. Because of the thickness of bamboo they were unable to land and were forced to hover to attempt the pick-up. As soon as they made the approach they started to take heavy fire. They thought they had them all, but Rodger was unable to get on. As Bill started to pull up under a veil of enemy fire, Rodger ran and leaped for the airplane, grabbing the rear right skid and hanging on by his arms. Bill cleared the bamboo and started to climb out. The door gunner reached for Rodger and tried to pull him on board, but he couldn't and a few seconds later Rodger fell into the bamboo. We never found his body. In the movies he would have made it.

'DUSTOFF 7-1-1. I'M HIT AND GOING DOWN' 27

1. Quang Tri

*T*HE first five medical evacuation (medevac) UH-1As arrived in Vietnam in April 1962 with the 57th Medical Detachment (Helicopter Ambulance). They were the first of the thousands of Hueys to serve in Vietnam and were sent in response to a request from the Special Forces for improved support in the evacuation of wounded. A year later the medevac aircraft were allocated their call-sign, 'Dust Off', and the name stuck for the rest of the war.

In those early days before the arrival of American combat troops, the South Vietnamese were the Dustoffs' main customer. They were not easy to work with. ARVN units often insisted that the Dustoffs fly out the dead, before the wounded, because of the sentiments, of the soldiers who believed that the soul lingers between this world and the next if not properly buried. In later years, Dustoffs would be mobbed by ARVN troops trying to escape combat, regardless of the wounded requiring evacuation. During Operation 'Lam Son 719', the Laos incursion of 1971, the problem was so great that the Dustoff crews had to grease their landing skids to prevent would-be deserters from hitching a ride.

As explained earlier, the evacuation of wounded was supposed to be carried out according to the seriousness of the wounds, and the casualties classed as Routine, Priority or Urgent. Many Dustoff crews, however, worked by their own categories of Urgent or Non-urgent. If it was urgent, they went in, any time or anywhere. Many a bullet-ridden Huey arrived at an aid station, full of wounded and with the medic and crew chief exhausted, but still working at their own priorities: 'Stop the bleeding and keep 'em breathing'. It was a decided boost to troop morale to know that they could be evacuated from a fire-fight and into an Army hospital more quickly than someone involved in an automobile accident on a highway back in the States. The red cross emblems on the Hueys made ideal aiming points for the enemy gunners and, being usually unarmed, the helicopters made tempting targets. The organic Eagle Dustoffs of the 101st Airborne and those of the 1st Cav took exception to this lack of respect for the Geneva Convention and mounted door guns to their aircraft.

Warrant Officer Phil Marshall arrived in Vietnam in July 1969 and was assigned to the 237th Medical Detachment at Quang Tri. He recalls the procedure that was used for getting into a landing zone as safely as possible:

When we approached an LZ, we would go to the ground troop frequency, which Operations had been given in the clear over our nationwide Dustoff frequency (which was sometimes jammed). About two minutes out, we would ask for smoke to be popped and we would identify the color. There were instances of the ground unit calling the color and several smokes of that color appearing, as the Viet Cong monitored our radio calls and tried to lure us into a trap. On one mission, we called for smoke and spotted two green, one yellow and one red smoke. The ground commander said the yellow was his, so that is where we landed, avoiding the other smokes. This procedure helped us determine wind direction too: as long as the last three feet of an approach were made into the wind, you could do just about anything you wanted to do with the aircraft, and we usually did! Now that was flying. See if you can visualize this:

110 knots and a few feet off the deck, flying downwind. You spot your smoke and just as you are about to fly directly over it you bottom the pitch, at the same time pulling up the nose of the aircraft. A split second later, you bank the aircraft into an almost vertical turn (literally) and kick in pedal using the lift of the rotor system to brake you as you pass over the LZ. About the time the helicopter begins to sink in, you've done a 180-degree turn and you pull up the nose and pitch, slowing the descent as you level the aircraft for the last three feet. All this takes a very few seconds and slows the aircraft down immediately without overstressing it, since the G force is down, from the top of the rotor system, which is actually pointing sideways. This also allows us to approach downwind and also to get in and out in a hurry.

I don't ever remember being misled by a ground commander: they were usually pretty good about calling us in, although I did hear stories of cold LZs turning hot. Our policy was to not land until we could see a ground guide standing in the middle of the LZ with his hands and his weapon held over his head. We figured that if the guy was confident enough to do that it was OK to land there. We even went one step further by landing so close to the ground guide that he had to back up, again figuring if it was safe enough for him to stand in that exact spot it was safe to put our skids there.

The busiest year for the air ambulances was 1969, when 140 Dustoffs were stationed around the country. Fifteen per cent belonged to the 101st Airborne and the 1st Cav, the rest to various medical detachments. Each aircraft was flying four missions per day and for such service someone had to pay. The bill was usually settled by the Dustoff crews. By the end of the war 88 pilots had been killed and around 380 wounded, with their crew chiefs and medics suffering accordingly.

On the night of 15 November 1969, Phil Marshall became one of the 380 Dustoff pilots to be wounded. He was dozing on his bunk in the alert hooch as the call for 'Dustoff!' came from the radio shack next door. Instantly awake, he leapt up and ran to the radio room to get the mission sheet as the co-pilot, crew chief

Above: Phil Marshall in the left seat of a UH-1 Dustoff helicopter, after passing his aircraft commander check flight. (Phil Marshall)

and medic ran to the Huey nearby. With the details of the location and the radio frequency of the unit requesting Dustoff in his hand, he emerged from the shack at a dead run.

Night scrambles were less traumatic than daytime, when the aircraft commander would often run from the mess tent shovelling food into his mouth, followed invariably by such examples of combat pilot humour as 'If you don't make it back, can I have your fan?'

The co-pilot's shout of 'Clear' and the slowly increasing whine of the turbine greeted Marshall as he jumped into the darkened left seat. Repositioning his 38-calibre revolver in its waist holster between his legs, for extra protection of the vital areas, he crammed the mission sheet into his shirt pocket. It joined the letter from his girlfriend that he had received that evening but had only been able to read three or four times.

He fastened his seat belt and shoulder harness and slid his armored chicken-plate under the shoulder straps. He pulled on his helmet and continued the engine *run-up to 6,600rpm while Don Study, the co-pilot, was now able to buckle up and put on his helmet. Marshall continues the story:*

Immediately upon reaching proper rotor speed, my intercom call of 'Coming up' was instantly answered by a 'Clear left' from the crew chief, Specialist Fourth Class Zeb Dulin, behind me and a 'Clear right' from the medic, Spec 4 Randy Love, on the opposite side. The crew always sat on armored pads on the floor, with their backs to our armored seats for maximum protection. Their rear-facing positions thus gave us 360 degrees of eyesight in any situation.

As we got the light on the skids and lost contact with the ground, Don informed Quang Tri tower of our departure and direction. A Dustoff aircraft on an urgent medevac was rarely questioned or asked to hold. A low-level departure generally gave us a chance to scan the area as we climbed to altitude and to stay under the traffic pattern until well away from the city.

Below: *The hospital ship* Repose *where Phil Marshall was taken after being wounded. (Phil Marshall)*

While departing, the copilot normally made a call to the artillery command center for clearance, or at least a report of where arty was firing from and where it was impacting, so that we could avoid or fly under the rounds. An artillery shell through the cabin could spoil your whole day.

As Don made the call, I noticed the dim glow of flares on the north-west horizon. I didn't even have to look at my map under the red lights – I knew where we were going. The 101st Airborne was making a night combat assault out near the fire-bases along the DMZ. The arty info was coming in over the radio, but it didn't register . . . my mind was about 40 clicks away.

The crew were quiet. We knew what we had to do. Here we were . . . a very green, 21-year-old aircraft commander, a 22-year-old copilot in-country for less than two months, a new crew chief all of 20 years old on his first trip to the field, and a 19-year-old medic who had a nice safe job back in some hospital in Da Nang but was bored and wanted to fly. Young as we were, we had already flown together two days without a hitch and it was as if we had known each other for years. We were professionals and we had a job to do.

When we arrived over the area we realized that things were kind of bad. The assault was still going on and gunships were trying to suppress the ground fire. The ground commander, Click 66, informed us that he had three wounded that he wanted evacuated; one had a sucking chest wound – the next worst thing to being dead – and time was running out.

We had trouble locating the correct LZ – there were flares going off and three or four strobe marking lights flashing at the same time. One of the gunships said he would fly over the correct LZ and switch his position lights on as he overflew it. This he did, but as we flared over the LZ I looked out of my left window and saw a slick making an approach at the same time. He was fifty feet away and coming straight in, so I pulled pitch and got out of there as fast as I could.

I asked Click 66 to turn his strobe light on and off and eventually we found the correct LZ, in a bomb crater on the side of a hill, amongst some defoliated trees. I could not land and had to hover about six feet above the ground, with the rotor blades turning within a foot of the trees. We got the wounded on board and departed the LZ to the south.

As Marshall cleared the LZ, one of the Viet Cong aimed his AK-47 assault rifle in the direction of the tell-tale 'wop-wop-wop' of the Huey rotor blades and fired off his whole clip. One of the rounds came through the left door, struck the armored seat and shattered, sending shrapnel from the seat and bullet into Marshall's left arm, severing the nerves:

My left arm went completely numb from the elbow down and my arm jerked upwards. The engine began to die as I rolled off the throttle and the low rpm audio warning began to sound. It felt like I had the whole of my left hand blown off and the explosion was so great that I thought we had been hit by an RPG. I looked across at Don Study and said 'I'm hit, I'm hit,' and he grabbed hold of the controls as the aircraft began to fall like a stone. Although my life did not begin to flash before my eyes, I thought 'This is it Phil' and I wondered how the folks back home were going to take it.

Don bottomed the pitch and rolled the revs back on as I tuned the radios from the ground to the gunship frequency. I called 'Mayday, mayday, Dustoff 7-1-1. I'm hit and going down.' We continued to descend and were heading for the ridgeline, although by now the power was beginning to return. We hit one tree going over the ridgeline and severely damaged both rotor blades, but thankfully they stayed together and we headed for the hospital ship *Repose*, followed by one of the 'Batman' gunships.

Don Study made a very good approach to the helicopter pad on the ship and the Navy medics rushed to take the wounded off. A doctor looked at Phil Marshall's arm and hold him that he would be home for Christmas. The paratrooper with the sucking chest wound died on the way in.

By 1969 two Dustoff pilots had won the Medal of Honor, Major Patrick H. Brady in 1968 and CW3 Michael J. Novosel in 1969. Statistics showed that Dustoff aircraft suffered 3.3 times more losses to hostile fire than all other types of helicopter. Air ambulance work was a good way to get killed. It was also very rewarding work. By the end of the war, some 390,000 Army patients had been evacuated by helicopter to a medical facility. Without the skill, devotion and bravery of the Dustoff crews the final number of American dead would have been significantly higher.

CRASH CARTER'S DIARY

28

1. Tay Ninh   2. Cu Chi
3. 25th Inf Div into
   Cambodia

O NE of the better surprises to be inflicted upon the author whilst researching this book was the discovery of Lawrence E. (Crash) Carter. Not only did he willingly respond to a request for assistance in the Newsletter of the Vietnam Helicopter Pilots' Association, but he freely offered the use of his photographs and four diaries that he filled whilst in Vietnam. Unfortunately, space limitations prevent the reproduction of the bulk of the contents of the diaries, but the events of five of the days are included here and provide an insight into Crash Carter's war.

I graduated with flight class 69–37 from Fort Rucker in Alabama and arrived in South Vietnam on 1 January 1970. I was assigned to the 25th Aviation Battalion, the organic aviation asset of the 25th Infantry Division. I was assigned to A Company, the Little Bears, whose three platoons of slicks were charged with general support. Our sister company, B Company, the Diamondheads, had one platoon of guns with Cobras, one with OH-6A scouts and one with slicks.

I was stationed at Cu Chi and Tay Ninh in III Corps during 1970 and at that time we were equipped with the UH-1H. The callsign, Little Bears, was derived from the physical appearance of the original commanding officer. He was short and stocky and had a large amount of body hair; thus he was referred to as a little bear. Somehow the name stuck, as names are prone to in aviation, and the callsign that started out as Red Carpet was changed to Little Bears.

From January to April I flew C and C (Command and Control), somewhat against my will, then was transferred to another platoon to fly general support. To configure a ship for C and C required the placement of two long whip antennas on the heel of each skid. Two steps were also placed over the skids for ease of entry for the Big Dogs who flew with us. A large radio console filled the cargo deck and consisted of multiple FM, UHF and VHF radios for the 'Codes' use. Brigade Commanders had an RTO (radio telephone operator) assigned to the aircrew permanently. For the General, his aide acted as the RTO. The Brigade Commanders further had an artillery liaison officer attached to the aircrew.

General support aircraft were assigned to single-ship missions sequenced one through twenty. Each aircraft would depart early in the morning and not usually return until sunset or later. We also had regular night missions, Division Ready and Night Hawk. Division Ready was a slick that was placed on five-minute alert for any emergency missions that might come up in the night. Night Hawk was a different job altogether. The aircraft was rigged out with a minigun, searchlight, starlight scopes and flares and flown as a single-ship mission. At one time there were three Nighthawks available for missions at any given time. One was sent north to Tay Ninh, one stayed at Cu Chi and the third one went to Bear Cat on a nightly basis. Nighthawk was a self-support mission, in that targets were found, fixed and attacked without support from other aircraft. In many instances, there were other aircraft that were flown in conjunction, such as the INFANT ship out of the 11th Aviation Group in Phu Loi.

When Lawrence Carter realized that he was going to Vietnam he was determined not to lose the experience to failed memory. He started his diaries when he arrived in San Francisco and continued them until he returned to the United States. It was to be a significant year, for, at last, the political restrictions were to be temporarily lifted and American troops were saddling up to invade the enemy sanctuaries in Cambodia.

30 January 1970
I should have known this morning, when we flew two clicks into Cambodia, that this was going to be one of those days. What tipped us off was the lack of bomb craters.

This afternoon a unit north of fire-support base Washington came into heavy contact in an area between Highway 22 and Highway 4 north of the six-zeros east–west line. That whole area is indian country . . . makes us nervous just to go up there. When we first arrived the 'Issue' FAC was directing an airstrike on the wood-line. The Air Force jets were orbiting at 5,000 feet above the clouds and making their runs east to west. The FAC was directly over the contact at about 2,500 feet, which by my map is X-ray Tango 2067. Air Traffic Control at JFK in New York must be a drag compared to what those FACs do here. This guy had two gun teams in race tracks to the southeast, making their gun runs from south to north with a west break. We were in a left-hand racetrack slightly to the west of the AH-1G's run-in headings.

This is the wildest air show I've seen to date. Delta troop of the three-quarter Cav had a Loach team doing visual recons down in the smoke and ground fire between gun runs. Pulling back between gun runs and incoming bombs or impacting artillery, we orbited at 2,000 feet for three and a half hours, adjusting our airspeed according to what was coming from which direction. Every aircraft was taking some sort of ground fire, which we ignored until our ship took a few hits.

Above: Lawrence E. 'Crash' Carter with the Night Hawk gunship that he flew while serving with the 25th Aviation Battalion during 1970. (Lawrence E. Carter)

The weather was alternately clear and closing in all afternoon. The haze cut down visibility to half a mile or so and we kept busy spotting and dodging fast-movers as they dropped out of the clouds on bombing runs. After dark we returned to Tay Ninh. It had started to rain, so it was time to go on instruments as we could not see past the windshield. Mac did a 180-degree turn to get out of the storm. Once out of the rain all we had to worry about was the dark. We dropped down to the deck so we could at least see the ground. We had been on a fuel light about five minutes when we found Highway 22. We finally broke over the base camp off the end of the active runway. Needless to say the next flight was canceled as the Colonel and his people no longer wished to view the contact from the air.

Tonight I was running back from the mess hall in the rain and dark and during an attempt to tiptoe across a large area of standing water I found myself swimming. Skin-diving is more like it. Some bozo is in the process of digging a large bunker and the hole had filled with rainwater.

I'm sure anybody who saw me wondered about the guy neck deep in water and laughing. Oh well, just another day in sunny Southeast Asia.

2 March 1970
Last night I took some balsa wood and styrofoam and made a phoney taxicab meter. When it was painted the thing looked like the real thing, so much so that JC wants one for his Loach. I mounted it this morning on the Colonel's command console. It really looks neat and is very much in keeping with the nature of our combat mission here in sunny Southeast Asia. I hung a sign next to it that says 'Where to?' There is a string attached to the bottom of the sign that, when pulled, flips the sign over, revealing a second message: 'Oh no! Not there!'

We took off for the top of the rock, Nui Ba Dinh, about 0830 hours. I was eating peanuts and tossing the shells out of the window, not really paying attention, and the slipstream was picking them up and depositing them upon the door gunner. It was more like he was sitting in a little whirlwind of peanut shells. Poor Butch was sitting in a storm of shells, so I did the only gentlemanly thing possible and ate the nuts all the faster.

O'1 Captain Cortney had a good case of heart failure while we were approaching the helipad on the top of the rock. His jumpseat collapsed, dumping him onto the floor and almost out of the door. Somehow he failed to see humor of our removing all of the retaining pins in his seat.

Poor Butch got a 'Dear John' letter from his girlfriend and he is very broken up about it. Apparently they had planned to marry when he got back to the world. Bill and I agreed that the letter was a really low stunt to pull.

We went to the Yellow Jackets' (the Loach platoon of the 116th AHC) famous or infamous stag flicks, hosted by the equally infamous Sergeant Miller. The movie was the tease type and it got active responses: everybody yelled and cheered for the hero. Whats more, everybody had very explicit suggestions for the actors, many of which must be physically impossible . . . but good fun to try. Every time the action started to get good, the guy would stop and do something else. This only resulted in a shower of beer cans rebounding off of the screen. All is quiet and I'm about to turn in . . . but it is not midnight yet.

6 May 1970
The 25th Division moved into Cambodia today, starting with large troop insertions about three miles inside the border. At first the grunts met little resistance, but as the day wore on the bad guys started to put up resistance. I saw at least eight Cobras on station with two C and C ships overhead and Loaches thick as flies down on the deck, throwing smokes and frags everywhere. The grunts got mortared soon after landing, and when the Cobras jumped the bad guys they started to receive 50-caliber

fire. Everybody, all of the Cobras and the Air Force jets, opened up on the grove of trees that the fire was coming from. One Cobra punched off all of its rockets on a single pass. The grove of trees became a boiling cloud of orange, black and brown and was totally flat and burning a few minutes later when all the smoke had cleared.

The scouts were spotting gooks faster than the Cobras could kill them, catching as large as company-sized formations in the open. What the Cobras couldn't handle the artillery was firing on. On one of our low passes over a village we were hosed with AK-47 fire, but we lucked out and took no hits. The whole day was spent flying around Cambodia, coming back to refuel and occasionally setting down so the General could check on ground units.

While we were up in the clouds I heard a call on our control push: 'Three-zero, if you will look out your left door at nine o'clock you will see a high performance aircraft.' We all looked and saw JC in his Yellowjacket Loach, to which we replied 'Tally-ho the football.'

We took some ABC newsmen from Cambodia to Cu Chi and, just for grins, low-leveled the whole way, flying down in the trees and rice stalks, just having a good ol' time. The General finally got tired of our high jinks and stated that he wanted to come up. I did the only thing decent, a cyclic climb up to about 2,500 feet. The guys in the back got very restless when the aircraft went weightless at the top of the climb. The General elected to terminate early. Life's tough when you're OD green.

A friend of mine who flies Loaches reported a strange thing. He spotted a group of about eight NVA moving down a road in formation hats, packs and guns, just like a parade. The gooks just looked up at them for a while before attempting to shoot them down. By then it was too late, there were a half dozen frags on the way down. He said that for the hunter-killer teams it was just like fishing at a fish hatchery.

8 May 1970

About five this evening, while we were preflighting our aircraft for night flying, someone came running past our bunker hunting for Major Marsh. He said that Littlebear Five had been shot down in Cambodia. A Nighthawk was scrambled to accompany the Major to help out with five. Captain Harrison and Captain Franke were flying when they were shot down about three clicks inside Cambodia, due west of Tay Ninh. A Blue Max gun team was on them immediately to provide cover while a unit of grunts pushed through the jungle to help them. A Dustoff aircraft picked up the three crewmen who were not injured, but a second ship was required to pick up Captain Franke who had a broken leg. Their aircraft was totally destroyed when it hit the trees. We have not heard, but we don't think it burned.

About 0100 hours Lieutenant Orr and Lieutenant Frasher were killed when their ship exploded and crashed right on the border. They were flying Division Ready, resupplying ammunition to units in Cambodia. No one knows whether they took any ground fire, just that the ship torched and crashed from a very low altitude. It burned, and the ammunition exploded on impact so that even if anybody survived the impact they wouldn't have survived the explosion and fire. The only survivor was the door gunner who was thrown clear on impact.

I'm getting tired of seeing my friends die. That kind of sh** gets old the first time. These are very brave men who go and fly every day knowing that this could be the day they get zapped. Getting used to getting shot at takes a whole lot of getting used to. The events in my *Dallas Morning News* do not make my life any easier. The big topics to seem to center on the campus protesting and the various leaders who are considered to be heroes. It's a shame we can't bring those heroes over here and see what kind of heroes they really are. Poor Gary and Merlin died for a country of which they are not citizens, and were not old enough to a have a say in the government of the country of which they are citizens.

8 June 1970

I was on Tay Ninh Nighthawk again, providing gun cover for the INFANT ship. We arrived in Tay Ninh just beating out an ungodly huge thunderstorm coming in from the west. While we played cards inside the O Club, the inhabitants of the Tay Ninh base camp must surely have been building an ark of wood. We could hardly hear each other bidding over the pounding of the rain on the roof. When we went outside at closing time we were all absolutely amazed, the sky was clear and a full moon was shining – not a cloud in the sky. Unfortunately, the mud was still with us.

We performed two routine sweeps of the roads, our ship low on the roads and the INFANT above and behind, covering us. We swept the rest of the blocks without sighting anything and returned to Tay Ninh.

At 0330 hours I was leaving the TOC to sack out on the ship when the duty officer told me that someone in Cambodia was reporting bad guys in their wire. I went back to the ship and woke the guys and were they happy about that. The INFANT ship came along with us just for laughs and on the off-chance that they might be able to kill somebody. As we climbed to altitude off the northern active we picked up GCA for a vector to the fire-support base in Cambodia. As we approached the border we could see all the night laagers being hit with all manner of incoming. The sky was lit up with flares in all directions. With the clear sky and full moon we were able to see our target a good ten to fifteen miles out. A firefight at night is a sight unlike any other I've ever seen. As much as I hate to see them, they are still weirdly fascinating, almost mesmerizing. The whole area was as though a red and green blossom, but it was a place where people were dying.

It is strange, whenever I see a firefight in the distance and I know that is where we are going, a whole shift in attitude takes place. I find myself tightening my seatbelts and chicken board and getting myself mentally prepared to concentrate on the task at hand. I don't recall ever discussing this with anybody else, but I'm sure that everybody else does the same thing. I've seen the others in the crew suddenly getting serious and quietly getting their tasks accomplished. The normal level of BS (bull****) on the intercom suddenly stops and everybody gets very businesslike.

Leo was flying and I was working the radios. I contacted the ground unit about ten minutes out and got them ready to shut off their mortars when we arrived overhead. I also got the arty shut off so we could work. The artillery flares continued to light the area until we arrived over the target. An aerial flare is a ghostly device, silent and shadowy, and it gives off an eerie light. In the air you can see the drifting smoke trail it leaves as it settles and the sight is all the more spooky when there are more than one of them.

We were the first aircraft on station and the INFANT ship had dropped down to cover us. The friendlies had already requested a Dustoff from Tay Ninh and we had relayed the message. We dropped to about 200 feet to locate the friendlies and give the starlight scope operator a better view of the wood-lines. The bad guys had stopped the heavy firing about the time we arrived overhead, although an occasional burst of small-arms fire could be heard. The night laager was set up in an open area of dried-up rice paddies about 150 meters from the tree-lines on all four sides. A small village about 400 meters to the southeast is where the first of the RPGs and recoilless-rifle fire had come from. Those little SOBs know that they can hide in the villages and we won't shoot at them for fear of hitting innocent civilians. On occasions like this it is very tempting to roll in and level the only defined targets to be seen.

A gun team of Cobras showed up just as we were getting set for our first run. Ernie had the gun working perfectly – not a single jam. We dropped to 100 feet and ran the length of the tree-line, about 300 meters, north and east of the friendlies. For the next five minutes we just ran the wood-lines shooting everything in sight. We had to move back and change ammo cans. When we pulled back the INFANT ship rolled in and unloaded a whole bunch of nails on each of the four primary targets.

At this time, just to our north, another night laager seemed to turn red because of the incoming rounds exploding. An AC-119 Shadow gunship overhead opened up with all of his 20mm cannon and all hell broke loose on the ground.

We had rearmed and moved back into position to hit the wood-lines again. All the time we had been on station, the ground units had been trying to get a Dustoff for their wounded without success. By this time we were running low on fuel and ammunition, so we told the friendlies that we would pick up the wounded and transport them to the 45th Surgical in Tay Ninh. On the last pass I set up the approach to the edge of the perimeter. We had all discussed the pickup among ourselves and the crew were just as eager to make the pickup. Just as we were turning on short final the Shadow popped a flare and the Cobras came in on gun runs to cover us. As soon as our skids touched, the gunner dumped the flares from the flare barrel, further lightening our load.

It is strange that the events should seem to be in slow motion, but it is so. I can visualize very clearly the flares being dumped onto the ground and the grunts carrying the wounded and placing them into the aircraft. We couldn't have been on the ground more than 45 seconds to one minute, although it seems like forever. At one point I remember looking out at the tree-line and thinking how close it was and what a nice target we must be making.

We took off immediately and headed for Tay Ninh. We alerted the Dustoff that was en route that we had picked up the wounded from this location. He thanked us and told us that he also had wounded at another contact and our trip would cut down on the waiting time of the second set of wounded.

As we were finally departing the area, I could see the gunships working out on the various targets over three separate locations. By this time the sky was alive with rotating beacons and anticollision lights. And off in the east I could see the first lightening of the sun rising on a new day. I could also see our aircrew in the cargo space tending to the wounded as best they could. We contacted the 45th and called about ten minutes ETA with the wounded.

FIRST OF THE NINTH 29

1. Phuoc Vinh
2. Song Be

*I*F one sat with a group of former Army helicopter pilots and asked them to decide which was the elite amongst the many helicopter units to serve in Vietnam, one would consume enough beer to float a Huey, listen to a lot of lies and never hear the same unit mentioned twice. True enough, there are many possible candidates – the First Cav, the Mad Dogs and the Blue Max to name but a few. However, the author, until persuaded otherwise, considers the 1st Squadron, 9th Cavalry, to be the elite of the elite.

The 'First of the Ninth', as it was known, arrived in Vietnam in the autumn of 1965 and was part of the new 1st Cavalry Division (Airmobile). This new concept of an airmobile division included an air cavalry squadron whose function would be to scout for and locate the elusive Viet Cong. The true measure of its work can be seen when one realizes that practically every major engagement fought by the First Cav was started with a contact by the scout helicopters of the First of the Ninth.

The First of the Ninth suffered tremendous losses in men and machines during the war. One of their pilots, Bill Frazer, saw and experienced enough war to last a lifetime. This is his story.

I went through flight school at nineteen and had turned twenty just prior to going to Vietnam in February 1970. I was assigned to the First Cavalry Division, or, to be more specific, an elite unit of the First Cav known as the First of the Ninth. I served with both Charlie Troop in Phuoc Vinh and Alpha Troop at Song Be, or Firebase Buttons.

The First of the Ninth operated primarily as a separate unit: we worked the hot-spots in our area in northern III Corps along the Cambodian border. I flew as a scout pilot, and my job primarily was to get up every morning at four-thirty, go through a quick briefing, pick up my codes for the day, go out to my aircraft, fly out to the AO (area of operations) up on the Cambodian border and shoot people.

Left: Bill Frazer in the right seat, about to pull pitch in a First of the Ninth Loach. (Bill Frazer)

I flew a Hughes OH-6 Loach scout helicopter and my job was to hover around above the trees, and when I say hover I mean hover: we didn't fly above 20 knots, and stayed just inside translational lift. We worked in an area that was primarily triple-canopy jungle where the trees were about 150 feet high.

I always had a cover ship, a Cobra, which flew circles above me at 3,500 feet, taking spot reports as I flew around and saw signs of enemy activity, whether it be trails, hooches or equipment. The copilot of the high bird would write the spot reports down on the plexiglass of the Cobra and later relay them to headquarters.

Because we covered the hot-spots there were very few days when we didn't take any fire. I can only remember a few times during the 370 days that I was in Nam when I didn't come under fire or get involved in a firefight. We flew from first light to last light and generally put in twelve to sixteen hours a day, seven days a week.

We usually flew in a Pink Team which comprised a Cobra from the Red Platoon and a Loach from the White Platoon. We would normally fly out to the AO at about 3,500 feet to stay above small-arms fire, and when we reached the AO I would put the Loach into a slip, kick it out of trim and let it fall like a rock, to decrease my exposure to small-arms fire between 3,500 feet and the tops of the trees. I would then recover power on top of the trees and start working in tight right-hand circles.

Our crew comprised three people, a warrant officer pilot, an observer (usually an enlisted man who sat on the left side in the front) and a crew chief. The observer carried an M-16 rifle and a smoke grenade to mark targets, and the crew chief, whom we called 'Torq,' sat on the floor in the back. In our unit we did not have bungee cords, seat belts or safety harnesses for the torq. We also took out everything we could to lighten the aircraft. This was so we could carry more frag grenades, 30-caliber ammunition for our machine gun, home-made bombs, white phosphorous grenades ('Willy Petes') and smokes.

If we saw a gook as we were flying in tight right circles, I would shout 'I got gooks.' Immediately, the crew chief in the back would lean out the doorway and pull the trigger on the machine gun. Now quite often he would not see the target until after the pilot had seen it, so his job was just to pull the trigger, ensure that we didn't fly into our own bullets, keep the bullets away from the main rotor and let the pilot walk the bullets into the target.

When you first start flying scouts, the pilot is pretty worthless. You can't see anything. You're a new pilot and so tied up trying to fly the aircraft and keep from hitting things that you haven't yet developed the highly skilled vision that it takes to pick up trails or individuals hiding on the ground and so forth. So for the first couple of months the crew chief does most of the work.

Our crew chiefs were probably some of the gutsiest people you could imagine. We reconned by target – we made ourselves such a real meaty target that the gooks on the ground could not resist shooting at us. They had the advantage because they could hear and see us before we could see them. Usually they would open up as we flew over the top of them and we would have to break and come around again. The only way you could cover yourself would be for the crew chief to step out onto the skids and hold on to the door rim with one hand and fire the M-60 with the other to cover your tail.

As we would make our break the observer would throw out a red smoke to mark the gooks' position. The Cobra would then roll in and saturate the area with rockets and minigun fire. After he made one or two passes we would move back into the area to do a BDA, a bomb damage assessment, to check the kills. Because we used point-detonating rockets and were working in triple-canopy jungle, many times the rocket fire from the Cobra was ineffective because it would blow up in the tops of the trees and the shrapnel would not penetrate to the ground. However, it did keep their heads down long enough, so we could come back in and shoot them. Our job was to stay on top of them, shoot them, or get shot down ourselves. It was as simple as that. When we got in a firefight we stayed there until it ended.

Many times when we hit a hot-spot like that we would work it for hours, sometimes an entire day. It would be a constant running battle and the only time we would break station would be to refuel or rearm. In these situations a second Pink Team would cover our breaks and we would relieve them when they had to leave. Often an Air Force OV-10 FAC would follow us out to the AO, because they knew that one of our troops would be getting into trouble that day. They would orbit around 5,000-7,000 feet and hope that they could direct a team of Air Force fighters into the area.

You couldn't ask for a better unit to be around than the First Cav or the First of the Ninth. I had heard back when I was stateside that if you've got to go to a combat unit the First Cav was a stand-up unit and they were that. The First of the Ninth lived up to that reputation. It's unbelievable some of the situations we got into and the fact that you never backed away from them. I can remember when I first got in-country just how scared I was. I was a 20-year-old kid and I couldn't imagine myself killing anybody, and the idea of someone trying to kill me during the 365 days of my tour was more than I could handle. I went through a period of about a month and a half when I was so scared I just couldn't handle it, but eventually you get used to it. Its amazing what the mind can adjust to. The only thing I can equate it to is a form of insanity, but it's an insanity that helps you survive. You literally become the meanest person out there.

The mortality rate amongst scout pilots was incredibly high, especially in units like the First of the Ninth or the Second of the Seventeenth with the 101st Airborne. Because of our missions and the areas that we worked pilots just didn't last long. Chuck Frazier and I finished our first six months as scout pilots at the same time. We were told by our platoon leader that we were only the fifth and sixth scout pilots in Charlie Troop ever to complete six months. Chuck and I went on to fly for a full year and were only number two and three to do so. There had only been one other pilot before us who had flown for a complete year and survived to tell the story.

My CO, Major Rosher, would not let me do an additional six months in scouts, because he was sure I would get killed. Instead, I was forced to attend Cobra school, and when I came back they put me in the red platoon as a copilot in a Cobra. I lasted two weeks there; I couldn't stand the job. We were flying around at 3,500 feet and shooting rockets at the trees, whereas in scouts we were looking the gooks in the face. The level of intensity was just like a drug. I can tell you there is nothing that can get you as high as that kind of life-and-death intensity on a day-to-day basis – when you are riding the thin edge of being wiped out, when they are shooting your helicopter up, and glass and crap is flying everywhere and tracers are flying in one door and out the other. The adrenalin high is such that there is not a dope or a booze made that can give you that kind of intense high.

All of us were that way in scouts. The ones who weren't like that you knew weren't going to make it. You needed that level of intensity. In my mind I would have damn near crashed the helicopter on top of them rather than let them get away. You wanted them so bad I felt sure that that desire radiated itself to the enemy and kept them scared and ducking, and I think this is the reason that I survived a year of nonstop battles.

After two weeks of flying Cobras I knew it was not for me. I had to get back down on the deck again. One day Major Harris, the CO of Alpha Troop, came into our squadron headquarters at Phuc Vinh. They had just moved from Tay Ninh to Firebase Buttons, up around Song Be. I asked him if he had a slot open for a scout pilot in his unit. It was a kind of stupid question because there was always a slot open for a scout pilot anywhere in the First of the Ninth. He couldn't believe it and said 'Pack your bags – you can come with me tonight.'

The accommodation at Firebase Buttons was the bottom of the heap. It was knee-deep in mud and we were living twenty men in a ten-man tent. We didn't have mess facilities, and if you couldn't steal C rations or had a care package from home you didn't eat! Everything stayed wet and had mold on it. We couldn't get water to shower or wash your clothes in. We would wear the same uniform for four or five days and we just stank. The only luxury we had was coffee in the morning, and we had to use it to brush our teeth with!

I can remember the day I joined the First of the Ninth at Phuc Vinh and went to my first scout meeting that night. Nothing impressed me more than walking in there and seeing these guys. They were grungy and haggard, and had a look in their eye that I had never seen before, a result of being in combat day in day out. In the previous five days they had lost seven pilots, either killed or badly wounded. My platoon leader had been shot down that day, got another aircraft and went out again and had two crew members injured – and that was all in a day's work.

As a new guy, or 'f***ing new guy' (FNG) as we were known, I sat in my newly pressed uniform and listened to them discuss the day's events. It scared the hell out of me. After the meeting I went back to my hooch and a couple of wild-looking crew chiefs came in and said, 'Is there a Mister Frazer in here?' I said 'Yeah, thats me.' They said 'Good to meet you Sir. My name's Neff and this is Rankin.' Then they said, 'Could we have your initials please?' I said 'Well, yeah, it's W. C. F.' They asked me to come over and stand next to the wall, and when I did so one of them pulled out a tape measure and he measured me. I said 'What in the hell are you doing?' He looked me right in the eye and said 'We're measuring you for a body bag motherf***er, 'cos you ain't goin' to make it!'

The first time that you kill somebody stands out in your memory for life. I can remember it vividly. As a new scout pilot they send you out on what are referred to as rat-f*** missions, in areas where you don't expect to see much. This is to keep the new pilots out of trouble until they learn the job and the aircraft. This day we were working an area to the east of Firebase Buttons close to an area known as Elephant Flats. Apparently there hadn't been much enemy activity up there for a while and they thought that was a safe place to put me.

My high-bird pilot that day was on his second tour in Vietnam and was not much less than an alcoholic. Nobody wanted to fly with him and they generally sent him on the rat-f***s so that no one would have to depend on him in a bad situation. We were working along a river surrounded with open fields and we came across what looked like a rocket pod jettisoned by a Cobra. As we came down to check it out I looked across the river and saw a sampan tied up in some trees. I told the high bird about it and went on over for a look. I assumed he was watching me and covering me, but what I didn't realize was that he was sitting over there messing about with that pod.

As I went on over to the sampan he told me 'If you see gooks, shoot 'em,' but I was new and did not want to open fire indiscriminately and shoot some innocent civilian. As I flew over the cornfield I saw two guys squatting down on their haunches, right next to two pottery kilns. It was a part of a VC base camp and these guys had their AK-47s beneath them, although I couldn't see this from 20–30 feet above them. I told the Cobra 'I have gooks,' and he replied 'Shoot 'em!' As I was thinking that they might be friendly they stood up, took aim and opened up at me.

We took about fifteen hits all over the aircraft and at that point my crew chief pulled the trigger on the machine gun. It fired about three rounds and then jammed. The observer got shook and dropped the smoke in the cabin and we went IFR with red smoke. He began to fish around trying to kick it out and I threw the aircraft out of trim to try to blow the smoke out of the door, so I could see where we were going. In all the confusion and hollering, my high bird, who hadn't been watching me (an unforgivable sin), spotted my red smoke. The pilot wasn't thinking straight and locked in on the red smoke. It didn't register that the smoke was flying along at 150 miles an hour, and he began shooting rockets at it!

Finally we got everything sorted out and I went back in again to try to find the two gooks who had now disappeared. I noticed a guy lying on the ground pointing an M-16 up at me, but before he could fire, my torq ran a path of bullets across the top of him. This was the first time I had seen a guy killed and it isn't like you see on TV: the guy kept crawling and looking up at me. My torq had been in Nam for two years and he knew he was dead. I could have sworn he was still alive; I hollered at him to shoot him again, but he said 'He's dead.' I said 'Bull**** – he's still moving: shoot him, just open up on him.' So he did and he put about thirty rounds into him, but he still kept moving.

I ended up killing ten people in the open that day – ten people. I can remember that my fuel-low warning light came on and we were just about out of ammo, but there was the one guy dressed in white who had been standing at the pottery kiln and I had not yet found him. We had just about given up on him and were ready to leave as soon as a team from the Blue Max arrived. Just then we flew over a clump of head-high vegetation, and standing in the middle of it was this guy. As he stuck his gun up in the air to shoot at us, we dropped a grenade on him and blew him to pieces.

For the next three or four nights I couldn't sleep. I would go over that entire battle time and time again in my dreams, but after that I became accustomed to it and it didn't bother me any more.

I remember a story that Chuck Frazier told about a mission he was on. He had stumbled across several gooks in the open and killed some of them, but over about an hour and a half period they would keep coming across them as they broke from cover to run. They were taking a little fire, but not much because the gooks were just ducking and hiding and running. Eventually they began to run out of everything. Torq was in the back, firing the machine gun, when it suddenly stopped. Chuck said 'What are you doing? Keep shooting at 'em.' Torq said 'I can't – I'm out of ammo.' So Chuck said 'Well, throw something at 'em.' Torq replied 'I can't – we're out of grenades.' He said 'Well, for Christ's sake shoot something at them,' thinking that he may have had an M-79 Chunker (grenade launcher) or something. He turned around and looked and the crew chief was standing out on the skids, shooting them the finger. It was all he had left. He told him 'Dammit, shoot something at them,' so he stood on the skids and flipped them the bird.

SMART BOMBS

30

1. Ubon
2. Thanh Hoa Bridge
3. Paul Doumer Bridge

*O*NE of the most important of the many mistakes made by the civilian war managers in Washington, DC, was to stop the bombing of North Vietnam in November 1968. President Johnson and his advisers naively believed that it would result in a peace agreement. However, in the following four years 25,000 more servicemen were to die as the United States and North Vietnamese negotiators agreed on little more than the shape of the conference table. Then, on 30 March 1972, the North Vietnamese invaded South Vietnam.

During the four-year bombing halt the North Vietnamese had repaired and strengthened their road and rail networks, in particular the vital Thanh Hoa and Doumer bridges. To the layman, destroying a bridge might seem an easy task, but in practice scoring a hit on a bridge with a bomb does not automatically destroy it. For example, between April and September 1967 the Navy flew 97 sorties against the Thanh Hoa bridge, and although they dropped 215 tons of bombs on it they only managed to render it temporarily unusable.

By the spring of 1972, when the bombing of targets in North Vietnam resumed, one factor had changed in the pilots' favour: they could discard their traditional iron 'dumb' bombs and use the new generation of 'smart' bombs. These weapons consisted of electro-optical guided bombs (EOGBs) and laser guided bombs (LGBs). The EOGB was a 2,000-pound bomb with a small television camera attached to the nose. The camera transmitted a picture of what it was viewing to a scope in the attack aircraft. The pilot would point the aircraft and bomb at the target area and the weapon systems officer (WSO) in the rear cockpit of the F-4 would find the target on the scope, refine the aiming point with the cross-hairs on the scope and designate the target to the weapon. Once this was done the pilot would release the bomb and quickly depart the target area, leaving the EOGB to guide itself toward the designated aim-point. Cloud cover over the target was always a problem, but if the weapon could see the target it would usually hit the aim-point.

The LGB was somewhat different. A laser sensor was fitted to the nose of a 2,000- or 3,000-pound bomb, which enabled it to guide itself toward a target illuminated with low-power laser energy. Such sensors were also fitted to 500-pound bombs, which were known as laser guided firecrackers. A pod mounted

Right: An Air Force
Phantom launching a
Mk 84 smart bomb in
November 1971. (US
Air Force)

*under the wing of the aircraft would illuminate the target with laser energy, its
optical viewing system and laser-illuminating capability controlled by the WSO in
the aircraft. The advantage of this system was that one aircraft could illuminate the
target for a number of others to bomb, with all weapons homing in on the same
illumination point.*

*The new weapons were given to the 8th Tactical Fighter Wing, the 'Wolfpack',
and between 6 April and 30 June 1972 their Phantoms destroyed 106 bridges in
North Vietnam, including the Doumer and Thanh Hoa, with the new guided bombs.
One of their WSOs was Harry Edwards.*

I was stationed at Ubon RTAFB from October 1971 to October 1972. During
this period I was assigned to the 433rd Tactical Fighter Squadron of the
'Wolfpack', as an F-4 weapon systems officer. Our squadron did much
of the laser-guided bombing and I either led, or was on, many missions,
including the Lang Chi hydroelectric plant, the Thanh Hoa bridge and
the Doumer bridge.

Laser systems employed by my squadron were the Paveway (optical)
and Pave Knife (TV). Since only six Pave Knife pods were ever built, and

two of these were lost the year I was there, few were available for training purposes after we started flying 'up North' on Christmas Day 1971. As a result the same people got to go day after day. Other missions we flew included low-altitude sensor drops, regular bombing, gravel, white phosphorous, napalm and CBUs. Gravel was our name for an anti-personnel explosive that looked like 2-inch square bean bags. They were frozen to an extremely low temperature and became active when thawed. When stepped on they would blow off a foot.

Paveway consisted of a set of optics mounted in the rear seat, alongside the right canopy. We looked through the optics through a three-power magnifying glass while in orbit at 9,000–11,000 feet. Paveway was a very effective system in low-threat areas. Orbiting at 9,000–11,000 feet in a high-threat area was not conducive to longevity. We used this system extensively in Southern Laos against gun sites.

The Pave Knife system consisted of a TV camera in a pod, mounted under the port wing of the F-4. A design defect caused what we saw in the rear cockpit 5-inch Sony TV to appear upside down and backwards! Therefore, when describing a hard-to-find target to someone looking in the TV, directions such as north, south, east and west could not be used; rather, easily located ground features were used as reference points to find more difficult ones.

Now for the controls. In the 'Acquire' position, I saw in my TV what the pilot saw in his pipper. Once I could identify the target I could select 'Track' on a switch by the radar tracking handle. This handle was utilized to move the picture, rather than the crosshairs on the TV. The TV moved via a roll rate gyro, i.e., the longer the tracking handle was held in a certain position the faster the picture moved. This fact, combined with the upside-down and backwards problem, meant that some training was required to become skilled. The training was best accomplished when the pods were off the aircraft and in the shop, connected to a TV there.

The picture movement caused serious problems at lower altitudes because it could not keep up with the speed at which the ground below was moving. We could, at least, illuminate for our own bombs as well as those of others. The eye of the bomb would open a couple of seconds after it left the aircraft and look for the reflected energy from the laser beam. The bomb had to be dropped within a 'box' 1,500 feet long and 500 feet wide, from the point the beam hit the ground, or the eye would not see the energy. This happened only rarely. Once the pilot saw the target he put it in the pipper, I found it in the TV, went to track and told the pilot I was tracking; he told the delivery aircraft 'Cleared to release,' and when they released they said 'Pickle, pickle, pickle.' I then had to make sure the target remained illuminated until I saw the bombs go off.

On the Thanh Hoa bridge mission I was flying with Captain D. L. Smith, who was later to become leader of the Air Force 'Thunderbirds' aerial demonstration team and was subsequently killed in an aircraft accident when he flew into a flock of birds and had an unsuccessful ejection. We had the Pave Knife system and one 2,000-pound Mk.84 bomb; our wingman had a Mk.84 and a 3,000-pound 'Fat Al.' Fat Al could not penetrate hard surfaces – it would break up – so it was always set to detonate at ground level or slightly above if the bomb carried a fuse extender.

We had about five-eighths cloud cover over the target area and it was covered with smoke and very difficult to see in my 5-inch black and white TV set. The bridge was very strong, with 18-foot abutments at the end, and it was very well protected with lots of antiaircraft guns. Our bombs scored a direct hit though, as later proven by aerial reconnaissance film and the film from the onboard camera which recorded what I saw on

Above right: *Weapon Systems Officer Harry Edwards standing next to the Pave Knife laser designator pod with a Mk 84 'Smart' bomb on his left. (Harry Edwards)*

Right: *The Lang Chi hydro-electric plant was destroyed by smart bombs on 10 June 1972. (US Air Force)*

SPILLWAY

HEAVY DAMAGE TO
TURBINES & GENERATORS
IN TRANSFORMER
BUILDING

TRANSFORMER

the TV during the tracking cycle. The western span of the bridge had been completely knocked off its 40-foot thick concrete abutment and the bridge superstructure was so critically disfigured and twisted that rail traffic would come to a standstill for at least several months.

I was also lead in the third and last four-ship flight that hit the Lang Chi hydroelectric plant on 10 June 1972. This target was particularly difficult because the huge dam was only about 30 feet away from the plant and was off-limits in this political war. Twelve of our F-4s were targeted against the plant, led by our Wing Commander, Colonel Carl Miller, and his backseater, First Lieutenant Wayne King. The second flight of four was from the 25th TFS and was targeted against the nearby transformer yard. Unfortunately they missed the target. The last flight was led by Lieutenant Colonel Hilton, the 433rd TFS commander, and I was in his pit (back seat).

The first flight scored a direct hit on the plant and blew off two-thirds of the roof with seven Mk.84s. Our flight put some of the bombs into the gaping hole and blew the rest of the roof off. We were able to dive in from about 23,000 feet, pickle off the bombs at about 14,000 feet and bottom out at 11,000 feet. At these altitudes we were above most of the ground fire, but there was a lot of it and I could see it in my small TV on the way down.

When we were not flying or at the squadron building near the flightline, we were at the 'party hooch.' I was in charge of this as an extra duty during my tour. We could order meals from the Thai restaurant on base and these were brought to the bar by a Thai on a bicycle. A favorite pastime for me and many others was going down to the 'hotsey bath' or 'rub n' scrub.' Here girls sat on bleachers and each had a pin with a large number pinned to her uniform. For three dollars you chose the one you wanted and got a one-hour bath and massage – the beer was extra. Also, there were many good restaurants in town. It was so good at Ubon that folks used to come from Vietnam for R and R!

Each squadron member also had his own patches, brass mug, scarf, party suit with lots of different patches unique to the war, and hat. Each new squadron member had to 'drink his hat' the first time he strode into the squadron bar with it on. This entailed filling it with everything behind the bar, including mustard, ketchup, bitters etc, and serenading the new guy while he stood on a pedestal drinking the concoction. After he finished everyone stomped on the hat to make it look as bad as possible. He then wore it for a year, dropping it over enemy territory from the speed brake of his Phantom on his last mission.

THE FASTEST SAVE OF THE WAR

31

1. Song Cai River

*T*HE Kaman HH-43 Huskie helicopter first arrived *in South-East Asia late in 1964. At that time the USAF Rescue Service lacked a helicopter suitable for search and rescue missions in jungles and mountains, where the inhabitants were not only hostile but armed with anti-aircraft weapons.*

The HH-43 was not really suitable for the role, having been designed for the local base rescue function and used primarily for fire-fighting and picking up pilots who had baled out near an air base. However, it was the only helicopter available at the time, and despite its limited range it had to fill the gap until newer models arrived.

By 1972 the Sikorsly HH-3 and H-53 had arrived and were primarily responsible for the rescue of downed airmen. It was, therefore, a surprise to the author to discover that the record for the fastest combat rescue of the war was held by an HH-43 'Pedro' and that the rescue took place on 23 November 1972. The story is told by James Moulton, one of the two Lieutenant pilots of 'Pedro 61', whose wish that the story of the HH-43 not be neglected has now been fulfilled.

The Song Cai River was a riddle. Twenty-four hours a day seemingly forever, fields of floating water hyacinths drifted with the lazy current – a beautiful conveyor garden of dark green, round, waxy leaves supporting vertical spike racemes of lavender flowers. This was a short river with headwaters in the near mountains. Many times we had weaved through those jungle-draped ranges in our Pedro, admiring the waterfalls and glimpses through foliage of foaming rapid streams. No hyacinths there. How they reproductively maintain the required recruitment to feed that moving floral carpet, or why they do not all flow out to sea, ridding the river of their cover, or why the oceans are not a teeming soup of salt poisoned hyacinths, are still questions that puzzle me. We were blowing them in our rotor wash. From a low-river hover, we could herd them like bobbing green cattle.

An Army pilot had told us that the Viet Cong float down the river concealed among the hyacinths. This was, he explained, how many of the Soviet 122-millimeter rockets were moved into the 'rocket belt' from

Above: An Air Force HH-43B with its fire-suppression kit slung underneath. The helicopter was designed for the local base crash-rescue function. (US Air Force)

which Da Nang took frequent poundings and which provided the town with its wartime label, 'Rocket City.'

'Just blow 'em across the surface,' he said. 'Any clump of weeds that don't blow, stitch it.' We were playing. It wasn't our job to stitch anything. We were rescue.

Nguyen was in the right seat. He reached above his head, placing his thumb on a toggle switch. Focusing on the path of the right rotor blade tip, he beeped in a tracking adjustment. Bill Latham was his real name. Some local girl had once said Nguyen was Vietnamese for William. Unfortunately she said it to Bill in the presence of fellow-pilots and he didn't have a chance. A pained expression betrayed his discomfort as we tested the nickname, but he was too wise to protest, knowing the folly of bleeding among sharks. Although still a Lieutenant, Nguyen was the most experienced and professional HH-43 pilot in the unit. He was fastidious about keeping the blades tracked and his crew enjoyed the resulting smooth ride. Inflight blade-tracking was one of several great features of 'Charlie' Kaman's HH-43 Huskie.

The hyacinths were rolling against one another as I maneuvered along the retreating wall. Suddenly, over the radio came 'Mayday, mayday, mayday – nail three-six, ah, lost one engine, ah, in trouble.' The distress call was loud and crisp, obviously not far from our position. I pulled collective and, as the Song Cai fell away beneath, Nguyen came on the controls.

'Damn,' he muttered on the intercom. 'We're the alert! Contact Rescue Ops.' I acknowledged the change of controls and leaned over the center console to dial up our operations, when Da Nang tower requested the distressed aircraft to identify itself and state intentions. I chose not to change frequencies just yet. We had accelerated to 100 knots, leveled at 300 feet and turned towards Da Nang. We had the equipment that would allow us to home in on the Guard channel, but it was designed for use with continuous broadcast, as with survival radios, and was of little value with short transmissions.

Nail three-six wasn't answering. We wanted to be in the right place, but didn't know where that was. 'Hoist circuit breaker – on' came a request from the cabin. Sergeants Gaskins and McCoy were busying themselves with the hoist operations checks. Like a trained retriever shivering with excitement over the smell of pheasants, we were ready. Knowing that we must let Rescue Ops know our position, I changed frequencies. Suddenly an aircraft caught my eye. 'Traffic, ten o'clock high – closing,' I said, pointing.

It was an OV-10 Bronco on a descending collision course with us. It billowed black smoke like from a Hollywood war movie as Nguyen hauled up the nose, attempting a quick stop. I watched with fascination the Bronco grow larger, until it was within 300 feet, approximately at our level and about to cross our twelve o'clock, when its cockpit burst with flame and pieces. 'Son of a bitch,' I exclaimed. My eyes followed the OV-10 through a hard, noseover maneuver that resulted in it striking a rice paddy in a near-vertical dive in front of and beneath our decelerating helicopter. I was stunned like one is after witnessing real death, for I now assumed that the pilot and crew, if any, had ridden it in and were now cooking in the growing orange fireball.

What appeared to me as a small explosion in the cockpit was really an ejection, and now, hanging in space before us, was the OV-10 pilot, suspended by his parachute. Concerned that our high-hover rotor-wash might pull the parachute into our thrashing machine, Bill bottomed the collective. We briefly entered autorotation. In formation, the parachute and Pedro descended to the rice paddy. A handful of collective to cushion our landing caught the parachutist and dragged him a little through the rice field. Sergeant McCoy bolted from the cabin and ran straight toward our survivor. McCoy's long strides left a string of circular sprays though the shallow water. The scene had an orange glow from the near-by burning wreckage. McCoy's boots weren't the only things kicking up sprays of water.

'Jesus, we're under fire,' I exclaimed. We grabbed our AR-15s and scanned nervously while McCoy pulled the downed pilot from the tar-like mud. He flipped open the pilot's riser covers and jerked the releases, freeing the soiled lieutenant from his chute. Next, McCoy grabbed the parachute harness chest strap and made a determined return to the helicopter with his pilot-survivor in tow.

Vietnamese were approaching from the nine and eleven o'clock position, about a hundred yards out, trotting along ditch-banks waving like approving fans. They wore the ubiquitous black pajamas and appeared to have no weapons. Water was still spraying up around the helicopter and the confusion was like bees buzzing in my head.

McCoy threw our survivor on board and scrambled in, shouting 'In and secure, get the hell out of here!' Nguyen pulled max torque and our Huskie strained to get airborne, but nothing happened. 'What the hell, over!' he exclaimed. As our 6,000-pound helicopter sat idling in the rice field, its tires had become anchors in the underlying muck. I slid down in my seat to take maximum advantage of the armor plating. This didn't look good. The cockpit filled with the stench of rot and night soil that McCoy and his survivor were wearing.

Nguyen ignored the transmission limits and pulled everything that the Lycoming could give and suddenly we broke free, springing upwards in a truly max-performance takeoff. Our new vantage point above the burning crater showed a ring pattern of impacts in the water around the wreckage, probably the result of burning ammunition, and, within the perimeter, the black marks of our tires, Sergeant McCoy's trail out and back, and a bright orange and white parachute. A parachute with enough nylon fabric to make shirts, pants and dresses for a lot of impoverished peasants – a coveted parachute . . . fear and confusion . . . and they nearly paid with their lives.

I transmitted 'Rescue Ops, Pedro Six-One has the survivor on board and secure. Returning to base.' 'Pedro Six-One, Rescue Ops, what survivor?' was their reply.

The rescue was determined to be the fastest combat save of the Vietnam War. It took one minute and thirty-two seconds from ejection to recovery.

TARGET HANOI 32

1. U-Tapao
2. B-52 Route from Guam 3. Hanoi

*A*FTER four years of negotiations in Paris with the North Vietnamese, Henry Kissinger's team finally decided that they were so near to a peace agreement that on 23 October 1972 they again ordered a halt to all bombing of North Vietnam above the 20th Parallel and Kissinger confidently announced that 'Peace is at hand'. He should have known better.

The enemy again took advantage of the bombing halt to repair the bridges and roads above the 20th Parallel and to increase the amount of supplies flowing South. By the middle of December the peace talks had broken down yet again, and with more MiG-21 fighters appearing at Gia Lam airfield and the monsoon season approaching, President Nixon decided that he had had enough. The President summoned Admiral Thomas Moorer, the Chairman of the Joint Chiefs of Staff, and told him, 'This is your chance to use military power to win this war'; he then added melodramatically, 'And if you don't, I'll hold you responsible'.

By 18 December Strategic Air Command had moved 155 Boeing B-52 Stratofortress bombers to Guam island in the Marianas and a further 50 to U Topao in Thailand. The briefing room on Guam was packed to overflowing when General McCarthy addressed the assembled crews with the simplest of opening statements: 'Gentlemen, your target for tonight is Hanoi'. For the rest of the briefing you could have heard a pin drop.

The restrictions had finally been lifted and the bomber crews were now being given the chance to do what seven years of war had failed to to – to bring Hanoi to its knees by the swift, massive application of air power against the heart of North Vietnam. Operation 'Linebacker II' was about to begin.

On 18 December 1972 129 B-52s arrived over Hanoi in three waves, four to five hours apart. They attacked the airfields at Hoa Lac, Kep and Phuc Yen, the Kinh No complex and the Yen Vien railyards. The aircraft flew in tight cells of three aircraft to maximize the mutual support benefits of their ECM equipment and flew straight and level to stabilize the bombing computers and ensure that all bombs fell on the military targets and not in civilian areas.

Captain Hal Wilson in the lead B-52 from U Tapao reported 'wall to wall SAMs up ahead' as he neared the outskirts of Hanoi. His B-52D was one of the three bombers hit by SAM missiles over their targets that night and destroyed. Despite

Right: North Vietnam's Premier Pham Van Dong inspects the wreckage of a US aircraft shot down over Hanoi. (Socialist Republic of Vietnam)

the 200 missiles fired at the bomber force, 94 per cent of the bombs were on target, and as the weary crews returned to their bases the bombers participating in the next day's raid were preparing to depart.

One of the aircraft commanders on day four, 21 December, was Peter Giroux. He was on his third mission of the Linebacker II operation and was designated as lead aircraft in his three-ship cell for the mission against storage facilities located near Bac Mai airfield. When the crew boarded their B-52 for the mission they noticed that the radar system had been written up for maintenance by the previous crew, as it had failed almost two hours after take-off. The write-up had been signed off as 'could not duplicate' by maintenance. Unfortunately, they were wrong.

All went well during the flight over Thailand and Laos, but as Captain Giroux in Scarlet One approached the IP (initial point) the radar began to deteriorate. Giroux instructed Scarlet Two to take the lead and began to drop back to take up position as number three in the cell. In this position they could take their release instructions from the tail gunner in the preceding aircraft.

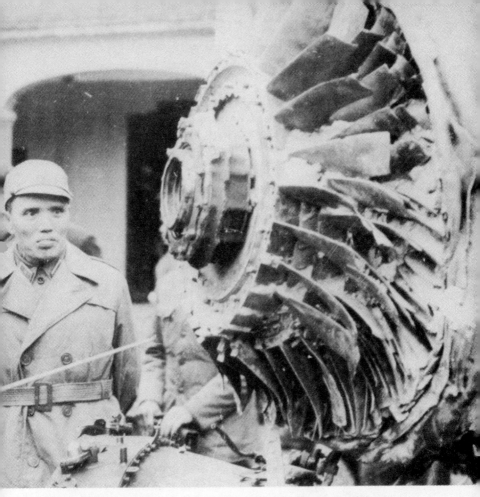

As Scarlet One rolled out into its new position the radar failed completely and, at about the same time, its gunner called for the 'TTR' maneuver. This was designed to counter enemy radar, but when the gunner asked for it, it meant MiGs. It could not have happened at a more inopportune moment. Giroux began the maneuver, realizing that it would back the bomber out of the cell slightly and affect the protective ECM shield. A second or two later the gunner called for flares and began shooting at the attacking MiGs. The flares were designed to lure the incoming infra-red missiles away from the heat signature of the eight engines and they worked. Two of the missiles passed under the aircraft as Giroux concentrated on the maneuver. The gunner yelled 'I've got one' over the interphone (not allowed as it was unverified) and continued to fire until the attackers broke away.

The reason for the MiGs' departure was soon to become obvious. Directly below were two SAMs, and they were heading right for Scarlet One. Giroux called the missiles to the crew, turned hard back to the right and said a short prayer. A few seconds later there was a sharp bang like a paper bag exploding, as the missile hit somewhere near the centreline and towards the front of the aircraft.

Another went by the tail but failed to explode.

Captain Giroux rolled the aircraft out on heading and took stock of the situation. Some shrapnel had hit him in the legs and in both wrists, but he was alright. The side panel was a mess, the interphone was out and the left wing was already on fire; engines five and six were burning, and the flames were reaching past the tail.

The aircraft began a bank to the right, probably because of the loss of engines on that side. The controls were not much help, and as the bank increased they experienced a complete electrical failure. Giroux looked at his co-pilot and reached for the 'Abandon' light on the rear of the centre console. One ejection seat fired immediately and two more followed as the aircraft depressurized. Giroux may have passed out from lack of oxygen, because the next thing he knew he was upside down in the aircraft as it began to fall to earth.

All I could see was the shattered window directly in front of me. I was hanging in the straps even though I had tightened them before the world had begun to come apart. I knew the seat would probably give me a compression when it hit me, but it was the least of my worries. I reached for the arming levers on the side of the seat near my knees and pulled them up and tried to squeeze the trigger to fire the seat. Nothing happened. My little finger was between the trigger and the arming lever. I squeezed again as hard as I could and the seat fired.

Peter Giroux woke up on the ground. It felt wet and muddy and someone had hold of him by the hair. He was surrounded by a crowd of North Vietnamese and was totally unable to move. As the pain flooded through his head, he mercifully fell unconscious again.

Two more brief periods of consciousness followed, once when Giroux awoke in a truck moving slowly down a road and once when he found himself on an operating table with a woman in a white coat trimming at the skin on his neck with a pair of scissors. He did not really come around until the 24th, two days after he had been shot down.

He was in the 'Hanoi Hilton', in a large, dark room with high windows and a bare light bulb hanging from the ceiling. Across the room was Louis LeBlanc, his gunner.

At first Louis did not recognize me, so I knew I looked bad. He related what had happened to him. His interphone was intermittent too and he had stayed on board until the right wing had finally burned through and started to fold over the top of the aircraft. He thought it was appropriate that he leave and he stepped out the back, having blown the turret earlier when he saw the abandon light flicker. He wasn't sure how long he had stayed until the wing broke – probably two or three minutes. I realized then that I must have gone unconscious when the aircraft depressurized, as my oxygen system had been damaged. Then, when the plane had rolled over, it was enough to bring me around and give me a last chance to eject. He said he could see another chute when he was coming down, but whoever was in it appeared to be unconcious. He told me both of us (I'll assume that was me) were getting shot at. He was captured immediately and taken to Hanoi.

The electronic warfare officer, Pete Camerota, had been the first one to eject. He was sitting on a hill about 25 or more miles to the south-west while his fellow crew members were speculating about his fate. He'd woken up in the chute at opening or a little lower. He came down through several cloud layers and landed in a rice paddy. He had seen three parachutes near him at about 3,000 feet, but that was the last he saw or heard of them. He took off immediately and reached some higher ground without being seen. Over a period of several days he finally reached the top of the hill and made contact on his survival radio on 29 December. A rescue that close to Hanoi would have been a miracle, and he was getting weak from lack of food and little water. After three or four days on the hill he reached the point where it took two hands to operate the radio, and he realized that he could either give up or die where he was. He surrendered on 3 January 1973.

Peter Giroux took stock of his wounds on Christmas Eve. His arm was in a brace, tied together with cloth strips, he was burned on the back of his hands and knuckles and on the ankles, and it felt like he had a broken rib. He was lucky to be alive, if only in the Hanoi Hilton.

On Christmas Day the bombing ceased and the North Vietnamese served their prisoners a special meal; rice wine, a salad, some duck with bones still in it (ap-

Below: Not all the B-52s made it home – a US crewman's jacket, papers, life-vest and survival radio on display in Hanoi. (Socialist Republic of Vietnam)

Above: An aerial view of targets struck during Operation 'Linebacker II'. They include Gia Lam airfield (3) and the docks and warehouses at (5) and (6).

propriately named 'dynamite duck' as the bones were all broken) and something sweet for dessert. It didn't take long to come back up, however.

On the 26th the bombing resumed with a great deal of intensity. SAC had finally changed its tactics, and all the bombers were tasked to hit their targets within a 15-minute time period. The approach and departure routes and altitudes were also varied to reduce losses, and only two of the 120 bombers failed to return home. The raids continued until 30 December, by which time most of *the worthwhile targets around Hanoi and Haiphong had been struck. The enemy were practically out of SAM missiles and they had at last got the message. The North Vietnamese wanted to talk again, and serious negotiations began again on 8 January.*

The treatment of the prisoners began to improve, and on 27 January the peace agreement was finally signed. On 12 February 1973 Operation 'Homecoming' began, and the first batch of 116 prisoners-of-war were released in Hanoi. Giroux recalls:

The morning of the 12th was brisk at first. We lined up near the main gate and then began to wait. I recognized Everett Alvarez, who was the first man captured in August 1964, and introduced myself. He thanked me for my efforts and I replied that he should thank the President who made the decision and that I thought the decision should have come sooner. He agreed. After a while we moved through the gates, past sullen and unsmiling crowds, to several small camouflaged buses. We drove through the city toward Gia Lam airfield.

The city reflected the French architecture in the tree-lined streets, and the buildings were unpainted and dirty. We crossed the Red River on a pontoon bridge next to the Paul Doumer bridge. The airport was soon in the distance on our left as some old prop transports became visible. We moved up a tree-shaded lane and got off to wait again in a small building. We were offered beer and pork-fat sandwiches. I took the beer; all I could think about was the hair on the first pork fat I had seen in the soup. We reboarded the buses and moved to the main part of the airport, just out of sight of some revetments that I was sure held MiG-21s.

The group formed up and reported in to an impressive looking Colonel in a good-looking blue uniform, and headed for the C-141. I climbed into a seat by the wall and watched. My sacrifice was of no consequence compared to these men. There had been no torture, no solitary, no anything. They were subdued until the plane lifted off the runway and the gear thunked into the well. Then it was pandemonium. I was thinking about the rest of my crew.

The three other members of Giroux's crew are still listed as missing in action. They are Jerry Alley, Waring Bennet and Joe Copack. This story is for them.

PRISONERS OF WAR AND MISSING IN ACTION

33

POW/MIA

1. Cambodia 84
2. Laos 549
3. Socialist Republic of Vietnam 1,782

BY the end of March 1973, Operation 'Homecoming' was over and 591 American prisoners-of-war had returned home from North Vietnam. Only nine came home from Laos, and these few had been captured by the North Vietnamese in Laos and passed on to Hanoi.

With America finally out of the war and President Nixon claiming that all POWs had been brought home, little thought was given to the almost 2,500 men still missing in action. The only people who still cared were the families and friends of the MIAs, and as the Nixon administration began to sink into the mire of Watergate little attention was paid to their plight. The intelligence community, namely the Central Intelligence Agency, the Defense Intelligence Agency and the National Security Agency, kept quiet. This was despite the fact that the NSA, who had monitored enemy radio traffic throughout the war, was aware that almost 300 men on its list of 'captured alive' pilots had not been repatriated. General Eugene Tighe, the former head of the DIA, put the number of those who expected to return, but did not, to be around 400–500.

At the time of writing 2,413 men are still missing. The majority belong to the Air Force (899), followed by the Army (702), Navy (480), Marines (289), civilians (42) and Coast Guard (1). Over half are believed to have been 'killed in action – remains not recovered'; the others are listed as 'prisoners of war/missing in action.'

As the last Operation Homecoming POW stepped on to American soil back in 1973, he was unaware that none of his comrades captured in Laos or Cambodia had been released. To date, 549 are still missing in Laos and 82 in Cambodia. The figure for Laos may be slightly higher, in view of the doubts expressed recently over the return of thirteen remains from one crash site. The majority of those missing are aviators, and most were lost over territory controlled by the North Vietnamese, in particular in the vicinity of the Ho Chi Minh Trail. From the remaining 1,782 men missing in North and South Vietnam, the majority of the Army and Marines MIA were lost in the South and those from the Navy and Air Force in the North.

Left: Operation 'Homecoming' – Captain Anshus, US Army, (right) with escort in March 1973 at Hanoi's Gia Lam Airport. (US Army)

As the war progressed and increasing numbers of US servicemen became lost in jungle fire-fights or ejected from their stricken aircraft over enemy territory, the intelligence community was tasked with the collection of information on the whereabouts of the POW/MIAs. To this end they were aided by captured documents, enemy POWs, 'ralliers' and refugee-interrogation reports, together with reports from their own agents, electronic radio traffic eavesdropping and photographs taken by spy-planes and satellites. The majority of the enemy POW camps were located and a list of men believed to be held captive was compiled.

The CIA practically ran the war in Laos and one of its classified reports in November 1970, using 'confirmed information', listed prisons in Laos where POWs were being held. These included Ban Na Kay Neua, a major enemy prison where as many as twenty US POWs reported; Khamkouane Prison Complex, where forty American or other foreign nationals were being held; and Hang Long, a prison in a cave containing American, Thai and Loa prisoners. The CIA also possessed aerial photographs of these places.

When Hanoi was asked for the return of the POWs in Laos in 1973, their reply was 'Go talk to the Pathet Lao'. At the time the United States did not recognize the Pathet Lao regime, and to date not one POW, aside from the nine captured

Below: Lieutenant Dieter Dengler, a US Navy pilot, survived torture at a prison camp located in Laos, operated by the Pathet Lao, but controlled by the North Vietnamese. He escaped and spent three weeks in the jungle before being rescued. (US Navy)

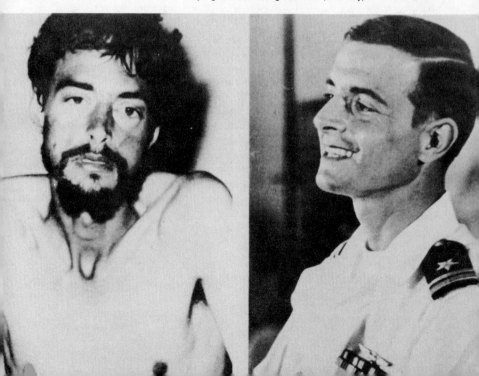

by the North Vietnamese and moved straight to Hanoi, has been repatriated by Laos.

The majority of the pilots were shot down over North Vietnam and, assuming that they survived the crash of their aircraft and were not killed by irate peasants on the ground, they were soon in the hands of the communist authorities. Most of the men eventually appeared in the prison system and were returned in 1973, less those who were killed or driven insane by torture or died in captivity because of inadequate medical care. A number, however, were known to have been captured alive but did not show up in the prison system.

There has been speculation, both during the war and over the years since, that some of the men were 'Moscow bound' – passed on to the Soviets, who wished to make use of their specialized knowledge. This idea cannot be summarily dismissed. Amongst the pilots and aircrew who floated down to enemy soil were electronic warfare experts, weapon system officers and operators of the latest technology, such as that used in the AC-130 gunships or the SAM-suppressor Wild Weasel F-105s. Harry Edwards, with his knowledge of the new 'smart' bombs, would have made a fine catch, as would the crews of the new F-111 swing-wing fighter-bomber. These weapons might some day be used against the Soviet Union, and it is naive to suggest that the Russians would not take advantage of the opportunity to interrogate some of these men.

Some of the pilots possessed other specialized knowledge that would have been of interest to the Soviets. Lieutenant Colonel Iceal Hambleton was a 53-year-old navigator in an electronic countermeasures EB-66 that was shot down just south of the DMZ in the midst of the enemy invasion of Easter 1972. He had been the assistant Deputy Chief of Operations of a Strategic Air Command Missile Wing before he went back to the cockpit, and he had a head full of top-secret war plans. He was so important to the US Command that the eleven-day operation to recover him before he fell into enemy hands formed the largest search and rescue mission mounted during the war.

Apart from the possibilities that prisoners-of-war may have been kept by the Soviets for their specialized knowledge, and by the Lao for possible political reasons, another factor must be considered – money. President Nixon informed the North Vietnamese that they would be given aid and reparations to the tune of three billion dollars. However, Congress would never approve the payment, and Nixon was soon out of office. The North Vietnamese no doubt kept an ace up their sleeves and retained some prisoners as insurance, in case the reparations were not forthcoming. If this was the case, the money is still in America and the prisoners, no doubt reduced in numbers by now, are still in what has now become the Socialist Republic of Vietnam.

Historically, communist nations have never released all their prisoners following the end of hostilities. The Russians did not do so in 1945, nor did the North Koreans or Chinese in 1953. Following the defeat of the French at Dien Bien Phu and their subsequent withdrawal from Indo-China, 13,000 French POWs had been returned by the end of 1954, but the French Command accused the North Vietnamese of witholding 9,500 more. The French knew who they were dealing with, and for the last thirty years have been paying millions of dollars annually for the return of remains and live POWs. There is no doubt that the same thing happened in 1973 and for the same reason – money.

In the eight years immediately after Operation Homecoming, the Nixon, Ford and Carter administrations paid little attention to the reports of live Americans still being held in Indo-China and even less attention to the families wishing to recover the remains of their loved ones. A small number of remains were returned and sent to the US Army Central Identification Laboratory in Hawaii (CIL-HI) for identification, prior to release to their families for burial.

The National League of POW/MIA families continued to press the various administrations to obtain the fullest possible accounting of the 2,413 Americans still missing, and at last, since 1981, the Reagan administration has accelerated

Below: Lieutenant-Colonel James Lindberg-Hughes being taken to a press conference in Hanoi after capture. (Author's Collection)

negotiations with the various communist governments in an effort to obtain a full accounting.

Whereas only 48 remains were returned between 1976 and 1980, since the current administration became involved 94 more remains have been returned. No live POWs have surfaced however, with the exception of a Marine who returned home in 1979 and was court-martialled and accused of collaborating with the enemy. He claims to have seen groups of American POWs in North Vietnam between 1973 and 1979.

Since the fall of South Vietnam, Laos and Cambodia, a wealth of intelligence information has appeared in the form of refugee reports. Vietnamese boat people escaping by sea and refugees trekking into Thailand have provided almost 1,000 first-hand sighting reports of Americans still alive in Indo-China after 1975. The Defense Intelligence Agency has dismissed 211 as untrue and claim to have resolved a further 641 as relating to individuals who have since left South-East Asia such as returned POWs, known missionaries and civilians detained after Saigon fell in 1975 and were later released, but 137 sightings are still unresolved and under investigation. Vice-President George Bush stated, in July 1985, 'If we can get hard evidence that Americans are still held in Vietnamese prisons, we're pledged to do whatever's necessary to get them out'. The statement hinges, of course, on the definition of 'hard evidence'. With the most sophisticated spy-planes, cameras and electronic eavesdropping equipment in the world available on its inventory, is such hard evidence so difficult to obtain?

If there is a lack of hard evidence concerning live POWs, there is no shortage of refugee reports. The following are two examples of sighting reports received by the National League of Families:

1. I was an [ARVN] officer and company commander, Marines, and was captured by the Viet Cong at the Thach Han River in June 1974. I want to provide to you information on a number of American prisoners which I knew of while I was in captivity in the Khe Sanh area near the Lao border. I escaped from the Viet Cong in 1978 and crossed the border [left Vietnam] in 1980, arriving in America just five months ago . . .

For your work of good will, I can possibly give you the names of two American prisoners still alive in the Viet-Lao border area, one a Lieutenant and one a Private First Class.

2. During the time I was imprisoned in Hanoi I knew of a number of American POWs. I have heard their voices and I have heard the cadremen say that they were downed pilots undergoing reeducation. They were held nearby, separated from me by a six-meter-high wall. I could not see them, but could hear their voices. [The source of this report spent fifteen years in communist prisons in North Vietnam, after serving as a CIA-trained Special Forces paratrooper.]

The source goes on to say that at the end of 1978 he and 130 American POWs were transferred to Thanh Hoa. While in Thanh Hoa, the former paratrooper said he saw about thirty Americans held in three separate camps about seven kilometres from each other. He adds that the Americans were divided into separate camps so that the communists could keep closer guard.

In conclusion, the source states:

The POWS I saw were very thin; they were covered with scabies – there was just skin and bones left on them. They could hardly walk, yet they were forced to carry wood from the forests distant about 500 meters. They often fell down. Sometimes they were beaten by the guards. These are things I saw with my own eyes.

Another interesting refugee report was received in late 1979 from a man who had been a mortician in Hanoi. He claimed that some 400 sets of remains upon which he had worked were being held by the Vietnamese government. The DIA had the information cross-checked and independently verified, including the address at which the remains were stored. The source also passed a polygraph test at the DIA. Five Congressmen travelled to Hanoi in January 1980 to confront the Vietnamese government regarding the remains. They went to the warehouse in Ly Nam De Street where the remains were supposed to be stored, but were denied entry. A couple of months later the Vietnamese allowed the press into the same warehouse. It was empty.

In the last couple of years, with an increase in the number of remains returned, the water now appears a little murky. At first the families accepted the remains of their loved ones in good faith and laid them to rest with full military honours. Some afterwards had doubts and had the remains exhumed for a second opinion. They found that, far from containing full skeletal remains, the contents of the coffins were quite small and in some cases comprised merely a handful of small pieces of bone.

One of the eminent anthropologists called in by some of the families was Professor Michael Charney PhD, the Director of the Forensic Science Laboratory at Colorado State University. He testified before a House Armed Services Subcommittee in September 1986 that of the twenty sets of remains that he had examined only two, or ten per cent of the total, could be positively identified. If those statistics are applied to all of the remains returned . . .

It would appear that overzealousness, amongst other accusations, on the part of the CIL-HI, combined with pressure from above, has led to the incorrect identification of a number of remains. The 'success' of the CIL-HI in identifying all the remains would certainly show the laboratory and the government in a good light, but having been checked by the top anthropologists in the country some of the identification reports must be viewed with suspicion.

Suspicion is a word that must certainly be used in the case of the returned remains of Captain Thomas Hart, the pilot of an AC-130 gunship that was shot down over Laos on 21 December 1972. In February 1985, a joint Lao/US excavation team examined the burnt-out wreck of the aircraft and therafter returned the remains of the thirteen crew members who had been listed as missing since the

Above: North Vietnamese militia inspecting the wreckage of a Navy fighter bearing the name 'LT. J. G. GREENE'. (Author's Collection)

crash. At this point, Ann Hart, the wife of the pilot, became even more suspicious than before.

There had, in fact, been sixteen men in the AC-130 when it was brought down. Two were picked up almost immediately and the other fourteen were presumed lost. An indigenous recovery team was inserted into the crash site the next day and they found and fingerprinted the remains of one of the crew before enemy fire drove them out of the area, without having identified or recovered any other remains. The fourteenth member of the crew was listed as killed in action, the other thirteen as MIA. However, all fourteen remains should still have been at the site, and the 1985 excavation should have yielded fourteen remains, not thirteen. It should also be mentioned that the combined weight of the alleged remains of the thirteen men amounted to only seven pounds.

What had aroused Ann Hart's suspicions before she went out to Laos with the excavation team in 1985? In July 1973, seven months after Thomas Hart's aircraft was shot down, and five months after the signing of the peace agreement, a US spy-plane photographed the letters and date 'TH 1973' freshly cut in elephant grass 250 miles from the crash site. Ann Hart was not told about this and only found out in 1983 when a reporter handed her a copy of the picture. Subsequently, two other sources have confirmed that similar symbols were found near the crash site, together with five parachutes. At the time of writing, Ann Hart and other family members are involved in a lawsuit against the government for the suffering caused to them by their government's handling of the plight of their missing men.

It is clear that the communist governments of the Socialist Republic of Vietnam, Laos and, to a lesser extent, Cambodia, know far more about the fate of the men still unaccounted for than they are willing to admit. Perhaps the price of that knowledge is higher than that which the current administration is willing to pay.

It is the opinion of the author that live Americans are still held as prisoners-of-war in South-East Asia and that the American government is well aware of that fact. If the government has to pay for their release or mount a rescue operation, then so be it. They owe it to the men who laid their lives on the line and for whom, like Thomas Hart, the war may not yet be over.

INDEX
OF NARRATORS AND STORY LOCATIONS